Practice and Homework Journal

Grade 4

Currency and Coins Photos Courtesy of United States Mint, Bureau of Engraving and Houghton Mifflin Harcourt

Printed in the U.S.A.

ISBN 978-0-358-11102-3

6 7 8 9 10 0928 28 27 26 25 24 23 22 21

4500824211 C D E F G

Unit 1

Place Value and Whole Number Operations

Module 1 Place Value of Whole Numbers

Module 2 Addition and Subtraction of Whole Numbers

Unit 2

Multiplication and Division Problems

Module 3 Interpret and Solve Problem Situations

Module 4 Mental Math and Estimation Strategies

Module 5 Multiply by 1-Digit Numbers

Unit 3

Extend and Apply Multiplication

Module 8 Multiply by 2-Digit Numbers

Module 9 Apply Multiplication to Area

Unit 4

Fractions and Decimals

Module 10 Algebraic Thinking: Number Theory

Module 11 Fraction Equivalence and Comparison

Module 12 Relate Fractions and Decimals

Module 13 Use Fractions to Understand Angles

Unit 5

Operations with Fractions

Module 14 Understand Addition and Subtraction of Fractions with Like Denominators

Module 15 Add and Subtract Fractions and Mixed Numbers with Like Denominators

Module 16 Multiply Fractions by Whole Numbers

Unit 6

Two-Dimensional Figures and Symmetry

Module 17 Two-Dimensional Figures

Module 18 Symmetry and Patterns

Unit 7

Measurement, Data, and Time

Module 19 Relative Sizes of Customary Measurement Units

Module 20 Relative Sizes of Metric Measurement Units

Module 21 Solve Problems with Time and Measurement

Name ____

LESSON 1.1
More Practice/ Homework

ONLINE
Video Tutorials and Interactive Examples

Understand Place Value Relationships

1 (MP) **Reason** There are 12,600 insects on display at the new Science Center exhibit. Explain how you can use base-ten blocks to show the value of the digit 2 in 12,600.

____

2 One painting shows 520 different types of ladybugs. Another painting shows 750 different types. How many times as great is the value of the digit 5 in 520 than the value of the digit 5 in 750? How do you know?

____

____

Write the number in the place-value chart. Then complete the chart to find the value of each digit.

3 4,817

THOUSANDS			ONES		
Hundreds	Tens	Ones	Hundreds	Tens	Ones
		4 thousands			
				10	

4 **Math on the Spot** How many models of 100 do you need to model 3,200? Explain.

____

____

Compare the values of the underlined digits. Then complete the sentence.

5 <u>8</u>0,000 and <u>8</u>,000 The value of the digit 8 in __________ is __________ times the value of the digit 8 in __________.

Test Prep

6 Which correctly completes the sentence?

The value of the digit 3 in 730,500 is ■ the value of the digit 3 in 73,050.

Ⓐ 2 times
Ⓑ 10 times
Ⓒ 100 times
Ⓓ 1,000 times

7 Which shows the correct place-value position of the underlined digit?

4<u>1</u>9,235

Ⓐ hundred thousands
Ⓑ ten thousands
Ⓒ thousands
Ⓓ hundreds

8 Which correctly shows the value of the digit 4 in 604,027?

Ⓐ 4 ten thousands
Ⓑ 4 hundred thousands
Ⓒ 4 thousands
Ⓓ 4 tens

Spiral Review

9 Bobby has 8 toy cars with 4 wheels on each car. How many wheels are there?

____

10 Write the related facts for the numbers 3, 6, 18.

_____ ÷ _____ = _____

_____ × _____ = _____

_____ ÷ _____ = _____

_____ × _____ = _____

Name ______________________

ONLINE
Ed
Video Tutorials and
Interactive Examples

Read and Write Numbers

1 The distance from the Earth to the Moon is two hundred thirty-eight thousand, nine hundred miles. Write the distance in standard form and expanded form.

____

2 (MP) **Attend to Precision** The expanded form for 300,684 can be written with only 4 addends. Explain how this is possible for a number with 6 digits.

____

____

3 Shelly wrote the following number in expanded form: 90,000 + 600 + 8. How would she write the number in word form?

____

Write the number in expanded form.

4 40,897

____

5 nine hundred two thousand, fifty-seven

____

6 twenty-four thousand, forty-two

____

7 **Math on the Spot** Sophia said that the expanded form for 605,970 is 600,000 + 50,000 + 900 + 70. Describe Sophia's error and give the correct answer.

____

____

____

Test Prep

8 Select all of the correct forms of 806,510.

Ⓐ 800 + 6 + 500 + 10
Ⓑ eight hundred six thousand, five hundred ten
Ⓒ 800,000 + 6,000 + 500 + 10
Ⓓ eight hundred six, five ten
Ⓔ 80,000 + 6,000 + 500 + 10

9 Which shows 90,000 + 400 + 60 + 5 in word form?

Ⓐ nine thousand, four hundred sixty-five
Ⓑ ninety thousand, four hundred sixty-five
Ⓒ ninety-four thousand, sixty-five
Ⓓ nine hundred forty thousand, six hundred five

10 What is four hundred thirty-two thousand, one hundred six written in expanded form?

____

11 Write the number in a different form.

200,000 + 70,000 + 3,000 + 500 + 80 + 4

____

____

Spiral Review

Multiply or divide.

12 _____ × 9 = 72 **13** 42 ÷ 6 = _____ **14** 48 ÷ 8 = _____

15 9 × 3 = _____ **16** 4 × 3 = _____ **17** $8\overline{)56}$

18 $9\overline{)63}$ **19** _____ × 9 = 81 **20** 9 × 6 = _____

Name ______________________________

LESSON 1.3
More Practice/ Homework

ONLINE
Video Tutorials and Interactive Examples

Regroup and Rename Numbers

1 **Use Structure** Miguel uses base-ten blocks to show that 3,200 people are at a museum. How can you regroup and rename the number 3,200?

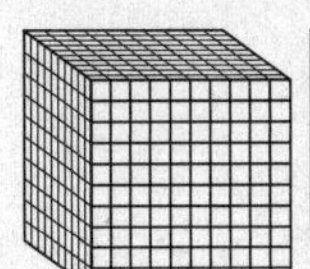 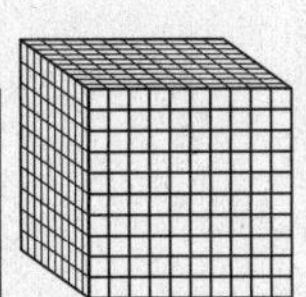 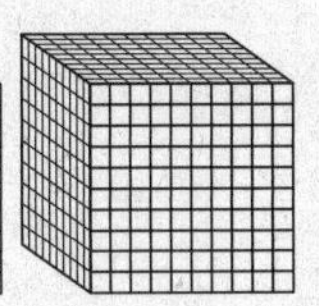 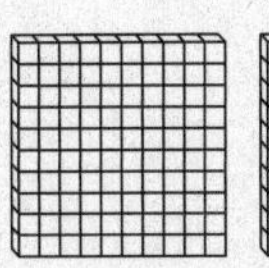

3,200 = _____ hundreds

2 Use the place-value chart to help you regroup and rename the number.

THOUSANDS			ONES		
Hundreds	Tens	Ones	Hundreds	Tens	Ones

83,000 = _____ hundreds

Regroup and rename the number.

3 5,300 = __________ tens

4 680,000 = __________ thousands

5 71 thousands = __________ hundreds

6 82 ten thousands = __________ thousands

7 Some students are playing a math game. Each of them must regroup and rename 47,000. Circle all of the ways that 47,000 is regrouped and renamed correctly.

47 ten thousands

47 hundreds

47 thousands

470 tens

470 hundreds

4,700 tens

8 **Math on the Spot** A toy store is ordering 3,000 remote control cars. The store can order the cars in sets of 10. How many sets of 10 does the store need to order?

____

Test Prep

9 Select all of the ways to regroup and rename 390,000.

Ⓐ 39 ten thousands
Ⓑ 390 tens
Ⓒ 39 thousands
Ⓓ 3,900 hundreds
Ⓔ 390 thousands

10 Which word correctly completes the sentence?

The number 65,000 can be regrouped and

renamed as 6,500 __________.

Ⓐ thousands
Ⓑ hundreds
Ⓒ tens
Ⓓ ones

11 Which number can be regrouped and renamed as 920 hundreds?

Ⓐ 920
Ⓑ 9,200
Ⓒ 92,000
Ⓓ 920,000

Spiral Review

Compare. Use <, >, or =.

12 $\frac{2}{4}$ ◯ $\frac{3}{4}$

13 $\frac{2}{3}$ ◯ $\frac{1}{3}$

14 $\frac{3}{8}$ ◯ $\frac{3}{8}$

15 $\frac{3}{8}$ ◯ $\frac{5}{8}$

16 $\frac{2}{6}$ ◯ $\frac{1}{3}$

17 $\frac{2}{4}$ ◯ $\frac{4}{8}$

18 $\frac{1}{4}$ ◯ $\frac{2}{8}$

19 $\frac{4}{6}$ ◯ $\frac{5}{6}$

20 $\frac{2}{3}$ ◯ $\frac{2}{9}$

Name

LESSON 1.4
More Practice/ Homework

ONLINE
Ed
Video Tutorials and Interactive Examples

Compare and Order Numbers

1 Explain how you know 671,287 > 617,827.

2 **Open Ended** Omar writes a number that is greater than 271,680 but less than 276,108. What number could he have written? Use <, >, or = to justify your answer.

3 MP **Attend to Precision** Write the numbers 108,567; 107,658; and 107,568 in order from least to greatest.

Compare. Write <, >, or =.

4 152,847 ◯ 152,848

5 105,050 ◯ 105,055

6 970,183 ◯ 970,183

7 98,604 ◯ 96,940

8 221,831 ◯ 212,831

9 28,045 ◯ 28,045

10 **Math on the Spot** What's the question? Compare: 643,251; 633,512; and 633,893. The answer is 633,512.

Test Prep

11 Write all of the digits that can replace the ■.

657,321 > 6■7,321 ______________

12 Which shows the numbers ordered correctly from least to greatest? Select all the apply.

Ⓐ 415,672; 416,672; 417,672
Ⓑ 928,013; 982,103; 982,130
Ⓒ 105,024; 150,421; 105,042
Ⓓ 97,210; 107,970; 170,826
Ⓔ 5,631, 5,642, 5,643

13 Melinda wrote 326,729 < 326,279. Which best describes her answer?

Ⓐ Melinda compared the numbers correctly.
Ⓑ Melinda should have written = because both numbers have 326 thousands.
Ⓒ Melinda should have written > because 7 hundreds is greater than 2 hundreds.
Ⓓ Melinda should have written > because 2 tens is greater than 7 tens.

Spiral Review

14 Ethan has a pencil. Circle the unit you would use to measure the mass of the pencil.

kilogram   gram

15 Draw a rectangle that has the same perimeter as the one shown, but with a greater area.

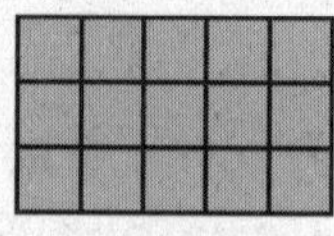

Name ______________________________

LESSON 1.5
More Practice/ Homework

Use Place Value Understanding to Round Numbers

1 (MP) **Use Repeated Reasoning** Use place value to round 314,609 to the nearest hundred thousand, to the nearest ten thousand, and to the nearest thousand.

____

2 (MP) **Attend to Precision** The sales department wants to place an order for 253,625 third grade math books for a region. Once the order is given, there is always a need for extra math books. How can the sales manager estimate the number of math books to be sure that there are more than enough?

____

____

3 Between which two hundred thousands is the number 185,104?

__________ and __________

4 **Math on the Spot** The number 2,■00 is missing a digit. The number rounded to the nearest thousand is 2,000. List all of the possibilities for the missing digit. Explain your answer.

____

____

____

____

Round to the place value of the underlined digit.

5 3<u>7</u>2,297 __________

6 <u>6</u>98,072 __________

7 1<u>5</u>,912 __________

Test Prep

8 Select all the numbers that round to 940,000 when rounded to the nearest ten thousand.

- Ⓐ 944,999
- Ⓑ 935,011
- Ⓒ 946,005
- Ⓓ 943,902
- Ⓔ 951,212
- Ⓕ 934,125

9 Devon lives in a city with an estimated population of 240,000 people. Which statement about this population is true?

- Ⓐ There are more than 300,000 people in this city.
- Ⓑ There are more than 250,000 people in this city.
- Ⓒ There are more than 245,000 people in this city.
- Ⓓ There are more than 200,000 people in this city.

10 An online report reads that about 120,000 copies of a book have been sold. What is the least number of books that could have actually been sold? What is the greatest number of books that could have been sold?

____

____

Spiral Review

11 **Write the value of the underlined digit.**

89<u>4</u>,356

____

12 **Write equations. Use letters for unknowns. Solve.**

Notecards cost $4 for a pack of 12. Jenna gives the cashier $16 to buy the notecards. She gets $4 in change. How many packs of notecards does Jenna buy?

____

____

Name ______________________________

ONLINE
Video Tutorials and
Interactive Examples

Add Whole Numbers and Assess Reasonableness

1 (MP) **Construct Arguments** On Saturday, 94,887 passengers rode on a local bus in Staten Island, and 11,107 passengers rode on the express bus. How many passengers rode on the two buses on Saturday? Explain how you know your answer is reasonable.

____

____

2 **STEM** The distance from the deepest point in the Marianas Trench to the surface of the Pacific Ocean is estimated to be 35,070 feet. The distance from Mount Everest, one of the highest mountain peaks, to sea level is estimated to be 29,029 feet. Imagine that Mount Everest was next to the Marianas Trench. What would the distance be from the top of the mountain to the deepest part of the trench?

____

Estimate. Then find the sum.

3 Estimate: __________

  8,214
+ 5,207

4 Estimate: __________

  295,657
+ 467,852

5 Estimate: __________

  12,548
+ 52,491

6 **Math on the Spot** What is the combined population of the three major Alaskan cities? Estimate to justify your answer.

Major Cities of Alaska	
City	**Population***
Anchorage	286,174
Fairbanks	35,252
Juneau	30,796

*2009 U.S. Census Bureau estimates

____

____

Test Prep

7 Which is the sum?

$$\begin{array}{r} 571{,}136 \\ 219{,}067 \\ +\ 16{,}995 \\ \hline \end{array}$$

(A) 588,131
(B) 790,203
(C) 807,198
(D) 951,198

8 Which unknown digit correctly completes the addition statement?

$$\begin{array}{r} 3\blacksquare 4{,}581 \\ +\ 149{,}906 \\ \hline 454{,}487 \end{array}$$

(A) 0
(B) 1
(C) 2
(D) 3

9 Find the sum. Then use an estimate to show your answer is reasonable.

$$\begin{array}{r} 741{,}852 \\ +\ 125{,}896 \\ \hline \end{array}$$

____

Spiral Review

10 Compare. Write <, >, or =.

27,394 ◯ 27,493

11 What is 3,980 rounded to the nearest thousand?

____

Name ___

LESSON 2.2
More Practice/ Homework

ONLINE
Video Tutorials and Interactive Examples

Subtract Whole Numbers and Assess Reasonableness

1 (MP) **Reason** A zoo had 11,287 visitors one weekend, and an aquarium had 5,159 visitors. How many more visitors did the zoo get than the aquarium? Use rounding as a strategy to show your answer is reasonable. Explain.

___

___

2 There are 85,740 seats in a sports stadium in New York. One year, 46,785 seats were sold to season ticket holders. How many seats were not sold to season ticket holders?

___

Estimate. Then find the difference.

3 Estimate: ___

834,924
− 358,172

4 Estimate: ___

38,207
− 28,278

5 Estimate: ___

7,496
− 6,028

6 **Math on the Spot** West Virginia has an area of 24,230 square miles. Texas has an area of 268,601 square miles. How much larger is Texas than West Virginia?

Read how Janice solved the problem. Find her error.

Texas: 268,601 sq mi
West Virginia: 24,230 sq mi

I can subtract to find the difference.

268,601
− 24,230
26,301

Solve the problem and correct her error.

___

___

Test Prep

7 Which is the difference?

$$\begin{array}{r} 460{,}025 \\ -\ 127{,}006 \\ \hline \end{array}$$

Ⓐ 33,302
Ⓑ 80,657
Ⓒ 333,019
Ⓓ 587,031

8 Which digit correctly completes the subtraction statement?

$$\begin{array}{r} 4\blacksquare5{,}692 \\ -250{,}017 \\ \hline 165{,}675 \end{array}$$

Ⓐ 0
Ⓑ 1
Ⓒ 2
Ⓓ 3

9 Find the difference. Then use an estimate to show your answer is reasonable.

630,741 − 236,907

____

____

Spiral Review

10 Order from least to greatest.

824,635; 842,635; 823,635

____

11 Regroup and rename the number.

8,400 = ______ hundreds

Name ______________________

Use Addition and Subtraction to Solve Comparison Problems

1 (MP) **Model with Mathematics** A school district has 9,352 students in elementary school and 4,794 students in middle school. How many more students are in elementary school than in middle school? Use a visual representation and an equation to model the problem. Then solve. ______________

2 **Math on the Spot** There were 574 hot air balloon pilots at a hot air balloon race. There were 1,465 more ground crew members than there were pilots. How many pilots and ground crew members were there?

____

3 In 1963, a conservation group estimated there were only 417 nesting pairs of bald eagles in the lower 48 states. After many years of conservation efforts, the group estimated there were 9,789 nesting pairs in 2007.

- According to the group's estimates, how many fewer nesting pairs were there in 1963 than in 2007?

  ____

- In 2007, the same group estimated that Minnesota had 1,312 pairs of eagles, Florida had 1,133 pairs, and Wisconsin had 1,065 pairs. How many pairs were found in the other states?

  ____

4 **Open Ended** Write and solve a comparison problem that matches the bar model.

8,501	
5,729	*n*

____

____

____

Test Prep

5 Select all the problems that could match this bar model.

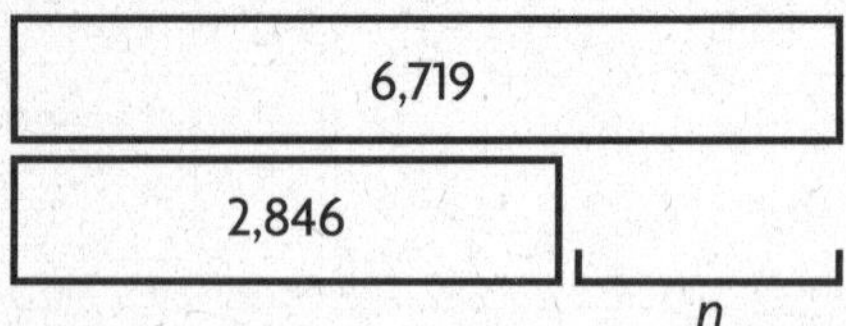

Ⓐ There are 6,719 people at a concert. Then 2,846 more people buy tickets. How many people are at the concert?

Ⓑ There are 6,719 visitors at the zoo who bought tickets for the day, and 2,846 who have season passes. How many more visitors bought tickets for the day than have season passes?

Ⓒ There are 2,846 cars in Lot A. There are 6,719 cars in Lot B. How many cars are in both lots?

Ⓓ There are 2,846 items for sale in the clothing department of a store. There are 6,719 items for sale in the electronics department of the store. How many more items are for sale in the electronics department than in the clothing department?

6 For the Friday night game, 3,782 tickets are sold. For the Saturday night game, 4,267 tickets are sold. How many fewer tickets are sold for the Friday night game than for the Saturday night game?

Write an equation to model the problem. Then solve.

____

__________ fewer tickets were sold for the Friday night game than for the Saturday night game.

Spiral Review

7 Compare. Write $<$, $>$, or $=$.

267,248 ◯ 276,248

8 What is 4,012 rounded to the nearest thousand?

____

Name ______________________________

ONLINE
Video Tutorials and Interactive Examples

Apply the Perimeter Formula for Rectangles

1 Gwen is starting a dog-walking business after school. The route she walks forms a rectangle. If the length of the route is 4 blocks and the width of the route is 3 blocks, what is the total distance of the route?

____

2 Jeffrey wants to put extra tape around the outer edge of his rectangular kite to make sure it does not rip. His kite is 1 meter wide and 2 meters long. How many meters of tape does Jeffrey need?

____

3 (MP) **Reason** The school wants to build a new trophy case. They know that the perimeter of the case will be 36 feet. They also know that the width can only be 3 feet. How would they find the length of their new trophy case?

____

____

4 **STEM** Energy can travel as electric currents through wiring made with conductive metals. If the electric company wants to install new wiring around the perimeter of a rectangular area that is 12 miles long and 8 miles wide, how many miles of wire does the electric company need?

____

5 Find the perimeter of a rectangle if the length is 10 yards and the width is 2 times as long as the length.

____

6 Find the perimeter of a rectangle if the width is 3 meters and the length is 3 times as long as the width.

____

Test Prep

7 Find the perimeter of a rectangle if the width is 4 feet and the length is 3 times as long as the width.

Ⓐ 14 feet
Ⓑ 22 feet
Ⓒ 32 feet
Ⓓ 48 feet

8 Joseph wants to string lights around the perimeter of the ceiling of his front porch. The ceiling is shaped like a rectangle. If the the ceiling of the porch is 9 meters long and 8 meters wide, how many meters of lights does he need?

Ⓐ 16 meters
Ⓑ 17 meters
Ⓒ 34 meters
Ⓓ 43 meters

9 Find the perimeter.

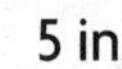

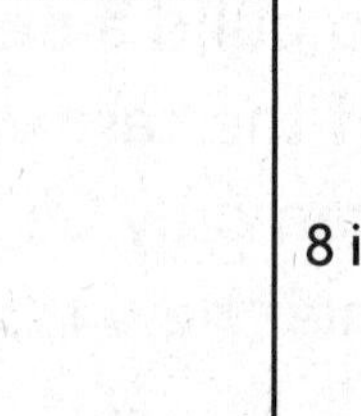

Ⓐ 40 inches
Ⓑ 26 inches
Ⓒ 22 inches
Ⓓ 13 inches

10 Find the perimeter of a rectangle if the width is 7 feet and the length is 4 feet longer than the width.

Ⓐ 22 feet
Ⓑ 28 feet
Ⓒ 36 feet
Ⓓ 77 feet

Spiral Review

Add or subtract.

11
$$\begin{array}{r} 268{,}401 \\ -\ \ 14{,}260 \\ \hline \end{array}$$

12
$$\begin{array}{r} 3{,}824 \\ +\ 9{,}452 \\ \hline \end{array}$$

13
$$\begin{array}{r} 28{,}489 \\ +\ 37{,}216 \\ \hline \end{array}$$

14
$$\begin{array}{r} 396{,}813 \\ -\ \ 45{,}015 \\ \hline \end{array}$$

Name ______________________

LESSON 3.1
More Practice/ Homework

ONLINE
Video Tutorials and Interactive Examples

Explore Multiplicative Comparisons

1 (MP) **Reason** Mikayla collects 4 silver coins in a video game. She collects 4 times as many gold coins as silver coins. How many gold coins does Mikayla collect? Draw a visual model to represent the problem.

Mikayla collects _____ gold coins.

2 (MP) **Use Tools** Ashley passes 6 rounds in a racing game. Danny passes 3 times as many rounds as Ashley. Complete the bar model to find how many rounds Danny passes.

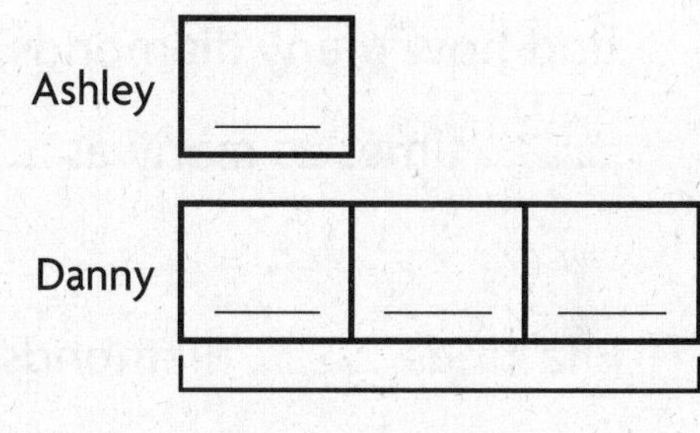

Danny passes _____ rounds.

(MP) **Model with Mathematics Write a multiplication equation to model the comparison.**

3 27 is 9 times as many as 3.

____

4 6 times as many as 7 is 42.

____

Interpret the multiplication equation as a comparison.

5 $32 = 4 \times 8$ ______________________

6 $5 \times 10 = 50$ ______________________

7 $63 = 7 \times 9$ ______________________

Test Prep

8 Anne has 2 pens. She has 5 times as many pencils as pens. Which visual model shows how many pencils Anne has?

Ⓐ

Ⓑ 

Ⓒ 

Ⓓ 

9 Brian finds 3 diamonds in a treasure game. Ella finds 4 times as many diamonds as Brian. Complete the bar model, comparison, and equation to find how many diamonds Ella finds.

_____ times as many as _____ is _____.

_____ × _____ = _____

Ella finds _____ diamonds.

10 How can you interpret the meaning of the equation $14 = 2 \times 7$ as a comparison? Select all the correct answers.

Ⓐ 14 is 2 more than 7.

Ⓑ 7 is 2 times as many as 14.

Ⓒ 14 is 2 times a many as 7.

Ⓓ 7 times as many as 2 is 14.

Ⓔ 14 is 2 fewer than 7.

Spiral Review

11 A pet store receives 4,592 cans of dog food and 8,246 cans of cat food. How many more cans of cat food than dog food does the store receive?

____

Name ______________________________

Distinguish Between Multiplicative and Additive Comparisons

1 Reese has 8 toy cars. Jena has 4 more cars than Reese. Nate has 4 times as many cars as Reese.

Draw a visual model to show how many cars Reese, Jena, and Nate each have.

2 Winnie has 6 feet of blue yarn and 5 times as many feet of yellow yarn as blue yarn. How many feet of yellow yarn does Winnie have?

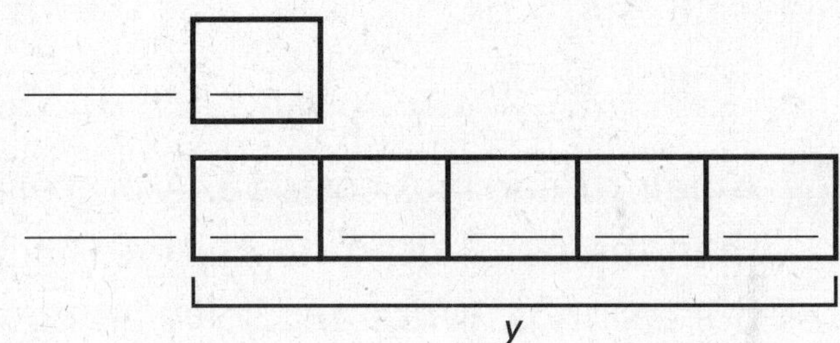

- Complete the bar model to show the problem.
- Write an equation to model the problem.

_____ × _____ = y

_____ = y

Winnie has _____ feet of yellow yarn.

3 Winnie has 5 more feet of red yarn than blue yarn. How many feet of red yarn does she have?

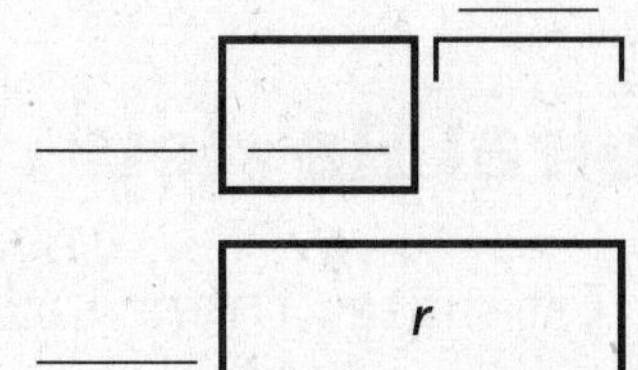

- Use the bar model to show the problem.
- Write an equation to model the problem.

_____ + _____ = r

_____ = r

Winnie has _____ feet of red yarn.

Test Prep

4 Jen has 3 cups of sand to make sand art. Shawn has 4 more cups of sand than Jen. Tavon has 4 times as many cups of sand as Jen. Which question is a multiplicative comparison problem?

(A) How many cups of sand does Shawn have?
(B) How many cups of sand does Jen have?
(C) How many cups of sand does Tavon have?
(D) How many more cups of sand does Shawn have than Jen?

5 Ian glues 4 buttons to decorate his picture. Kelsey glues 6 times as many buttons as Ian to decorate her picture. Which equation can be used to model the number of buttons Kelsey glues on her picture, *b*?

(A) $6 + 4 = b$
(B) $b \times 4 = 6$
(C) $b + 4 = 6$
(D) $6 \times 4 = b$

6 A pair of earrings costs \$8. A bracelet costs \$5 more than the earrings. A necklace costs 3 times as much as the earrings. Write and solve an equation to find how much a bracelet and a necklace each cost. Use *n* for the unknown in each equation.

Bracelet: ____________________

Necklace: ____________________

Spiral Review

7 Estimate. Then find the sum.

Estimate: ____________________

$$\begin{array}{r} 25{,}943 \\ +\ 28{,}302 \\ \hline \end{array}$$

8 Mr. Gordon is running for mayor in his town. He receives 37,024 votes. His opponent receives 9,202 fewer votes. How many votes does Mr. Gordon's opponent receive?

____

Name ______________________________

ONLINE
Video Tutorials and Interactive Examples

Use Division to Solve Multiplicative Comparison Problems

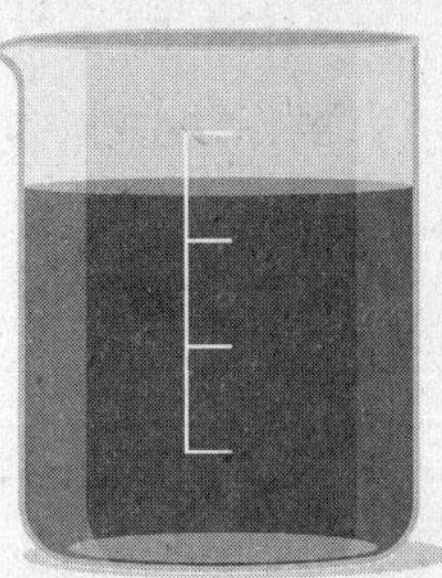

1 **STEM** The students in the science club are testing a chemical change, which is when two substances are mixed together to form something new. They use 12 cups of hot water. This is 4 times as much vinegar as they use. How many cups of vinegar do the students use?

- Complete the bar model to show the problem.
- Write an equation to model the problem. Use n for the unknown.

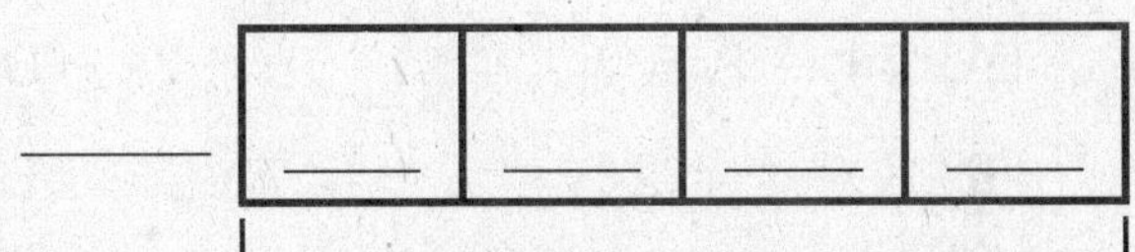

Problem: _____ times as many as n is _____.

Equation: _____ $\times n =$ _____

- Use the inverse operation to solve the problem.

_____ $\div$ _____ $= n$

_____ $= n$

The students use _____ cups of vinegar.

2 (MP) **Model with Mathematics** Todd has 35 soccer badges and 7 soccer banners. How many times as many badges as banners does Todd have?

Write multiplication and division equations to model and solve the problem. Use m for the unknown.

Todd has _____ times as many badges as banners.

Test Prep

3 This year, there are 30 students in the math club. That is 5 times as many as last year. How many students were in the math club last year?

Ⓐ 6
Ⓑ 7
Ⓒ 25
Ⓓ 35

4 Chris buys 24 strawberries and 8 kiwis. How many times as many strawberries as kiwis does Chris buy? Let t represent the unknown number. Select all the equations that model this problem.

Ⓐ $24 - 8 = t$
Ⓑ $8 + t = 24$
Ⓒ $24 \div t = 8$
Ⓓ $24 \div 8 = t$
Ⓔ $t \times 8 = 24$
Ⓕ $24 \times t = 8$

5 Tyrone has 16 model airplanes on his shelf. He has 4 times as many model airplanes as model trains. How many model trains does Tyrone have?

Write multiplication and division equations to model and solve the problem. Use m for the unknown.

____

____

Spiral Review

6 How many times as great is the value of the digit 3 in 143,600 than the value of the digit 3 in 25,300? How do you know?

____

____

____

7 Regroup and rename the numbers.

590 = ______ tens

2,700 = 27 ______

63,000 = 63 ______

480,000 = ______ ten thousands

Name ______________________________

ONLINE
Video Tutorials and Interactive Examples

Use Comparisons to Solve Problem Situations

1 (MP) **Use Tools** Henry buys bananas and oranges for a soup kitchen. He buys 10 pounds of bananas and twice as many pounds of oranges as bananas. How many pounds of oranges does Henry buy?

- Draw a bar model to represent the problem.

- Write an equation to model the problem.
  Let *n* represent the unknown number.

  ____ ◯ ____ = ____

- Find the value of *n* to make the equation true.

  ____

  Henry buys ____ pounds of oranges.

2 (MP) **Model with Mathematics** Dave and Sara deliver meals to people's homes. Dave delivers 13 meals and Sara delivers 5 meals. How many more meals does Dave deliver than Sara? Write an equation to model the problem. Let *m* represent the unknown number.

____ ◯ ____ = ____

Find the value of *m* that makes the equation true.

____

Dave delivers ____ more meals than Sara.

3 **Open Ended** Write a multiplicative comparison word problem where the unknown is how many times as many.

____

____

____

Test Prep

4 Jen uses 4 cups of raisins to make trail mix. She uses 6 times as many cups of granola as raisins. Which equation can be used to find how many cups of granola Jen puts in the trail mix, t?

Ⓐ $4 + 6 = t$

Ⓑ $4 \times t = 6$

Ⓒ $6 \times 4 = t$

Ⓓ $t - 6 = 4$

5 Ronnie bakes 3 more lemon tarts than raspberry tarts. He bakes 9 lemon tarts. Write an equation to find how many raspberry tarts Ronnie bakes. Use r for the unknown.

____

6 The visual model shows the number of stamps Andrea and Jose have.

Andrea □□□□□

Jose □□□□□□□□□□□□□□□

How many times as many stamps does Jose have as Andrea? Write an equation to model the problem. Use n for the unknown.

____

Spiral Review

7 Write the number shown in the place-value chart in expanded form.

MILLIONS			THOUSANDS			ONES		
Hundreds	Tens	Ones	Hundreds	Tens	Ones	Hundreds	Tens	Ones
				6	0,	5	8	4

____

Name ______________________________

LESSON 3.5
More Practice/
Homework

ONLINE
Video Tutorials and Interactive Examples

Solve Multistep Problems with Multiplication and Division

1 (MP) **Use Tools** Simone buys a shirt and hat. The hat costs \$6. The shirt costs 5 times as much as the hat. How much more does the shirt cost than the hat?

Break up the problem into smaller steps. Use a bar model and equation to complete each step.

- Find how much the shirt costs, *s*.

  ____ × ____ = *s*

  ____ = *s*

  The shirt costs ____.

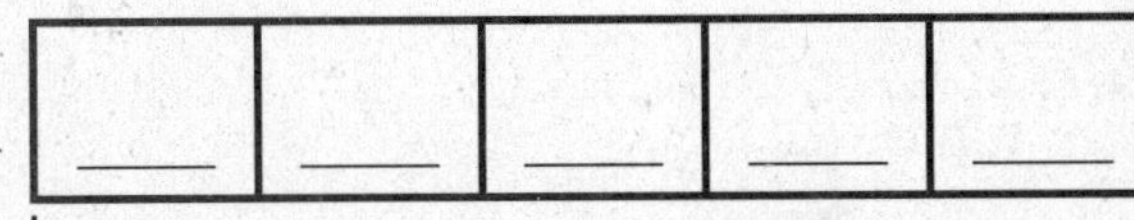

s

- Find how much more the shirt costs than the hat, *m*.

  ____ + *m* = ____

  m = ____

  The shirt costs ____ more.

m

2 (MP) **Model with Mathematics** This year, 63 students ran the 5K race. That is 7 times as many as ran last year. How many students ran the 5K in the last two years?

Write equations to model and solve the problem.

Let *s* = the number of students last year.

Let *b* = the number of students the last two years.

____

____

____

Test Prep

3 Lisa sees 10 birds during a birdwatching trip. Cheyanne sees 6 times as many birds as Lisa. How many birds do Lisa and Cheyanne see?

Ⓐ 16 Ⓑ 60 Ⓒ 66 Ⓓ 70

4 Ivana makes 40 muffins. That is 4 times as many muffins as Hayden makes. How many muffins do Ivana and Hayden make? Write equations to model and solve the problem. Use letters for the unknowns.

____

____

____

5 Jon cycles 28 miles on Saturday. That is is 4 times as many miles as he cycles on Sunday. How much farther does Jon cycle on Saturday than on Sunday?

Ⓐ 7 miles Ⓑ 14 miles Ⓒ 21 miles Ⓓ 24 miles

6 Tingyi swims 25 backstroke laps. She swims 10 more freestyle laps than backstroke. She swims 5 times as many freestyle laps as butterfly. How many laps of butterfly does Tingyi swim?

Ⓐ 10 Ⓑ 7 Ⓒ 5 Ⓓ 3

Spiral Review

7 Estimate. Then find the sum.

Estimate: ______________

$$\begin{array}{r} 513{,}567 \\ +362{,}249 \\ \hline \end{array}$$

8 Round to the place value of the underlined digit.

5<u>1</u>7,264 __________

23<u>8</u>,155 __________

Name ______________________

Explore Multiplication Patterns with Tens, Hundreds, and Thousands

1 MP **Use Structure** There are 6,000 people at a soccer game. Each game ticket costs $5. What is the amount of the ticket sales? Complete the patterns to solve.

5 × 6 ones = __________ ones   5 × 6 = __________

5 × 6 tens = __________ tens   5 × 60 = __________

5 × 6 hundreds = __________ hundreds   5 × 600 = __________

5 × 6 thousands = __________ thousands   5 × 6,000 = __________

The ticket sales are __________.

2 A store has 2,000 boxes of frozen yogurt bars for sale. Each box contains 4 bars. How many yogurt bars are for sale?

4 × 2 = __________

4 × 20 = __________

4 × 200 = __________

4 × 2,000 = __________

__________ yogurt bars are for sale.

3 A truck is carrying 3,000 boxes. Each box weighs 6 pounds and contains a laptop and power cord. What is the weight of all the boxes?

6 × 3 = __________

6 × 30 = __________

6 × 300 = __________

6 × 3,000 = __________

All the boxes weigh __________ pounds.

4 Susanna makes bead necklaces for 9 of her friends. She uses 200 beads for each necklace. How many beads does she use for the 9 necklaces? Show your work.

____

____

Test Prep

5 Select all of the equations that have a product of 2,400.

Ⓐ $8 \times 300 = ■$

Ⓑ $3 \times 800 = ■$

Ⓒ $2 \times 1{,}000 = ■$

Ⓓ $6 \times 4{,}000 = ■$

Ⓔ $6 \times 400 = ■$

Ⓕ $3{,}000 \times 8 = ■$

6 A train can carry 9,000 passengers each day. How many passengers can the train carry in 7 days?

Ⓐ 3,600

Ⓑ 6,300

Ⓒ 36,000

Ⓓ 63,000

7 Draw lines to match each multiplication problem with its product.

2×2 •	• 4,000
2×200 •	• 4
$2 \times 2{,}000$ •	• 400
2×20 •	• 40

8 What is the product of 6 and 900?

____

Spiral Review

9 Write the number in expanded form.

35,842

____

10 Estimate. Then find the difference.

Estimate: ____________

$$\begin{array}{r} 598{,}876 \\ -\ 112{,}543 \\ \hline \end{array}$$

Name ______________________

ONLINE
Ed Video Tutorials and Interactive Examples

Explore Division Patterns with Tens, Hundreds, and Thousands

1 (MP) **Use Structure** Brian makes 2,400 grams of trail mix. He puts an equal amount of trail mix into 4 containers. How many grams of trail mix are in each container? Complete the patterns to solve.

24 ones ÷ 4 = ________ ones

24 tens ÷ 4 = ________ tens

24 hundreds ÷ 4 = ________ hundreds

24 ÷ 4 = ________

240 ÷ 4 = ________

2,400 ÷ 4 = ________

________ grams of trail mix are in each container.

2 A theater has 2,700 seats in 9 sections. Each section has the same number of seats. How many seats are in each section?

27 ÷ 9 = ________

270 ÷ 9 = ________

2,700 ÷ 9 = ________

________ seats are in each section.

3 Jim earns $2,000 for working 4 weeks. He earns the same amount each week. How much does Jim earn each week?

20 ÷ 4 = ________

200 ÷ 4 = ________

2,000 ÷ 4 = ________

Jim earns ________ each week.

4 Natalie has 480 star stickers. She gives the same number of star stickers to 8 players on her soccer team. How many star stickers does each player get?

____

5 **Math on the Spot** Chip collected 1,730 dimes. Sue collected 1,870 dimes. They divided all their dimes into 6 equal stacks. How many dimes are in each stack?

____

____

Test Prep

6 Manuel wrote 3,500 ÷ 7 = 50. Which best describes his answer?

Ⓐ Manuel divided correctly.

Ⓑ Manuel should have written 3,500 ÷ 7 = 5 because 35 hundreds ÷ 7 = 5 ones.

Ⓒ Manuel should have written 3,500 ÷ 7 = 500 because 35 hundreds ÷ 7 = 5 hundreds.

Ⓓ Manuel should have written 3,500 ÷ 7 = 5,000 because 35 hundreds ÷ 7 = 5 thousands.

7 Draw lines to match each division problem with its quotient.

3,000 ÷ 3 •	• 90
8,100 ÷ 9 •	• 1,000
810 ÷ 9 •	• 100
81 ÷ 9 •	• 9
300 ÷ 3 •	• 900

8 Write a number to make each equation true.

4,800 ÷ ☐ = 600 480 ÷ 6 = ☐

4,000 ÷ 8 = ☐ 5,000 ÷ ☐ = 1,000

9 What is the quotient of 2,400 divided by 3?

____

Spiral Review

10 Compare. Write <, >, or =.

342,910 ◯ 324,901

11 Round to the place value of the underlined digit.

4<u>6</u>2,349 __________

Name ______________________________

Estimate Products by 1-Digit Numbers

1 Kai runs for 7 days in a row for 22 minutes each day. About how many minutes does she run in those 7 days?

____

2 A carnival has 9 rides. Each ride can carry 792 people each day. The carnival manager says that 5,818 people can ride each day. Is this reasonable? Explain why or why not.

____

____

3 Mr. Appleton has 6 science classes, and each class has 32 students. He wants to give an insect sticker to each student in his class. He has 175 stickers. Does Mr. Appleton have enough stickers? Use estimation to justify your answer.

____

____

____

Use rounding to estimate the product.

4 4×284

____

5 $8 \times 3,469$

____

Find two estimates that the product is between.

6 6×72

The product is between ________ and ________.

7 $5 \times 4,691$

The product is between ________ and ________.

Test Prep

8 A gymnastics coach buys 3 new exercise mats. Each mat costs \$483. Which of the following best estimates the total cost of all the new mats?

Ⓐ It is between \$400 and \$500.
Ⓑ It is between \$900 and \$1,200.
Ⓒ It is between \$1,200 and \$1,500.
Ⓓ It is between \$1,500 and \$1,800.

9 Select the two problems that could be used to estimate the product 7 × 362.

Ⓐ 7 × 300
Ⓑ 7 × 30
Ⓒ 7 × 3,000
Ⓓ 7 × 40
Ⓔ 7 × 4,000
Ⓕ 7 × 400

10 A truck carries 6 crates. Each crate has 2,360 boxes of cereal. Which is the best estimate for the number of boxes of cereal the truck carries?

Ⓐ about 6,000
Ⓑ about 12,000
Ⓒ about 18,000
Ⓓ about 24,000

Spiral Review

11 On Monday, stadium cashiers sold 4,237 tickets to a baseball game. By Tuesday night, they had sold a total of 6,158 tickets. How many tickets did they sell on Tuesday?

____

12 Oliver read 36 pages in his book Sunday night. That is 4 times as many pages as he read on Monday night. How many pages did he read on Monday night?

____

Name ______________________________

LESSON 4.4
More Practice/
Homework

ONLINE
Video Tutorials and
Interactive Examples

Estimate Quotients Using Compatible Numbers

1 Mr. Howard buys 656 apples for his summer camp. There are 8 cabins of campers. He says that he can give each cabin 82 apples. Is this reasonable? Explain why or why not.

____

____

____

2 **Financial Literacy** Mr. Howard plans his budget for snacks at his summer camp. He can spend $4,450 for 7 days of camp. He says he can spend $825 each day on snacks. Is this reasonable? Use estimation to justify your answer.

____

____

____

Use compatible numbers to estimate the quotient.

3 459 ÷ 9

______

4 1,506 ÷ 3

______

5 5,465 ÷ 7

______

6 3,762 ÷ 6

______

Find two estimates that the quotient is between.

7 2,108 ÷ 4

The quotient is between

______ and ______.

8 5,316 ÷ 6

The quotient is between

______ and ______.

Test Prep

9 Paulina plants 328 flower bulbs in a garden. She plants the bulbs in 8 rows. Which is the best estimate for the number of bulbs Paulina plants in each row?

Ⓐ about 20
Ⓑ about 40
Ⓒ about 60
Ⓓ about 80

10 Imani has 5,562 baseball cards to put into 9 binders. Which of the following best estimates the number of cards she can put in each binder?

Ⓐ It is between 60 and 70.
Ⓑ It is between 500 and 600.
Ⓒ It is between 600 and 700.
Ⓓ It is between 5,000 and 6,000.

11 Draw a line to match each division problem with the best way to use compatible numbers to estimate the quotient.

4,308 ÷ 6 •	• 3,600 ÷ 6
3,846 ÷ 6 •	• 5,400 ÷ 6
4,792 ÷ 6 •	• 4,200 ÷ 6
5,284 ÷ 6 •	• 4,800 ÷ 6

Spiral Review

12 Joelly has 8 feet of pink string and 3 times as many feet of purple string. Write an equation to find *f*, how many feet of purple string Joelly has. Then find the value that makes the equation true.

____

____

13 A pair of dress pants costs $60. That is 3 times as much as a pair of sweatpants. How much do the sweatpants cost? Write multiplication and division equations to model and solve the problem. Use *s* for the unknown.

____

____

Name ______________________

ONLINE
Video Tutorials and
Interactive Examples

Use Mental Math Strategies for Multiplication and Division

Use mental math to find the product or the quotient. Tell what strategy you used.

1 Chrystal helps her grandmother plant seeds in the garden. They plant squash, corn, sunflower, and tomato seeds. They plant 6 rows of each type of seed, and they plant 20 seeds in each row. How many seeds do they plant?

Find $4 \times 6 \times 20$.

____

2 Hunter and Grace pick 5,400 grams of walnuts. They put the same amount of walnuts in 6 baskets. How many grams of walnuts are in each basket?

Find $5{,}400 \div 6$.

____

Use mental math to find the product or the quotient. Tell which strategy you used.

3 5×24

____

4 $2{,}400 \div 8$

____

5 $369 \div 9$

____

6 $80 \times 4 \times 3$

____

Test Prep

7 Lonnie has 3 sticker books. Each book has 7 pages, and there are 10 stickers on each page. How many stickers does Lonnie have altogether?

Ⓐ 73 Ⓒ 213

Ⓑ 210 Ⓓ 703

8 Select all the ways you can use mental math to find the quotient.

$3{,}200 \div 4$

Ⓐ Think: $4 \times 8 = 32$, so $4 \times 80 = 3{,}200$.

Ⓑ Think: 32 hundreds $\div$ 4 = 8 hundreds

Ⓒ Think: $32 \div 4 = 8$, so $3{,}200 \div 4 = 8{,}000$.

Ⓓ Think: What times 4 equals 3,200?

Ⓔ Think: 32 thousands $\div$ 4 = 8 thousands.

9 Use the numbers to show a true equation that finds the quotient.

$636 \div 6 = ■$

3	6	6	30	36	106	136	600

(____ $\div$ ____) + (____ $\div$ ____) = ____

Spiral Review

10 Nina works 15 hours at the store this week. That is 5 times as many hours as she worked last week. How many hours did Nina work at the store last week?

____

11 A stadium holds 2,000 people. Tickets to a football game at the stadium cost \$4. If all of the tickets are sold, how much money will be made selling tickets?

____

Name ______________________________

Represent Multiplication

1 (MP) **Reason** Jeremy burns 65 calories each mile he walks. How can you use base-ten blocks to show how many calories he burns by walking 4 miles?

____

2 There are 480 sheets of paper in a short ream. How can you use base-ten blocks to show the number of sheets in 2 short reams?

____

Use base-ten blocks to show the product. Draw a quick picture to show your work.

3 2×426

4 3×67

Write the multiplication equation represented by the base-ten blocks.

5

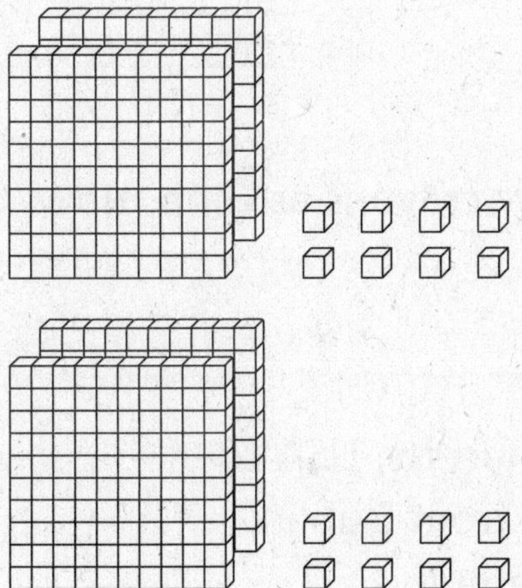

____

6

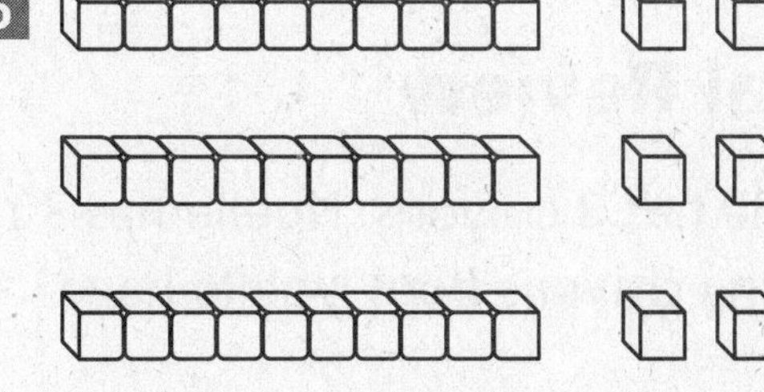

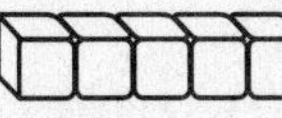

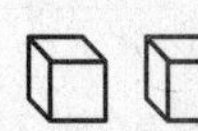

____

Test Prep

7 Which shows 2 × 16?

(A)

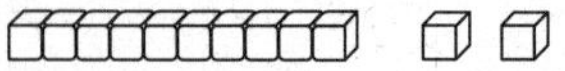

(B)

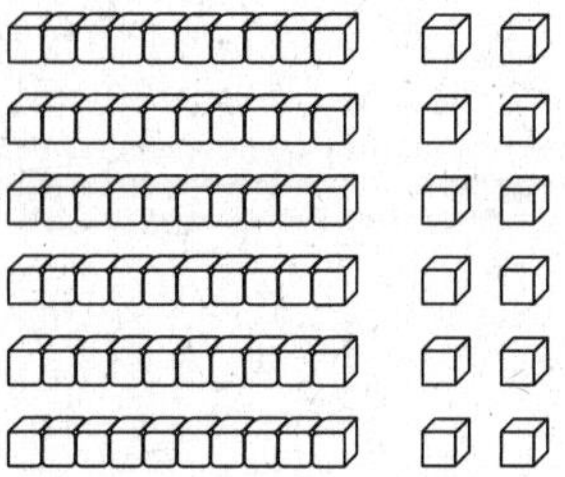

(C)

(D)

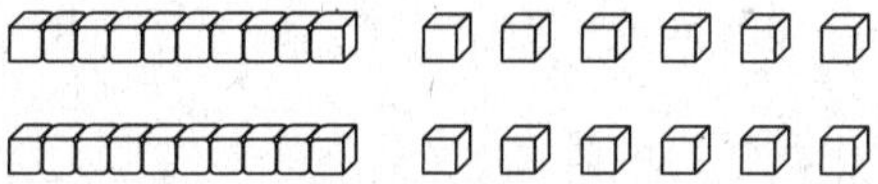

8 Which shows the product 84? Select all that apply.

(A) 3 × 21

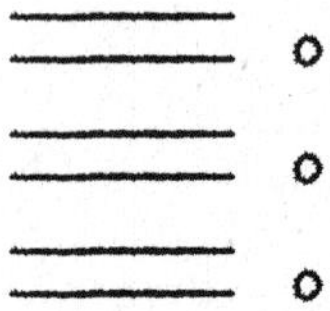

(B) 21 × 4

(C) 2 × 42

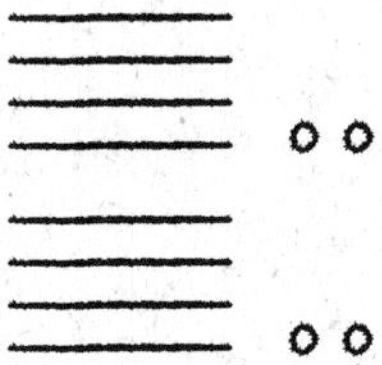

(D)

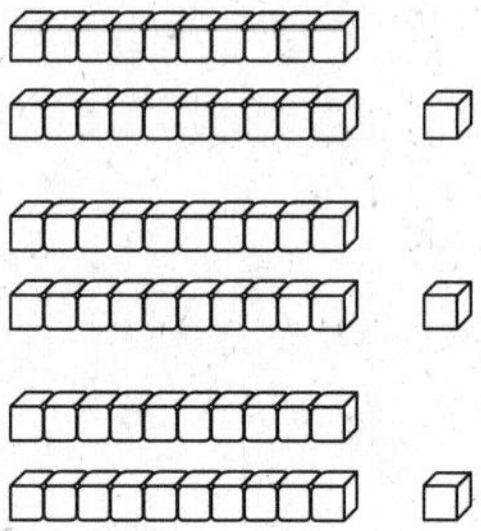

(E)

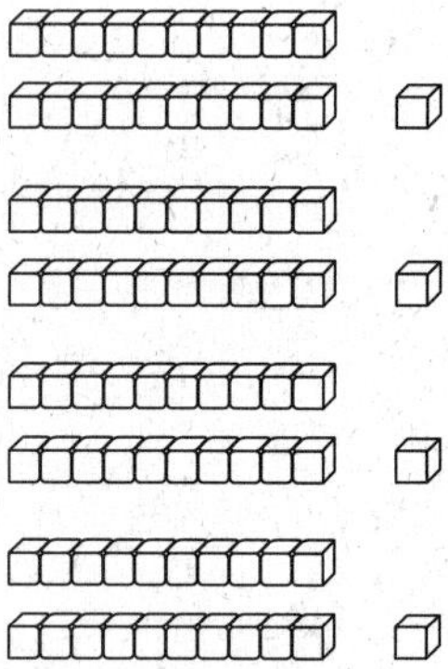

(F)

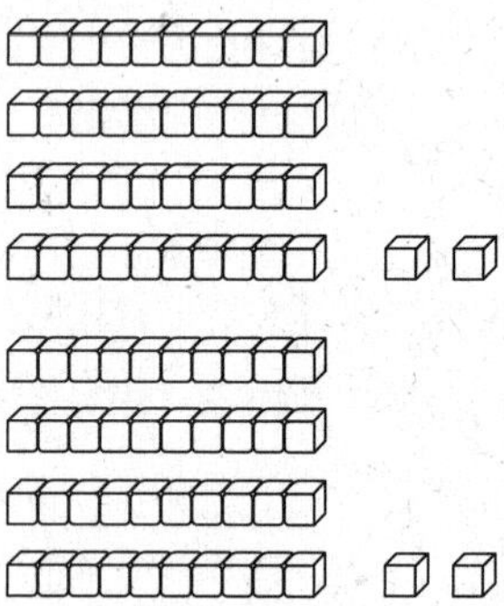

Spiral Review

9 Gina has 8 crayons. Noelle has 3 times as many crayons as Gina. How many crayons does Noelle have?

____

10 A plane flies 2,993 miles from Boston, Massachusetts, USA to Dublin, Ireland. Then the plane flies 901 miles from Dublin, Ireland to Madrid, Spain. How far does the plane fly?

____

Test Prep

8 Which is shown with the base-ten blocks?

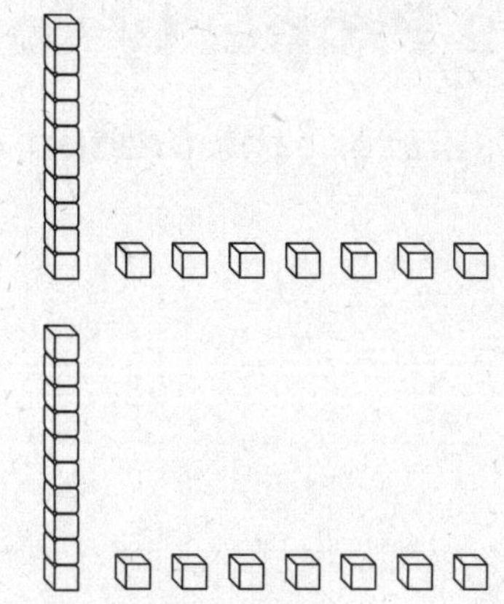

Ⓐ 2 × 17

Ⓑ 1 × 17

Ⓒ 1 × 34

Ⓓ 2 + 17

9 Which shows an area model for 3 × 16? Select all that apply.

Ⓐ 6 | 10, side 3

Ⓑ 10 | 6, side 3

Ⓒ 10 | 3, side 6

Ⓓ 10 | 9, side 3

10 Find the product.

18 × 6 = ______

Spiral Review

11 Find the sum.

$$\begin{array}{r} 319{,}587 \\ +\ 167{,}259 \\ \hline \end{array}$$

12 Order 314,899, 341,998, and 314,989 from least to greatest.

____

Name ______________________

LESSON 5.2
More Practice/ Homework

ONLINE
Ed
Video Tutorials
Interactive Exa

Use Area Models and the Distributive Property to Multiply

1 How can you represent the product on the grid?

7 × 18 = _____

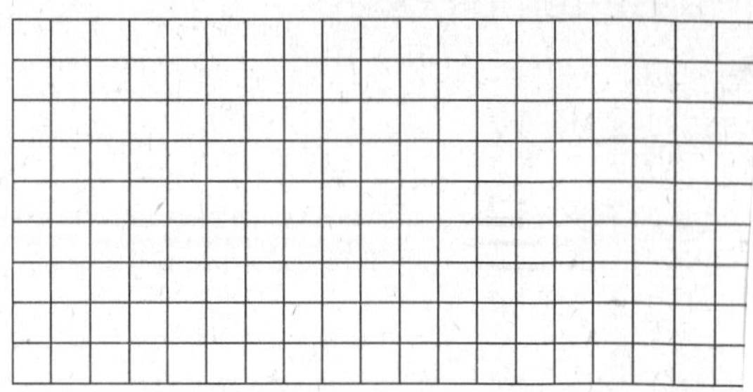

____

____

____

____

____

Draw an area model to represent the product. Record the product.

2 4 × 13 = _____

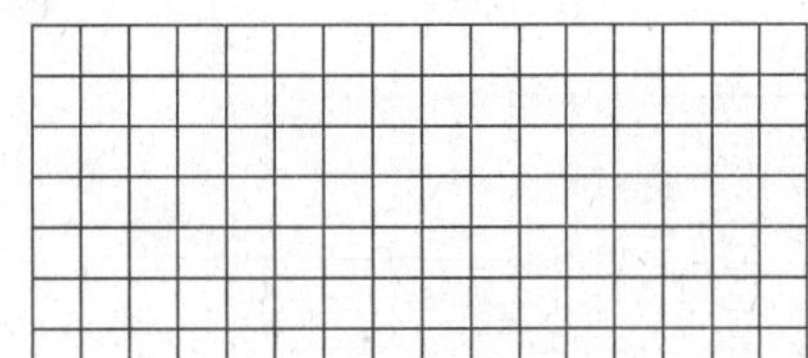

3 5 × 14 = _____

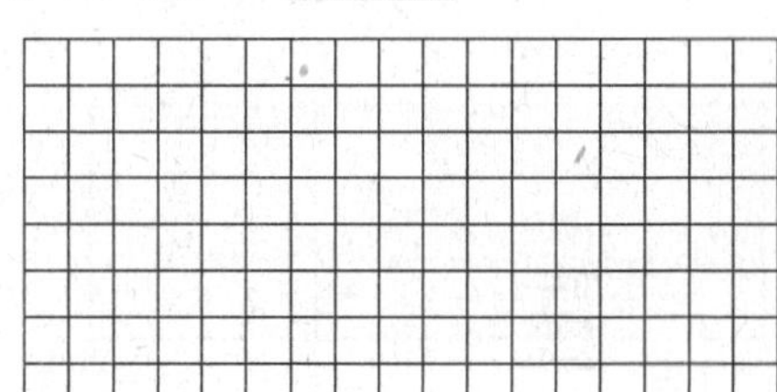

4 6 × 16 = _____

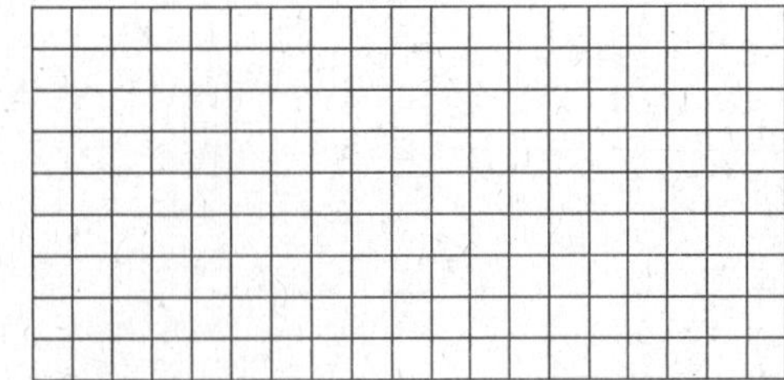

5 2 × 15 = _____

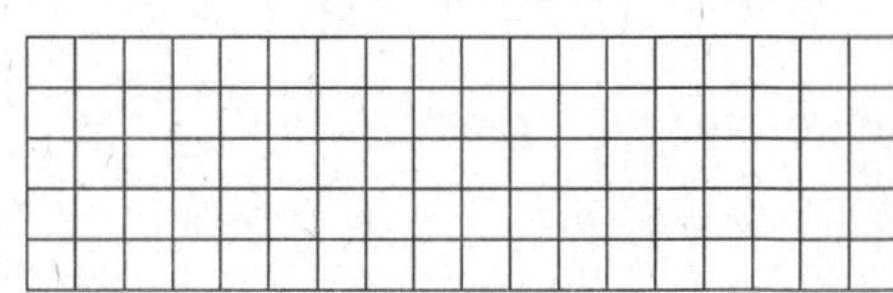

Find the product.

6 7 × 17 = _____

7 3 × 14 = _____

Name ______________________________

ONLINE
Ed
Video Tutorials and
Interactive Examples

Multiply Using Expanded Form

1 Marty has 6 bottles of water. Each bottle has 128 ounces in it. How many ounces of water does Marty have?

____

2 MP **Reason** Jefferson Elementary School has 379 students and 37 staff members who are going on a field trip. If they have 6 buses that each seat 65, will they have enough room for all the students and staff? Explain.

____

____

3 **Open Ended** Use the digits 3, 4, 8, and 9 to write a 3-digit by 1-digit multiplication problem. Then find the product.

____

____

4 Micah multiplies 8 × 267 and gets the following partial products: 16 + 48 + 56. What could you tell Micah about his work? Find the product 8 × 267.

____

____

____

Find the product.

5 8 × 780 = __________

6 8 × 137 = __________

7 5 × 102 = __________

8 5 × 226 = __________

9 7 × 716 = __________

10 9 × 321 = __________

Test Prep

11 Which shows finding 4 × 657 using expanded form and the Distributive Property?

Ⓐ (4 × 6) + (4 × 5) + (4 × 7)
Ⓑ (4 × 60) + (4 × 50) + (4 × 70)
Ⓒ (4 × 600) + (4 × 50) + (4 × 7)
Ⓓ (4 × 600) + (4 × 500) + (4 × 700)

12 Jerry's Bakery makes 144 muffins daily. How many muffins do they make in 7 days?

Ⓐ 108
Ⓑ 1,008
Ⓒ 1,080
Ⓓ 1,800

13 Five computers each have 128 gigabytes of storage. How many gigabytes do they have? Use expanded form to help you find the product. Show your work.

____

____

14 What is 7 × 842?

Ⓐ 598
Ⓑ 5,489
Ⓒ 5,844
Ⓓ 5,894

Spiral Review

15 Estimate. Then find the difference.

Estimate: __________

  697,103
−194,136

16 At the zoo, there were 82,725 guests in the summer, 62,286 guests in the fall, and 15,296 guests in the winter. How many fewer guests were there in the winter than in the summer?

____

Name ______________________________

LESSON 5.4
More Practice/ Homework

ONLINE
Video Tutorials and Interactive Examples

Multiply Using Partial Products

1 While at the beach, Amanda takes 48 photos of waves. She takes 5 times as many photos of shells. How many photos of shells does she take?

____

Estimate. Then use partial products to find the product.

2 Estimate: __________

$$\begin{array}{r} 72 \\ \times\ 4 \\ \hline \end{array}$$

3 Estimate: __________

$$\begin{array}{r} 2{,}519 \\ \times\ \ \ \ 3 \\ \hline \end{array}$$

4 Estimate: __________

$$\begin{array}{r} 368 \\ \times\ \ 9 \\ \hline \end{array}$$

Estimate. Then rewrite the problem and use partial products to find the product.

5 Estimate: __________

6×76

6 Estimate: __________

8×435

7 Estimate: __________

$4 \times 3{,}129$

8 **Math on the Spot** The sum of a 3-digit number and a 1-digit number is 138. The product of the numbers is 536. If one number is between 130 and 150, what are the numbers?

____

Test Prep

9 Which are partial products for 8 × 362? Select all that apply.

Ⓐ 3,200
Ⓑ 2,400
Ⓒ 480
Ⓓ 240
Ⓔ 42
Ⓕ 16

10 Which is the product 4 × 2,159?

Ⓐ 8,456
Ⓑ 8,636
Ⓒ 8,960
Ⓓ 12,236

11 Kennedy uses partial products to find a product. Which statement best describes her error?

$$\begin{array}{r} 847 \\ \times \quad 3 \\ \hline 2{,}400 \\ 1{,}200 \\ + \quad 21 \\ \hline 3{,}621 \end{array}$$

Ⓐ Kennedy writes the incorrect partial product for 3 × 800.
Ⓑ Kennedy writes the incorrect partial product for 3 × 7.
Ⓒ Kennedy writes the incorrect partial product for 3 × 40.
Ⓓ Kennedy adds the partial products incorrectly.

12 What is 9 × 92? __________

Spiral Review

13 Find the product.

6 × 8,000 = __________

14 Estimate the product.

4 × 976

____

Name ______________________________

LESSON 5.5
More Practice/
Homework

ONLINE
Video Tutorials and
Interactive Examples

Use Place Value to Multiply 2-Digit Numbers

1 A maple tree is 62 feet tall. Michael reads about a coastal redwood tree that is 5 times as tall as the maple tree. How tall is the redwood tree?

____

Estimate. Then find the product.

2 Estimate: __________

$$\begin{array}{r} 51 \\ \times\ 8 \\ \hline \end{array}$$

3 Estimate: __________

$$\begin{array}{r} 27 \\ \times\ 9 \\ \hline \end{array}$$

4 Estimate: __________

$$\begin{array}{r} 54 \\ \times\ 7 \\ \hline \end{array}$$

Estimate. Write the problem vertically to solve.

5 Estimate: __________

3×98

6 Estimate: __________

4×32

7 Estimate: __________

6×79

8 (MP) **Reason** Olivia practices piano for 45 minutes Monday though Thursday. Ben practices cello for 35 minutes Monday through Friday. Who practices playing their instrument for more minutes? Explain your thinking.

____

____

____

9 **Math on the Spot** The sum of two numbers is 31. The product of the two numbers is 150. What are the numbers? __________

Test Prep

10 In which problems do you regroup ones as tens? Select all that apply.

Ⓐ 2×48

Ⓑ 4×54

Ⓒ 3×23

Ⓓ 2×34

Ⓔ 3×65

11 Which is the product 7×43?

Ⓐ 281 Ⓑ 292 Ⓒ 301 Ⓓ 2,821

12 What is the product 6×87?

____

13 Kaedon thinks he made a mistake solving the problem.

$$\begin{array}{r} {}^{3} \\ 78 \\ \times \ \ 4 \\ \hline 282 \end{array}$$

Which statement best describes Kaedon's mistake?

Ⓐ Kaedon did not regroup the ones as 3 tens 2 ones.

Ⓑ Kaedon did not add the 3 regrouped tens.

Ⓒ Kaedon did not multiply the tens.

Ⓓ Kaedon did not record the 3 regrouped tens.

Spiral Review

14 Estimate. Then find the difference.

Estimate: ______________

$$\begin{array}{r} 518{,}112 \\ -\ 295{,}763 \\ \hline \end{array}$$

15 Regroup and rename the number.

580,000 = 58 ______________

Name ______________________

LESSON 5.6
More Practice/ Homework

ONLINE
Ed
Video Tutorials and Interactive Examples

Multiply 3-Digit and 4-Digit Numbers

Solve. Show your work.

1 A square city block has a side length of 563 yards. What is the perimeter of the block?

____

Estimate. Then find the product.

2 Estimate: __________

$$\begin{array}{r} 923 \\ \times \quad 2 \\ \hline \end{array}$$

3 Estimate: __________

$$\begin{array}{r} 923 \\ \times \quad 4 \\ \hline \end{array}$$

4 Estimate: __________

$$\begin{array}{r} 5{,}715 \\ \times \quad 7 \\ \hline \end{array}$$

5 A landscaper uses 764 gallons of water each week for a local park. Estimate the amount of water the landscaper will use in 4 weeks. Then find the amount of water used. Show your work.

____

____

Estimate. Then write the problem vertically and find the product.

6 Estimate: __________

3 × 754

7 Estimate: __________

5 × 6,821

8 Estimate: __________

9 × 4,932

9 **STEM** It takes Jupiter approximately 4,330 Earth days to revolve around the sun one time. How many Earth days does it take Jupiter to revolve around the sun 5 times? Show your work.

____

Test Prep

10 What is the product of 7 and 132?

Ⓐ 700 Ⓑ 724 Ⓒ 914 Ⓓ 924

11 Mailee brings 4 gallons of lemonade to a picnic. One gallon contains 128 fluid ounces. How many fluid ounces are in 4 gallons?

Ⓐ 32 fluid ounces
Ⓑ 132 fluid ounces
Ⓒ 256 fluid ounces
Ⓓ 512 fluid ounces

12 David's school has 1,358 students. Sophia's school has 3 times as many students as David's has. How many students are in Sophia's school?

Ⓐ 512
Ⓑ 1,361
Ⓒ 2,716
Ⓓ 4,074

13 Which is the product 9×912?

Ⓐ 2,808 Ⓒ 8,208
Ⓑ 8,028 Ⓓ 8,802

Spiral Review

14 A bookstore orders 3,000 new books. The store orders the books in sets of 10. How many sets of 10 does the store order?

____

15 Find the product.

$6 \times 353 =$ _______

Name ______________________

LESSON 5.7
More Practice/ Homework

ONLINE
Video Tutorials and Interactive Examples

Use Equations to Solve Multistep Problems

1 (MP) **Model with Mathematics** Kito saved \$18 over the summer. Nia saved three times that amount. How much money did they save? Show your work.

____

Use the order of operations to find the value of *n*.

2 $34 + 12 \times 3 = n$

3 $8 \times 7 - 4 \times 6 = n$

4 $5 \times 15 + 42 - 8 = n$

5 $610 - 9 \times 12 + 7 \times 3 = n$

6 The Brown family is driving to Junction City, which is 426 miles away. The family drives 60 miles for each of the first 3 hours. Then they drive 55 miles for each of the next 4 hours. How far are they from Junction City after driving 7 hours? Show your work.

____

____

____

Test Prep

7 A softball league has 17 teams. Eight of the teams have 12 players each. The rest of the teams have 13 players each. How many players are in the league?

Ⓐ 29
Ⓑ 170
Ⓒ 213
Ⓓ 270

8 Sean and Rick go to a garden to pick tomatoes. Sean fills 8 boxes with tomatoes. He puts 14 tomatoes in each box. Rick picks 4 times as many tomatoes as Sean picks. How many tomatoes do they pick?

Ⓐ 46
Ⓑ 112
Ⓒ 448
Ⓓ 560

9 Which shows the value of n?

$70 \times 2 - 5 \times 9 - 10 = n$

Ⓐ 85
Ⓑ 88
Ⓒ 92
Ⓓ 95

10 Which shows the value of n?

$342 - 30 + 7 \times 38 = n$

Ⓐ 556
Ⓑ 578
Ⓒ 580
Ⓓ 785

Spiral Review

11 Mrs. Stevens orders 215 packs of notebooks for the new school year. There are 9 notebooks in each pack. How many notebooks does she order?

____

12 Find the product.

$3 \times 11 =$ ____________

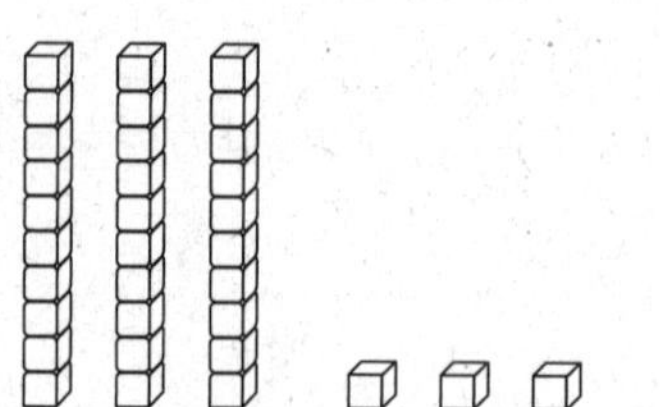

Name ____________________

ONLINE

Video Tutorials and Interactive Examples

Represent Division

1 **Health and Fitness** Our bodies use protein to build and repair cells. For this reason, nutritionists recommend that people aged 9–13 get at least 36 grams of protein each day. To reach that goal, how much protein should a person eat at each of 3 meals? Draw a visual model to represent 36 ÷ 3. Then solve.

2 (MP) **Model with Mathematics** Mr. Jay divides 66 students into 6 equal teams for a tug-of-war competition. He draws this quick picture to represent how many students are on each team. Write a division equation to model the problem. Then solve.

3 (MP) **Use Tools** There are 28 people participating in a boat race. Each boat has 2 people on it. How many boats are in the race? Draw a visual model and write an equation to model the problem. Then solve.

4 **STEM** The speed of an object is determined by the distance it travels in a unit of time. A robot moves a distance of 84 feet in 4 minutes. What is the robot's speed in feet per minute? Draw a visual model to represent 84 ÷ 4. Then solve the problem.

Test Prep

5 There are 77 fluid ounces of juice left over from a party. How many 7-fluid-ounce containers does Maria need to store the juice?

Ⓐ 14 Ⓒ 11

Ⓑ 12 Ⓓ 8

6 Which division equation models the problem that this quick picture represents?

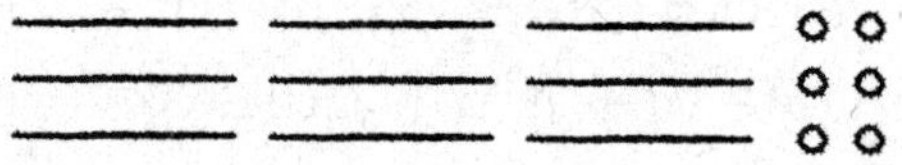

Ⓐ $96 \div 3 = 32$

Ⓑ $48 \div 3 = 16$

Ⓒ $63 \div 3 = 21$

Ⓓ $72 \div 3 = 24$

7 Malia has 72 pictures to place in her photo album. She places 6 pictures on each page. How many pages does she use?

Ⓐ 7

Ⓑ 8

Ⓒ 12

Ⓓ 14

Spiral Review

8 A farmer uses 50-pound bags of feed for her cows. What is the weight of 7 bags of feed?

$7 \times 50 = ■$

____

____

9 At a boat dock, 6 identical boats are lined up. The total weight of the boats is 6,000 pounds, How much does each boat weigh?

$6{,}000 \div 6 = ■$

____

____

Name ______________________________

ONLINE
Video Tutorials and
Interactive Examples

Investigate Remainders

(MP) **Attend to Precision Use the space at the right to draw a visual model to represent the problem. Then solve.**

1 Camille has 26 pieces of ribbon for making cards. She needs 4 pieces of ribbon for each card. How many cards can Camille make? How many pieces of ribbon will be left over?

____

2 Mae has 36 orange slices. She will fill each of 7 bags with the same number of orange slices. How many slices will be in each bag? How many slices will be left over?

____

3 Percy has 50 flowers. He will put 8 flowers in each centerpiece. How many centerpieces can Percy make? How many flowers will be left over?

____

Write the whole-number quotient and remainder.

4 $43 \div 5$

whole-number quotient ________

remainder ________

5 $29 \div 9$

whole-number quotient ________

remainder ________

6 (MP) **Reason** Does the division $25 \div 6$ have a remainder? How do you know?

____

____

Test Prep

7 Which visual model represents 32 ÷ 6?

Ⓐ 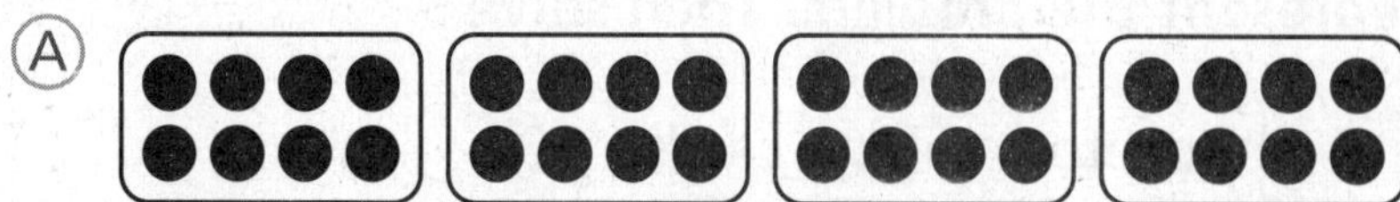

Ⓑ 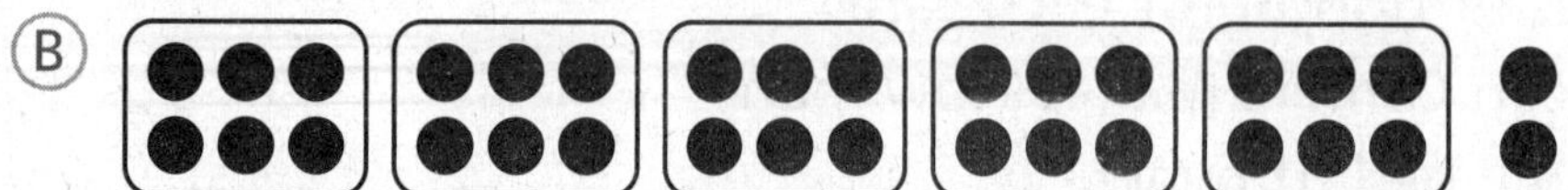

Ⓒ 

Ⓓ 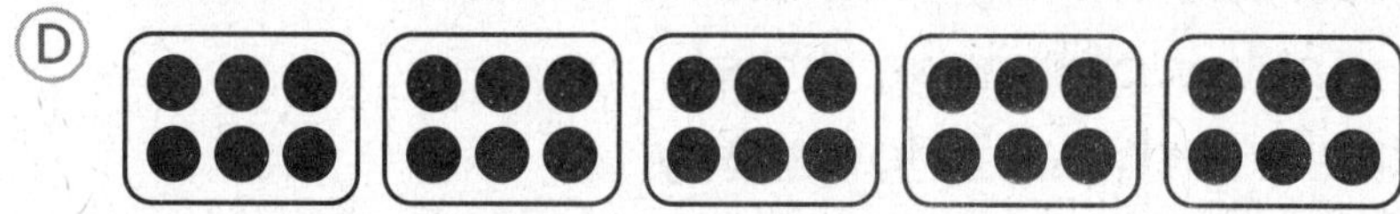

8 What does the visual model show about arranging 23 robots in a display? Select all the correct answers.

Ⓐ When you put 23 robots in 7 equal groups, there are 3 in each group, and 2 are left over.

Ⓑ When you put 23 robots in groups of 3, there are 2 groups, and 7 are left over.

Ⓒ When you put 23 robots in 7 equal groups, there are 2 in each group, and 3 are left over.

Ⓓ When you put 23 robots in groups of 3, there are 7 groups, and 2 are left over.

Ⓔ When you put 23 robots in 3 equal groups, there are 7 in each group and 2 are left over.

Spiral Review

9 Use mental math to find the product. Tell what strategy you used.

$5 \times 7 \times 40 =$ ______

______

10 A rectangular pool is 25 meters long and 10 meters wide. What is the perimeter of the pool?

______

Name ______________________________

Interpret Remainders

MP Use Tools Use objects or draw visual models to represent the division problem. Then explain how you interpreted the remainder to solve the problem.

1 Vick is putting batteries in toys. He needs 45 batteries. How many of these packs does Vick need to open in order to have enough batteries for all the toys?

____

____

____

2 Asia has 47 pencils to put in the pencil boxes she makes to sell at a fair. She puts 5 pencils in each box. How many boxes can Asia fill?

____

____

____

3 Isabel makes 64 cups of trail mix. She will put an equal amount of the mix in each of 6 bins. How many cups of trail mix will Isabel put in each bin?

____

____

____

4 **Math on the Spot** Juan has a piano recital next month. Last week he practiced for 4 hours in the morning and 9 hours in the afternoon. A full practice session is 2 hours long. How many full practice sessions does Juan complete?

____

____

Test Prep

5 There are 56 glasses. Each table gets 6 glasses when set. How many tables can be fully set with glasses?

Ⓐ 5 Ⓑ 6 Ⓒ 9 Ⓓ 10

6 Myra wants 48 stickers for an art project. The stickers come in packs of 9. How many packs of stickers will Myra need to buy?

Ⓐ 5 Ⓑ 6 Ⓒ 4 Ⓓ 7

7 The course for a bike race covers 38 miles. The course is divided into 5 sections of the same length. How long is each section?

Ⓐ $5\frac{1}{5}$ miles Ⓑ $7\frac{3}{5}$ miles Ⓒ $7\frac{5}{3}$ miles Ⓓ $8\frac{2}{5}$ miles

8 There are 55 people waiting in line for a carnival ride. Each car on the ride can hold 8 people and is filled before people get into another car. All the people in line get into a car. How many people are in the car that is not full?

Ⓐ 1 Ⓑ 6 Ⓒ 7 Ⓓ 8

Spiral Review

9 **Use base-ten blocks to show 2 × 421. Draw a quick picture to show your work.**

10 **Use expanded form to find the product.**

$6 \times 319 =$ ______

$8 \times 275 =$ ______

Name ______________________

LESSON 6.4
More Practice/
Homework

ONLINE
Video Tutorials and Interactive Examples

Use Area Models and the Distributive Property to Divide

1 (MP) **Use Tools** Shelly picks 84 pumpkins. She packs 6 pumpkins in each crate. How many crates does Shelly use to pack all of the pumpkins she picked? Complete the area model to find 84 ÷ 6.

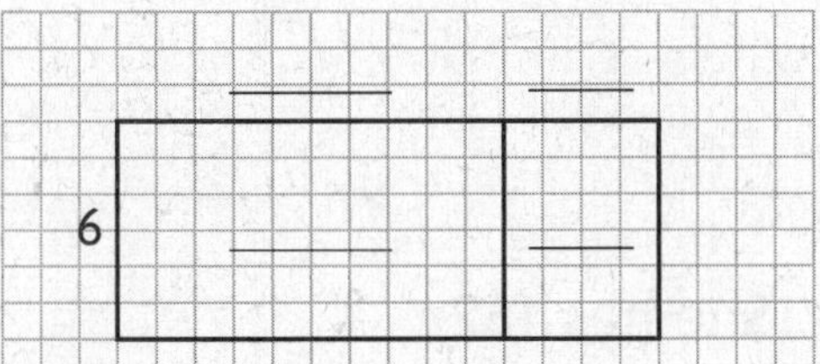

____

2 (MP) **Use Structure** Rebecca is sorting her pin collection. She has 136 pins and puts the same number of pins in each of 8 boxes. How many pins are in each box? Use the area model and the Distributive Property to find 136 ÷ 8.

136 = _____ + _____

136 ÷ 8 = (_____ + _____) ÷ 8

136 ÷ 8 = (_____ ÷ 8) + (_____ ÷ 8)

= _____ + _____

= _____

_____ + _____

8 | _____ | _____

____

Divide.

3 76 ÷ 4 = _____

4 112 ÷ 7 = _____

5 215 ÷ 5 = _____

Test Prep

6 Select all the problems that have a whole-number quotient of 23.

Ⓐ $138 \div 6$
Ⓑ $(120 \div 4) + (12 \div 4)$
Ⓒ $(120 \div 6) + (18 \div 6)$
Ⓓ $132 \div 4$
Ⓔ $(60 \div 6) + (48 \div 6)$

7 Mrs. Echine is packing ornaments in boxes. She has 152 small ornaments that fit 8 in a box. How many boxes of ornaments will Mrs. Echine fill?

Ⓐ 21 Ⓑ 19 Ⓒ 18 Ⓓ 16

8 Shira uses the Distributive Property to divide $168 \div 4$.

$168 = 16 + 8$

$168 \div 4 = (16 \div 4) + (8 \div 4)$

$= 4 + 2 = 6$

What error did Shira make?

Ⓐ Shira added 4 and 2 instead of multiplying 4 and 2.
Ⓑ Shira wrote 8 instead of 80 when she broke apart 168.
Ⓒ Shira incorrectly divided 16 by 4.
Ⓓ Shira wrote 16 instead of 160 when she broke apart 168.

Spiral Review

9 Jerome's basketball team scores 36 points in a game. In the same game, Russ's team scores twice as many points. How many points does Russ's team score?

____

10 If one gaming system costs \$238, how much will 5 gaming systems cost?

____

Name ______________________________

Divide Using Repeated Subtraction

1 (MP) **Model with Mathematics** Sylvia has $70 to buy plants for a garden. Each plant costs $6. How many plants can Sylvia buy?

- Write a division equation to model the problem.

  ____

- Use repeated subtraction to solve.

Sylvia can buy _____ plants.

2 (MP) **Model with Mathematics** Rob has 85 football cards. He can put 9 cards on each page of an album. How many album pages can he fill?

- Write a division equation to model the problem.

  ____

- Use repeated subtraction to divide.

Rob can fill _____ pages.

Use repeated subtraction to divide.

3 $65 \div 5$ _____

4 $46 \div 7$ _____

Test Prep

5 Use repeated subtraction to divide 74 ÷ 8.

For 74 ÷ 8, the whole-number quotient is _____ and the remainder is _____.

6 What happens when you use repeated subtraction to divide 36 ÷ 8? Select all of the correct answers.

Ⓐ You subtract 8 from 36 five times.
Ⓑ You get a remainder of 4.
Ⓒ You subtract 8 times to find the whole-number quotient.
Ⓓ You subtract 8 from 36 four times.
Ⓔ You get no remainder.

7 There are 7 people in the cooking club. They share 91 small pretzels that they bake. How many pretzels does each person get?

Ⓐ 9 Ⓑ 12 Ⓒ 13 Ⓓ 15

8 Geno makes 48 fruit bars for a party. He divides the fruit bars equally among 3 plates. How many fruit bars are on each plate?

Ⓐ 12 Ⓑ 14 Ⓒ 16 Ⓓ 18

Spiral Review

Estimate. Then find the product.

9 Estimate: _____

$$\begin{array}{r} 31 \\ \times\ 4 \\ \hline \end{array}$$

10 Estimate: _____

$$\begin{array}{r} 63 \\ \times\ 7 \\ \hline \end{array}$$

11 Estimate: _____

$$\begin{array}{r} 72 \\ \times\ 8 \\ \hline \end{array}$$

Name ___________________________________

LESSON 6.6
More Practice/ Homework

ONLINE
Video Tutorials and Interactive Examples

Divide Using Partial Quotients

1 (MP) **Use Tools** Gina has 396 photos. Her photo album can hold 3 pictures on each page. How many pages can Gina fill?

Use the area model and partial quotients to find 396 ÷ 3.

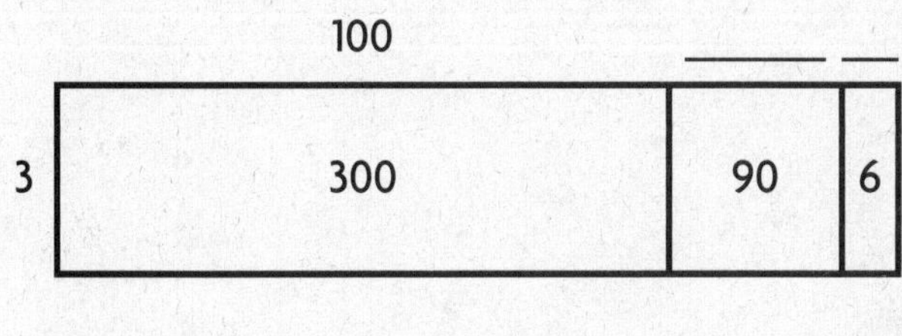

$$\begin{array}{r} 3\overline{)396} \\ -\ 300 \\ \hline \end{array} \quad 3 \times 100$$

$3 \times$ ______

$3 \times$ ______

100 + ______ + ______ = ______

Gina can fill ______ pages in her album.

2 (MP) **Attend to Precision** A teacher has 4,830 stickers and 4 classes. He will use the same number of stickers for each class. How many stickers can the teacher use for each class? Use partial quotients to divide. Show your work.

$$\begin{array}{r} 4\overline{)4{,}830} \\ -\ \underline{\qquad} \end{array} \quad 4 \times 1{,}000$$

The teacher can use __________ stickers for each class.

Use partial quotients to divide.

3 175 ÷ 5 ________ **4** 546 ÷ 6 ________ **5** 195 ÷ 8 ________

Test Prep

6 How can you break apart 4,872 into smaller parts that are multiples of 6? Select all of the correct answers.

Ⓐ 48 + 72

Ⓑ 4,800 + 72

Ⓒ 4,000 + 800 + 70 + 2

Ⓓ 4,800 + 60 + 12

Ⓔ 4,000 + 872

7 Josh scores 2,515 points in 5 rounds of a video game. He scores the same number of points in each round. How many points does Josh score in each round?

Ⓐ 53

Ⓑ 503

Ⓒ 530

Ⓓ 5,003

8 A gardener plants 246 flowers in 6 rows in the city park. She puts the same number of flowers in each row. How many flowers are in each row?

_____ flowers

Spiral Review

9 Complete the pattern.

40 ÷ 5 = _____

40 tens ÷ 5 = 8 tens

40 hundreds ÷ 5 = _____________

40 thousands ÷ 5 = _____________

10 Use compatible numbers to estimate the quotient.

352 ÷ 7

____

Name

Represent Division with Regrouping

1 (MP) **Use Tools** Shen puts all of his red marbles in 3 jars. He puts the same number in each jar. How many red marbles are in each jar? Use base-ten blocks to represent the division. Then draw a quick picture to show your work.

Shen's Marbles	
Color	**Number**
Yellow	57
Red	78
Blue	92
Green	43

2 (MP) **Attend to Precision** Bridget has 56 quarters. There are 4 quarters in 1 dollar. How many dollars does Bridget have? Draw a quick picture to show your work.

(MP) **Use Tools Use base-ten blocks or quick pictures to represent the division. Record the results.**

3 48 ÷ 3 ________ **4** 74 ÷ 7 ________ **5** 39 ÷ 8 ________

Test Prep

6 Janeka cuts out pictures of dogs to make posters. She puts an equal number of German shepherd pictures on 4 posters. How many pictures are on each poster?

Dog Pictures	
Breed	**Number**
Labrador retriever	62
German shepherd	52
Husky	28
Jack Russell terrier	44

Ⓐ 13 Ⓒ 11

Ⓑ 12 Ⓓ 9

7 Which quick picture represents 69 ÷ 4?

Ⓐ Ⓒ

Ⓑ 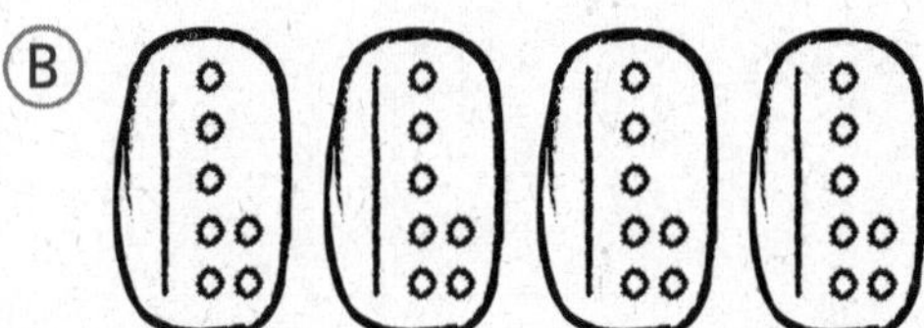 Ⓓ

8 Match the division problem to its quotient.

	13	14	17	18
51 ÷ 3	☐	☐	☐	☐
65 ÷ 5	☐	☐	☐	☐
84 ÷ 6	☐	☐	☐	☐
72 ÷ 4	☐	☐	☐	☐

Spiral Review

9 A rancher uses 40-pound bales of hay for his horses. What is the weight of 8 bales of hay?

____

____

10 A truck carries 6 telephone poles that have the same weight. The total weight of the poles is 6,000 pounds. How much does each telephone pole weigh?

6,000 ÷ 6 = __________

Name ______________________

LESSON 7.2
More Practice/ Homework

ONLINE
Ed
Video Tutorials and Interactive Examples

Use Place Value to Divide

MP **Use Tools Use base-ten blocks to represent the division. Then record the results.**

1 Frieda places 732 ribbons on 6 wreaths. Each wreath has the same number of ribbons. How many ribbons are on each wreath?

____

2 There are 378 almonds in a large snack bag. Arjun wants to divide them equally into 7 smaller bags. How many almonds will Arjun put in each bag?

____

3 Jolie uses this box of small nails to build 3 props for a play. She uses the same number of nails on each prop. How many nails does Jolie use on each prop? How many nails are left over?

____

MP **Reason Tell how many digits in the whole-number quotient.**

4 $174 \div 6$ ________

5 $358 \div 3$ ________

6 $136 \div 4$ ________

MP **Reason Tell where to place the first digit in the whole-number quotient.**

7 $4\overline{)364}$ ________

8 $8\overline{)841}$ ________

9 $6\overline{)173}$ ________

Divide.

10 $8\overline{)283}$

11 $3\overline{)375}$

12 $4\overline{)108}$

Test Prep

13 There are 858 seats in a theater. There are 6 sections with an equal number of seats in each section. How many seats are in each section?

Ⓐ 164 Ⓑ 152 Ⓒ 149 Ⓓ 143

14 Marvin sells bumper stickers at a festival. Each sticker costs $4. He records his sales each day. How many stickers did Marvin sell on Sunday?

Bumper Sticker Sales	
Day	**Amount**
Thursday	$64
Friday	$72
Saturday	$104
Sunday	$92

Ⓐ 12 Ⓑ 16 Ⓒ 20 Ⓓ 23

15 Tell where to place the first digit in the whole-number quotient. $6\overline{)825}$

____

16 How many digits does the whole-number quotient have?

627 ÷ 4

Ⓐ 4 Ⓑ 3 Ⓒ 2 Ⓓ 1

Spiral Review

17 Pria trains for a bike race. She rides her bike 85 miles every week. How many miles does Pria ride her bike in 9 weeks?

____

18 There are 105 days until basketball season starts. Melanie says the season starts in 15 weeks. Is this reasonable? Use estimation to justify your answer.

____

____

____

____

Name ______________________________

LESSON 7.3
More Practice/ Homework

ONLINE
Video Tutorials and Interactive Examples

Divide by 1-Digit Numbers

1 **Geography** The continental United States stretches from the Atlantic Ocean in the east to the Pacific Ocean in the west. A truck driver plans to drive 3,080 miles across the continental United States in 7 days. If she drives the same distance each day, how many miles will she drive each day?

____

2 **Math on the Spot** Four teachers bought 10 origami books and 100 packs of origami paper for their classrooms. They will share the cost of the items equally. How much should each teacher pay?

The Craft Store	
Item	**Price**
Origami Book	$24 each
Origami Paper	$6 each
Origami Kit	$8 each

____

Attend to Precision Divide and check.

3 $6\overline{)7,284}$

4 $3\overline{)8,296}$

5 $7\overline{)829}$

6 $5\overline{)2,965}$

Test Prep

7 An acting group pays $2,442 to rent a theater for 6 nights. The rent is the same for each night. How much does it cost to rent the theater each night?

Ⓐ $470 Ⓑ $407 Ⓒ $370 Ⓓ $307

8 Which is the answer for 4,915 ÷ 9?

Ⓐ 546 Ⓑ 546 r1 Ⓒ 646 Ⓓ 646 r 1

9 Divide and check.

$4\overline{)8{,}327}$

10 April helps her teacher divide 298 students into 9 groups. Her teacher wants the groups to be as equal as possible. Which grouping should April suggest?

Ⓐ 9 groups of 33 and 1 group of 27
Ⓑ 8 groups of 33 and 1 group of 34
Ⓒ 9 groups of 32 and 1 group of 10
Ⓓ 8 groups of 34 and 1 group of 33

Spiral Review

11 Use base-ten blocks to show 2 × 342. Draw a quick picture to show your work.

12 Use expanded form to find the product.

7 × 217 = ________

9 × 652 = ________

Name

ONLINE
Ed Video Tutorials and Interactive Examples

Solve Multistep Multiplication and Division Problems

1 (MP) **Reason** There are 8 markers in a pack. Mrs. Corey wants each of the 26 students in her class to have 3 markers. How many packs of markers should she buy?

2 **Math on the Spot** Ms. Johnson bought 9 bags of balloons. Each bag has 25 balloons. She fills all the balloons and puts 5 balloons in each bunch. How many bunches can she make?

3 (MP) **Attend to Precision** Six friends buy 4 of these boxes of pretzel bites. They share the pretzel bites equally. How many pretzel bites does each friend get?

4 **Music** The tempo, or speed, of music is measured in beats per minute (BPM). To find the BPM of her favorite song, Lisa counts 29 beats in 15 seconds of the song. Then she multiplies by 4 to find the song has a tempo of 116 BPM. An app on Lisa's phone says the song's tempo is 140 BPM. If the app is correct, how many beats does Lisa miss in her 15-second count?

Test Prep

5 There are 6 boxes of oranges for a race. Each box has 65 oranges. The same number of oranges are placed at each of the 3 first aid stations on the race course. How many oranges are at each station?

Ⓐ 140 Ⓑ 95 Ⓒ 135 Ⓓ 130

6 A tour group fills 8 minibuses. Each minibus holds 12 passengers. The tour group stops for lunch and the passengers are seated at round tables that fit 5 people each. How many tables do they need?

Ⓐ 11 Ⓑ 12 Ⓒ 19 Ⓓ 20

7 A tour boat has 248 seats arranged in rows of 8 seats each. During today's tour, the first 176 seats from the front of the boat are filled. Select all of the statements about the seats that are correct.

Ⓐ 8 rows are empty.
Ⓑ 8 rows are full.
Ⓒ 9 rows are empty.
Ⓓ 9 rows are full.
Ⓔ 22 rows are empty.
Ⓕ 22 rows are full.

Spiral Review

8 Marty's volleyball team scores 16 points in a tournament. In the same tournament, Jen's team scores twice as many points. How many points does Jen's team score?

____

9 One new set of team uniforms costs $146. How much do 5 sets of uniforms cost?

____

Name ____________________

LESSON 8.1
More Practice/ Homework

ONLINE
Ed
Video Tutorials and Interactive Examples

Multiply with Tens

Choose a method to solve the problem.

1 (MP) **Reason** There are 30 soccer teams with 16 players on each team. How many soccer players are there?

____

____

2 Cyclists in a road race must drink a lot of water. By the end of the race, they drank 40 cases of water. Each case contains 32 one-liter bottles. How many liters of water did they drink?

____

____

3 (MP) **Reason** Jeremy is going on a road trip in his new car. His gas tank holds 20 gallons of gasoline. The car can travel 19 miles on each gallon of gas. How many miles can Jeremy's new car travel on one tank of gas?

____

____

4 The new theater downtown has 90 rows with 12 seats in each row. Are there enough seats for 1,000 people? Explain.

____

____

____

Choose a method. Then find the product.

5 $14 \times 60 =$ ________

6 $30 \times 42 =$ ________

7 $54 \times 80 =$ ________

8 $20 \times 43 =$ ________

9 $74 \times 30 =$ ________

10 $50 \times 37 =$ ________

Test Prep

11 Keira buys 40 packs of balloons for the party. There are 16 balloons in each pack. How many balloons does Keira have?

Ⓐ 580 Ⓒ 620
Ⓑ 600 Ⓓ 640

12 Alonso is making 30 gallons of his favorite soup. Each gallon is enough to fill about 23 bowls. How many bowls of soup does Alonso make?

Ⓐ 1,210 Ⓒ 690
Ⓑ 960 Ⓓ 660

13 Mike drove a total of 20 hours during his trip. He drove 63 miles each hour. How many miles did he drive?

Ⓐ 1,480 miles Ⓒ 1,145 miles
Ⓑ 1,260 miles Ⓓ 830 miles

14 What is the product 87×60?

Ⓐ 5,280 Ⓒ 5,250
Ⓑ 5,210 Ⓓ 5,220

Spiral Review

15 Dimitri used 84 flowers to make 4 flower arrangements. How may flowers are in each arrangement?

____

16 A new bike company sells 5,513 bikes in its first year of business. The next year, the same bike company sells 7,302 bikes. How many more bikes were sold the second year than the first year?

____

Name

Estimate Products

1 (MP) **Reason** Mila swims 42 laps each time she goes to the pool. Last month she went to the pool 27 times. About how many laps did Mila swim last month?

____

2 (MP) **Construct Arguments** Jan wants to save $450 to buy a new TV. She earns $16 each week for walking the neighbor's dog. She estimates that if she saves for 18 weeks, she will have enough money. What does your estimate tell you?

____

____

3 **Math on the Spot** If Mel opens his refrigerator door 43 times every day, about how many times will it be opened in April? Will the exact answer be greater than or less than the estimate? Explain.

____

____

____

Estimate the product. Choose a method.

4 56 × 23 ______________________

5 32 × 24 ______________________

6 17 × 42 ______________________

7 79 × 68 ______________________

Test Prep

8 Choose a method. Estimate the product.

57×85 Estimate: ________

9 Michael earns $26 each week doing chores at home. He saves his earnings for 28 weeks. Using compatible numbers, about how much does Michael save?

Ⓐ about $850
Ⓑ about $750
Ⓒ about $600
Ⓓ about $400

10 Gena will run a marathon in 34 weeks. She runs an average of 45 miles each week to prepare for the race. Using rounding, about how many miles will she run to prepare for the race?

Ⓐ about 1,200 miles
Ⓑ about 1,500 miles
Ⓒ about 1,600 miles
Ⓓ about 2,000 miles

11 Todd is practicing free throws for 75 minutes each day for 28 days. What is an estimate for the number of minutes Todd will practice?

Ⓐ 150 minutes
Ⓑ 225 minutes
Ⓒ 2,250 minutes
Ⓓ 2,475 minutes

Spiral Review

12 Jess has 100 patches to sew on 8 pairs of jeans. Each pair of jeans will get the same number of patches. How many patches will be used on each pair of jeans and how many will be left over?

____

____

13 At the library, 43,284 books were checked out in March, 27,814 books were checked out in April, and 15,347 books were checked out in May. How many fewer books were checked out in April and May than in March?

____

Name ______________________________

LESSON 8.3
More Practice/ Homework

ONLINE
Ed
Video Tutorials and Interactive Examples

Relate Area Models and Partial Products

1 (MP) **Use Tools** Complete the area model. Write and solve an equation for the area model.

_____ × _____ = _____

	10	2
10	____	____
8	____	____

2 The craft center has 23 cans of markers with 16 markers in each can. How many markers are at the craft center?

____

(MP) **Use Tools** **Draw an area model to represent the product. Then record the product.**

3 $12 \times 17 =$ __________

4 $23 \times 27 =$ __________

Test Prep

5 Which equation does the area model represent?

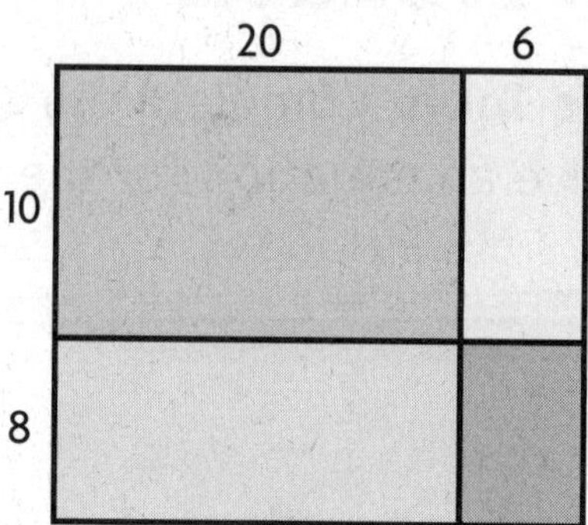

Ⓐ 18 + 26 = 44
Ⓑ 26 − 18 = 8
Ⓒ 18 × 26 = 468
Ⓓ 10 × 20 = 200

6 Helen wants to find the product 25 × 17. Which shows how she could use the Distributive Property to find the partial products?

Ⓐ (20 × 10) + (20 × 7) + (5 × 10) + (5 × 7)
Ⓑ (20 + 10) + (20 + 7) + (5 + 10) + (5 + 7)
Ⓒ (20 × 10) × (20 × 7) × (5 × 10) × (5 × 7)
Ⓓ (20 + 10) × (20 + 7) × (5 + 10) × (5 + 7)

7 What is the product 15 × 14?

Ⓐ 58
Ⓑ 120
Ⓒ 190
Ⓓ 210

8 What is the product 26 × 23?

Ⓐ 760
Ⓑ 598
Ⓒ 490
Ⓓ 418

Spiral Review

9 Ms. Burt's class of 25 students will be divided into 6 groups for the city tour. How many students should be in each group so that everyone is with a group?

10 Josh has 350 seeds to plant in a community garden. He plants the seeds in 7 rows with each row having an equal number of seeds. How many seeds are in each row?

Name ______________________________

LESSON 8.4
More Practice/ Homework

ONLINE
Ed Video Tutorials and Interactive Examples

Multiply Using Partial Products

1 (MP) **Attend to Precision** Moira has 46 tickets left to sell for the show. Each ticket costs $34. How much will it cost to buy all of the remaining tickets?

____

2 (MP) **Reason** Jason works out at the gym 16 hours each week for 36 weeks a year. How many hours does he work out at the gym in one year?

____

3 **Math on the Spot** Each person in the United States eats about 112 bananas each year, or about 28 pounds of bananas. Based on this estimate, how many pounds of bananas do 3 families of 4 eat each year?

____

Estimate. Then use partial products to find the product.

4 Estimate: ______

$$\begin{array}{r} 78 \\ \times\ 36 \\ \hline \end{array}$$

5 Estimate: ______

$$\begin{array}{r} 45 \\ \times\ 23 \\ \hline \end{array}$$

6 Estimate: ______

$$\begin{array}{r} 64 \\ \times\ 17 \\ \hline \end{array}$$

Rewrite the problem. Then use partial products to find the product.

7 $92 \times 38 =$ ______

8 $47 \times 53 =$ ______

9 $29 \times 87 =$ ______

Test Prep

10 There are 64 small squares on a checkerboard. How many squares are on 27 checkerboards? Write the problem and solve.

11 Mr. Tad delivers 94 copies of the newspaper to each of the 57 stores on his newspaper route. How many copies of the newspaper does he deliver to stores on his route?

Ⓐ 5,358
Ⓑ 4,791
Ⓒ 4,358
Ⓓ 1,128

12 What is the product 42×74?

Ⓐ 2,108
Ⓑ 3,008
Ⓒ 3,108
Ⓓ 3,118

13 What is the product 16×35?

Ⓐ 4,160
Ⓑ 560
Ⓒ 200
Ⓓ 51

Spiral Review

Find each quotient.

14 $144 \div 8 =$ ______

15 $135 \div 5 =$ ______

16 $138 \div 6 =$ ______

Estimate. Then find the product.

17 Estimate: ______

$$\begin{array}{r} 21 \\ \times\ 4 \\ \hline \end{array}$$

18 Estimate: ______

$$\begin{array}{r} 62 \\ \times\ 7 \\ \hline \end{array}$$

Name ____________________

LESSON 8.5
More Practice/ Homework

ONLINE
Video Tutorials and Interactive Examples

Multiply with Regrouping

1 There are 79 calories in a single breakfast bar.

How many calories are in a box of 24 bars? __________

2 (MP) **Construct Arguments** Mr. Lutz counted 15 boxes of 12 pencils in the school store. Sage says that is about 200 pencils. Is her answer reasonable? Explain.

____

____

3 (MP) **Construct Arguments** Mr. Franklin is buying 45 chairs for the meeting room at a community center. Each chair costs $27. What is the total cost of the chairs? Explain how you found your answer.

____

____

Estimate. Then find the product.

4 Estimate: __________

$$\begin{array}{r} 46 \\ \times\ 24 \\ \hline \end{array}$$

5 Estimate: __________

$$\begin{array}{r} 83 \\ \times\ 72 \\ \hline \end{array}$$

6 Estimate: __________

$$\begin{array}{r} 77 \\ \times\ 58 \\ \hline \end{array}$$

7 Estimate: __________

$$\begin{array}{r} 73 \\ \times\ 25 \\ \hline \end{array}$$

8 Estimate: __________

$$\begin{array}{r} 35 \\ \times\ 42 \\ \hline \end{array}$$

9 Estimate: __________

$$\begin{array}{r} 94 \\ \times\ 66 \\ \hline \end{array}$$

Test Prep

10 Mack makes 26 dozen muffins for the luncheon. How many muffins does Mack make?

Ⓐ 460
Ⓑ 380
Ⓒ 312
Ⓓ 286

11 Which would provide a reasonable estimate for the product 38×26? Select all that apply.

Ⓐ 40×30
Ⓑ 30×10
Ⓒ 40×25
Ⓓ 30×20
Ⓔ 50×30
Ⓕ 40×40

12 What is the product 32×68?

Ⓐ 21,376
Ⓑ 21,176
Ⓒ 2,376
Ⓓ 2,176

13 What is the product 14×79?

Ⓐ 1,427
Ⓑ 1,310
Ⓒ 1,106
Ⓓ 1,105

Spiral Review

14 Use repeated subtraction to solve. Show your work.

$46 \div 5$

______

15 There are 1,760 yards in a mile. Nikita runs 3 miles. How many yards does she run?

______

Name ______________________________

LESSON 8.6
More Practice/ Homework

ONLINE
Ed Video Tutorials and Interactive Examples

Choose a Multiplication Strategy

1 (MP) **Use Tools** Tina makes $25 a week babysitting. How much money will she make if she babysits for 39 weeks?

- Use partial products to find the product.

  39 × $25 = ______

- Draw a picture to check your work.

2 (MP) **Reason** There are 27 students in Mrs. George's class. If she starts the year with 500 pencils, will she have enough to give each student 15 pencils? Explain your answer.

____

____

Estimate. Then choose a method to find the product.

3 Estimate: ______

$$\begin{array}{r} 39 \\ \times\ 47 \\ \hline \end{array}$$

4 Estimate: ______

$$\begin{array}{r} 67 \\ \times\ 15 \\ \hline \end{array}$$

5 Estimate: ______

$$\begin{array}{r} 83 \\ \times\ 98 \\ \hline \end{array}$$

6 Estimate: ______

$$\begin{array}{r} 37 \\ \times\ 25 \\ \hline \end{array}$$

7 Estimate: ______

$$\begin{array}{r} 84 \\ \times\ 16 \\ \hline \end{array}$$

8 Estimate: ______

$$\begin{array}{r} 59 \\ \times\ 48 \\ \hline \end{array}$$

Find the unknown digits. Complete the problem.

9

$$\begin{array}{r} 4\ \square \\ \times\ 5\ 6 \\ \hline 2\ 8\ 8 \\ 2,\square\ 0\ 0 \\ \hline 2,\ 6\ 8\ 8 \end{array}$$

10

$$\begin{array}{r} 7\ 7 \\ \times\ 3\ \square \\ \hline 7\ 7 \\ \square,3\ 1\ 0 \\ \hline \square,3\ 8\ 7 \end{array}$$

11

$$\begin{array}{r} 9\ 6 \\ \times\ \square\ 2 \\ \hline \square\ \square\ \square \\ 5,\ 7\ 6\ 0 \\ \hline 5,\ 9\ \square\ \square \end{array}$$

Test Prep

12 Freddie buys 36 packs of paper plates. There are 28 plates in each pack. How many paper plates does Freddie buy?

Ⓐ 960
Ⓑ 1,008
Ⓒ 1,012
Ⓓ 1,103

13 Select all the ways to show 33×14.

Ⓐ $(30 + 3) + (10 + 4)$
Ⓑ $(33 \times 10) + (33 \times 4)$
Ⓒ $(30 \times 10) + (30 \times 4) + (3 \times 10) + (3 \times 4)$
Ⓓ $(30 \times 14) + (3 \times 10) + (3 \times 4)$
Ⓔ $(3 \times 10) + (3 \times 4)$

14 The model shows 24×75. What is the unknown partial product?

	70	5
20	1,400	100
4		20

Ⓐ 350
Ⓑ 280
Ⓒ 240
Ⓓ 210

Spiral Review

15 There are 1,615 people seated in a concert hall with 5 seating sections. If the same number of people are seated in each section of the concert hall, how many people are seated in each section?

____

16 Jacob sorted a package of 64 plastic animals into 2 containers so each container has the same number of plastic animals. How many plastic animals are in each container?

____

Name ______________________________

LESSON 8.7
More Practice/ Homework

ONLINE
Video Tutorials and Interactive Examples

Solve Multistep Problems and Assess Reasonableness

1 (MP) **Reason** Isla made 35 beaded necklaces. Each necklace sells for $27. She spent $385 on supplies to make the necklaces. How much money did Isla make?

____

2 (MP) **Reason** For the fourth-grade trip, there are 18 chaperones. There are 16 times as many students as chaperones going on the trip. The buses can each hold 60 people. How can you divide the students evenly among 7 buses? Interpret the problem and the remainder for this situation.

____

____

____

3 (MP) **Model with Mathematics** A crane operator moves 6 shipping containers that weigh 215 tons each onto a barge. The same crane operator loads 4 more shipping containers that weigh 194 tons each onto the barge. How many tons of shipping containers did the crane operator load onto the barge?

- Write an equation to model the situation and solve.

____

____

- How can you check if your answer is reasonable?

____

____

____

____

Test Prep

4 A large container of laundry detergent costs $17. A washing machine costs 34 times as much. How much does a washing machine and 2 containers of detergent cost?

Ⓐ $578
Ⓑ $595
Ⓒ $612
Ⓓ $646

5 At a store, there are 11 shelves with 27 picture books and 12 shelves with 21 chapter books. How many fewer chapter books than picture books does the store have?

Ⓐ 45
Ⓑ 71
Ⓒ 435
Ⓓ 549

6 Casey has a collection of 39 amusement park pins. The pins are from an amusement park in Florida and an amusement park in Virginia. There are twice as many pins from the Florida amusement park than from the amusement park in Virginia. How many pins are from the amusement park in Virginia?

Ⓐ 78
Ⓑ 37
Ⓒ 19 r1
Ⓓ 13

Spiral Review

7 Gina has 3 rolls of game tickets for the fair. Each roll has 64 tickets. She says that she has a total of 192 tickets. Is this total reasonable? Explain.

8 A dance group raised $4,480 for their competition trips by selling pizzas. They made $8 for each pizza they sold. The group's director says that they sold 560 pizzas. Is this amount reasonable? Explain.

Name ______________________________

LESSON 9.1
More Practice/
Homework

Apply the Area Formula to Rectangles

1 (MP) **Construct an Argument** Lorena has a square piece of fabric. She measures one side and finds that it is 9 inches long. Does Lorena have enough information to find the area of the fabric piece? Explain your answer.

____

____

____

Find the area.

2

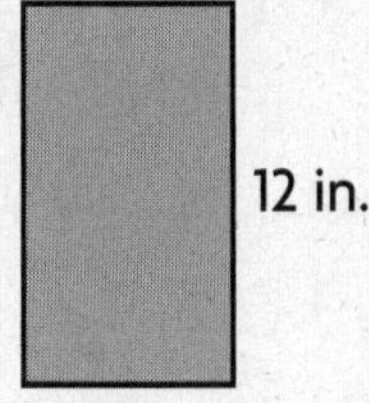

____

3

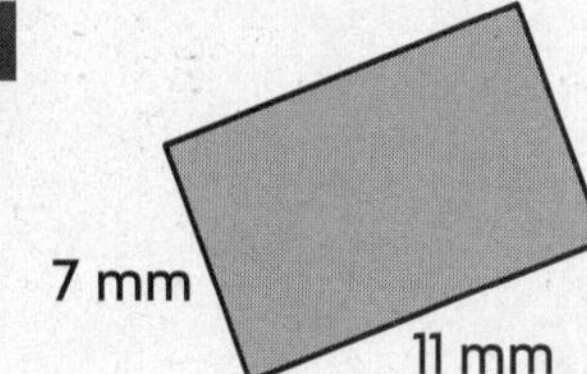

____

4

____

5

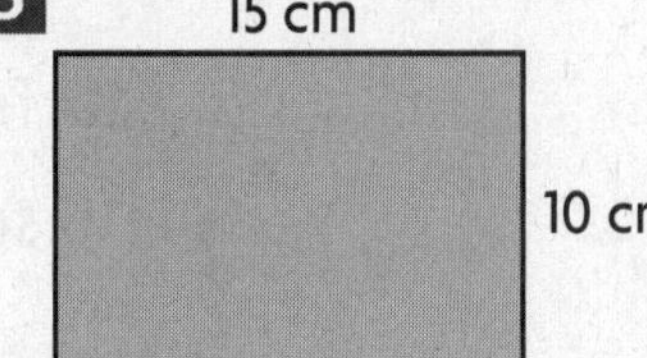

____

6 **Math on the Spot** Nancy and Luke are drawing plans for rectangular flower gardens. In Nancy's plan, the garden is 18 feet by 12 feet. In Luke's plan, the garden is 15 feet by 15 feet. Who drew the garden plan with the greater area? What is the area?

The area of Nancy's garden is __________.

The area of Luke's garden is __________.

__________ garden has the greater area.

Test Prep

7 What is the area of the rectangle?

Ⓐ 12 sq cm
Ⓑ 20 sq cm
Ⓒ 22 sq cm
Ⓓ 24 sq cm

8 What is the area of the square?

5 yd

Ⓐ 5 sq yd
Ⓑ 10 sq yd
Ⓒ 20 sq yd
Ⓓ 25 sq yd

9 The square rug in a bedroom covers 64 square feet. What is the length of one of the sides of the rug?

Ⓐ 8 feet
Ⓑ 8 square feet
Ⓒ 16 feet
Ⓓ 16 square feet

Spiral Review

10 Ken goes to a store with $27. He buys 4 packages of sports socks. Each package costs $6. How much money does Ken have now? Show your work.

____

____

____

____

11 One ticket to the new amusement park costs $74. How much do 6 tickets cost?

____

Name ______________________

ONLINE
Video Tutorials and
Interactive Examples

Find the Area of Combined Rectangles

1 MP **Attend to Precision** Melinda is painting part of a mural. The diagram shows the shape she will paint. A small can of paint covers 25 sq ft. Can Melinda complete her part of the mural with just 1 can of paint? Explain.

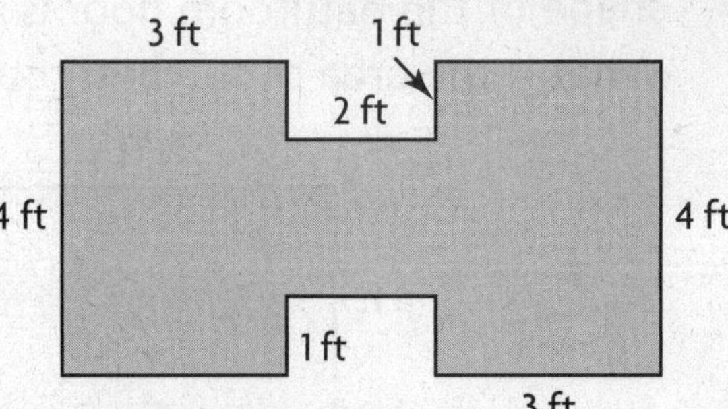

____

____

____

MP **Use Structure** Find the area of the shaded part of the figure.

2

8 mm
2 mm
6 mm
5 mm
4 mm
3 mm

3

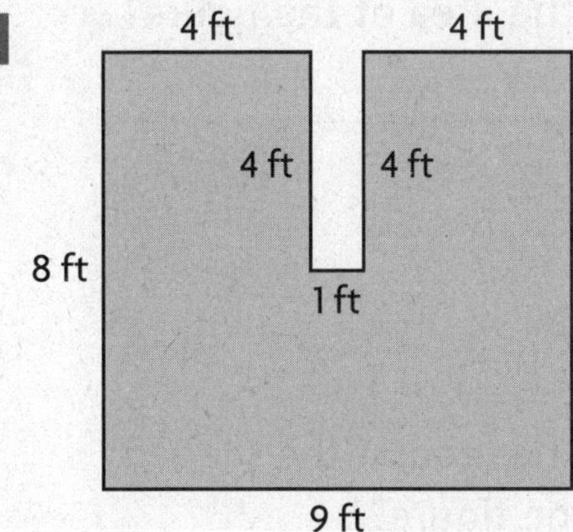

______________________ ______________________

4 **Math on the Spot** The diagram shows the layout of Mandy's garden. The garden is the shape of combined rectangles. What is the area of the garden?

____

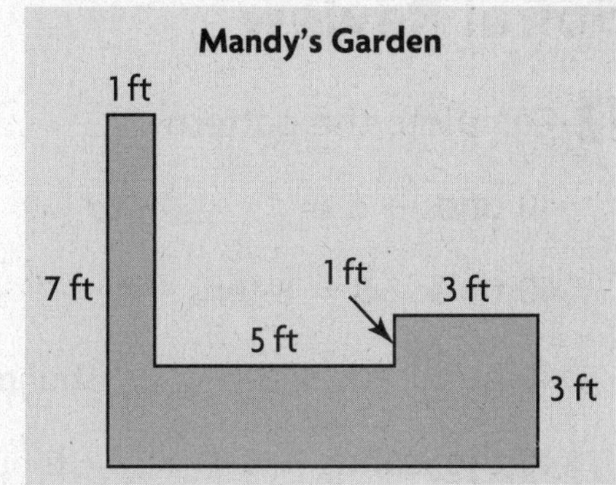

Test Prep

5 Jared is putting a new tile floor in a bathroom. The shape of the bathroom floor is shown in the diagram. What is the area of the bathroom floor?

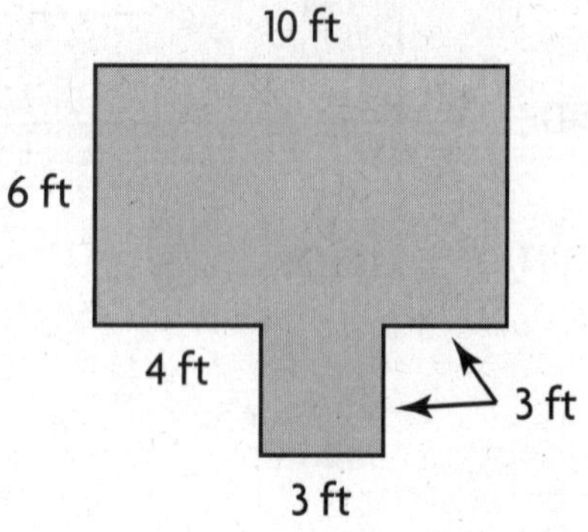

Ⓐ 60 sq ft
Ⓑ 69 sq ft
Ⓒ 81 sq ft
Ⓓ 90 sq ft

6 What is the area of the figure?

____

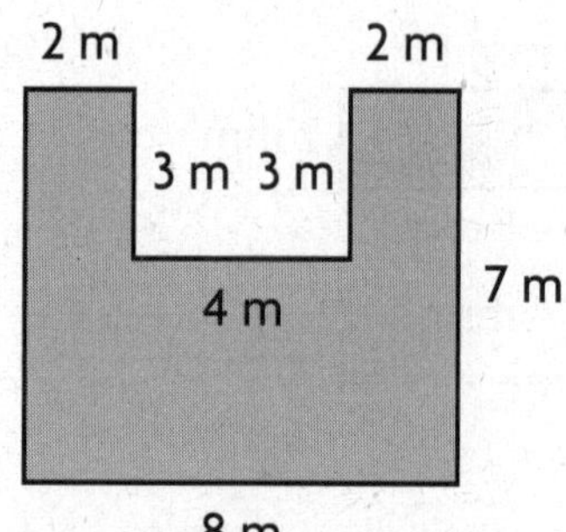

7 What is the area of the shaded part of the figure?

____

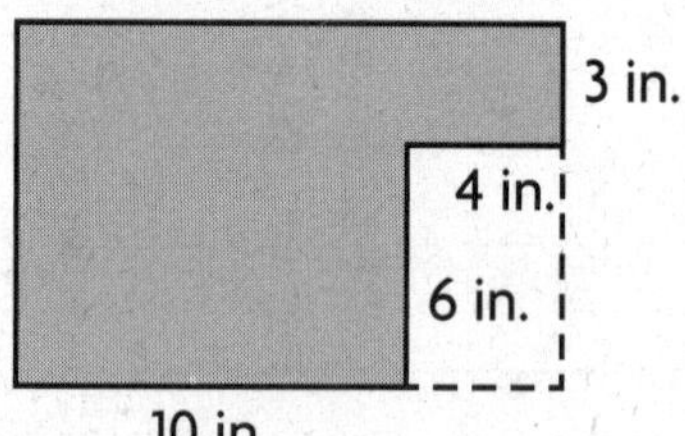

Spiral Review

8 Complete the pattern.

40 ones ÷ 5 = ______ ones

40 tens ÷ 5 = 8 tens

40 hundreds ÷ 5 = ______ hundreds

40 thousands ÷ 5 = ______ thousands

9 Use compatible numbers to estimate the quotient.

473 ÷ 6
Estimate: ______

1,282 ÷ 4
Estimate: ______

Name ______________________

ONLINE
Video Tutorials and
Interactive Examples

Find Unknown Measures

1 The area of a window is 63 square feet. The height of the window is 7 feet. What is the length of the base?

____

2 The perimeter of a vegetable garden is 48 feet. The width of the garden is 10 feet. What is the length of the garden?

____

MP **Use Structure** **Use the area or perimeter formula to find the unknown measures.**

3 Perimeter = 32 sq yd; side: 8 yd; base: n

$n =$ ______

4 Area = 54 sq m; side: 6 m; base: n

$n =$ ______

5 MP **Reason** A square has an area of 49 square centimeters. What is the length of one side? Explain how you got your answer.

____

____

____

6 **Math on the Spot** A male mountain lion has a rectangular territory with an area of 96 square miles. If his territory is 8 miles wide, what is the length of his territory?

____

Test Prep

7 A rectangular picture frame has an area of 24 square inches. The width of the frame is 6 inches. What is the length of the frame?

Ⓐ 4 inches
Ⓑ 6 inches
Ⓒ 12 inches
Ⓓ 18 inches

8 A square mirror has an area of 100 square centimeters. What is the length of one side of the mirror?

Ⓐ 10 centimeters
Ⓑ 25 centimeters
Ⓒ 96 centimeters
Ⓓ 400 centimeters

9 A rug is a rectangle that has a perimeter of 28 feet. The width of the rug is 4 feet. Which shows how you can use a formula to find the length of the rug?

Ⓐ $28 = 2 + n \times 2 + 4$
Ⓑ $28 = 4 + 2 \times n$
Ⓒ $28 = 4 \times n$
Ⓓ $28 = 2 \times n + 2 \times 4$

10 A photograph has an area of 48 square inches. The length of the photograph is 6 inches. Which shows how you can use a formula to find the width of the photograph?

Ⓐ $48 = 2 \times 6 + 2 \times w$
Ⓑ $48 = 4 \times 6 \times w$
Ⓒ $48 = 6 \times w$
Ⓓ $48 = 2 \times 6 \times w$

Spiral Review

11 Cole has 96 World Cup player cards. He has 3 player cards for each of the teams that are participating. How many teams are participating?

____

12 Estimate. Then find the difference.

Estimate: ____________

$$\begin{array}{r} 326{,}891 \\ -\ 112{,}430 \\ \hline \end{array}$$

Name ______________________________

LESSON 9.4
More Practice/ Homework

ONLINE
Ed Video Tutorials and Interactive Examples

Solve Area Problems

1 (MP) **Reason** There is a rectangular shaped pond with a path around it, as shown. What is the area of the path? How do you know?

path
pond
11 yd
15 yd
6 yd
10 yd

____

____

____

Find the area of the shaded part of the rectangle.

2

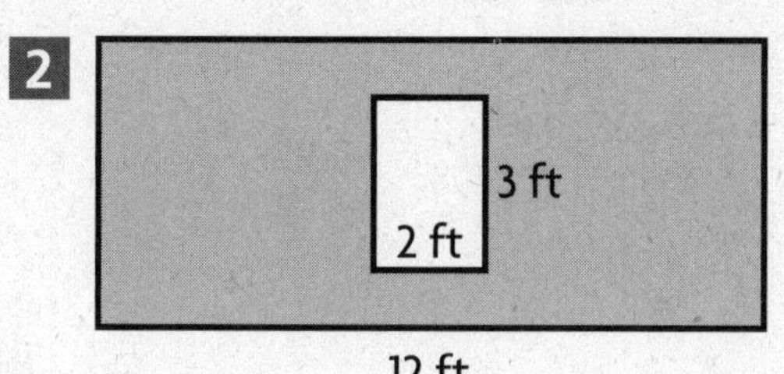

Area = ________

3

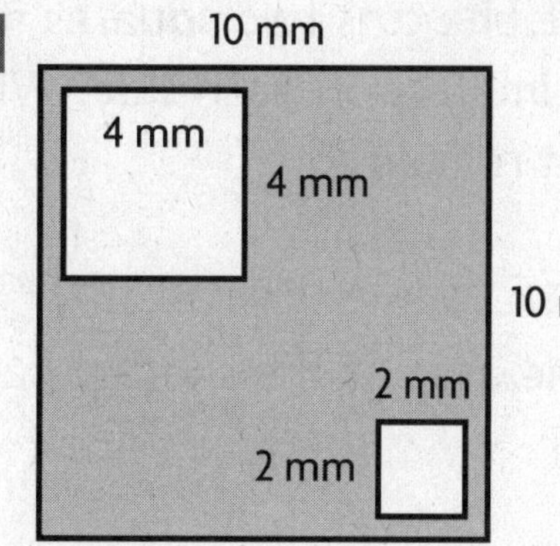

Area = ________

4 (MP) **Use Structure** A rectangular envelope has a clear window for the address to show. The measure of the envelope is 7 inches by 4 inches. The clear window is 4 inches by 1 inch. What is the area of the front of the envelope not including the clear window?

____

5 **Math on the Spot** Mr. Foster is covering two rectangular pictures with glass. One is 7 inches by 5 inches and the other one is 6 inches by 6 inches. Does he need the same number of square inches of glass for each picture? Explain.

____

____

Test Prep

6 Nick wants to paint a wall in his home. The rectangular wall measures 10 feet by 13 feet. There is a rectangular door in the wall that measures 7 feet by 3 feet. What is the area of the wall that Nick wants to paint?

Ⓐ 21 sq ft
Ⓑ 109 sq ft
Ⓒ 130 sq ft
Ⓓ 151 sq ft

7 Aisha has a sheet of construction paper that is 23 centimeters long and 8 centimeters wide. For an art project, she cuts two squares from the paper that are 4 centimeters on each side. What is the area of the paper that remains?

____

8 What is the area of the shaded part of the rectangle?

____

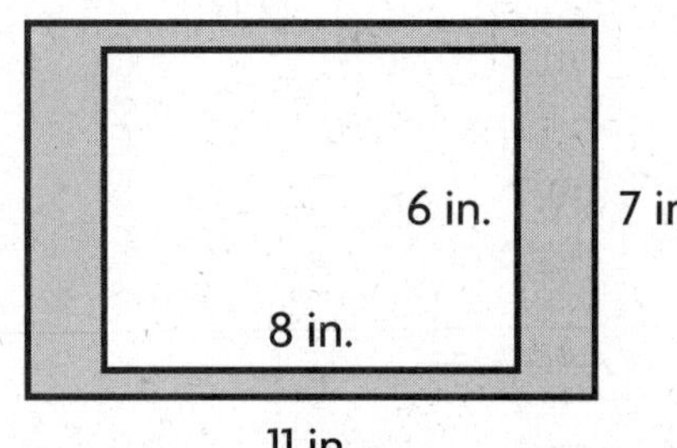

Spiral Review

9 Charisse has 42 beads to make friendship pins to sell at an event on Friday. She will use 5 beads on each pin. How many friendship pins can she make? How many beads will be left over?

____

____

10 At the aquarium, 73,384 tickets were sold in June, 34,319 tickets were sold in July, and 16,537 tickets were sold in August. How many fewer tickets were sold in July and August than in June?

__________ fewer tickets

Name ______________________

Investigate Factors

1 (MP) **Use Tools** The 28 cheerleaders will stand in equal rows. Use 28 square tiles to make as many different arrays as you can. Describe the arrays.

____

____

Write all the factor pairs for 28. ______________________

List all the factors of 28. ______________________

How many factors does 28 have? ______________________

How many different ways can the cheerleaders stand in equal rows?

____

2 Nick uses 16 cards for a math game. He will place them in a rectangular arrangement on the table. Use area models to show all the different ways Nick can place the cards.

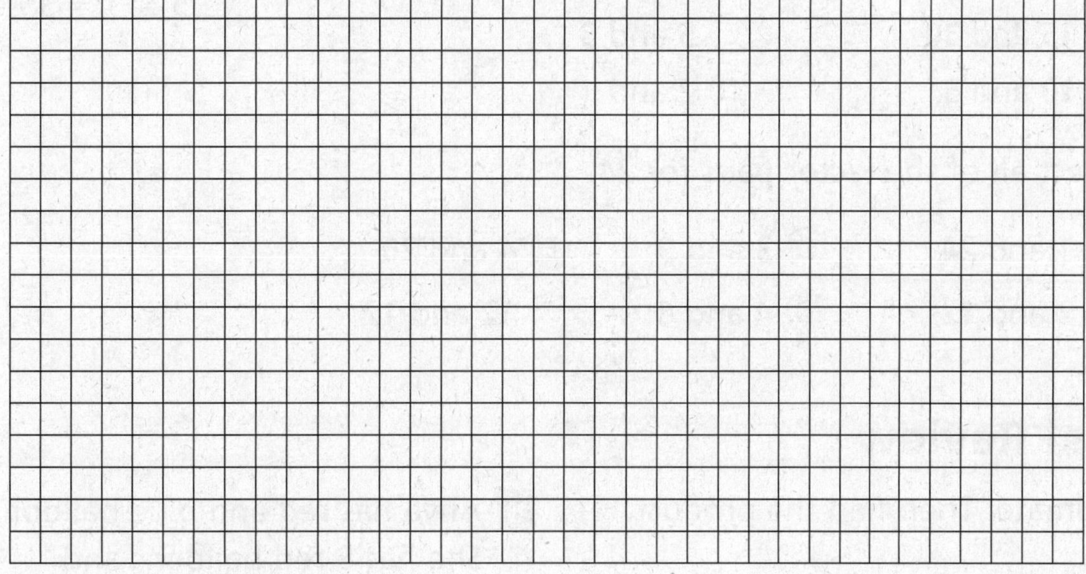

Write all the factor pairs for 16. ______________________

List all the factors of 16. ______________________

How many factors does 16 have? ______________________

How many different ways can Nick arrange the cards? ____________

Test Prep

3 Lou wants to arrange 18 carpet squares in equal rows. Which arrays show how he can arrange the carpet squares? Select all the correct answers.

Ⓐ 

Ⓑ

Ⓒ 

Ⓓ

Ⓔ 

4 Carrie writes these equations to model all the area models for 35. How many factor pairs does 35 have?

$1 \times 35 = 35$

$5 \times 7 = 35$

$7 \times 5 = 35$

$35 \times 1 = 35$

Ⓐ 2 Ⓑ 3 Ⓒ 4 Ⓓ 8

5 Which is a factor pair for 15?

Ⓐ 15 and 30
Ⓑ 10 and 5
Ⓒ 5 and 3
Ⓓ 2 and 1

6 Select all of the factor pairs for 24.

Ⓐ 1 and 24
Ⓑ 2 and 12
Ⓒ 3 and 9
Ⓓ 4 and 6
Ⓔ 4 and 20
Ⓕ 12 and 12

Spiral Review

7 Estimate. Then find the product.

Estimate: ______________

$$\begin{array}{r} 36 \\ \times\ 49 \\ \hline \end{array}$$

8 Anya has red and blue balloons. She has 8 red balloons and 4 times as many blue balloons as red. How many balloons does Anya have?

____

Name

ONLINE
Video Tutorials and Interactive Examples

Identify Factors

1 (MP) **Use Tools** There are 29 desks in a classroom. Can all the desks be placed in 3 equal rows?

- Use square tiles to represent the problem. Then draw the array to show your work.

- Can all the desks be placed in 3 equal rows? Use factors or divisibility to explain.

2 Use division to answer and explain.

Is 5 a factor of 58?

$5\overline{)58}$

3 Use divisibility rules to answer and explain.

Is 3 a factor of 75?

4 **Math on the Spot** Dirk bought a set of stamps. The number of stamps in the set he bought is divisible by 2, 3, 5, 6, and 9. Which set is it?

Stamps Sets	
Country	**Number of stamps**
Germany	90
Sweden	78
Japan	63
Canada	25

Test Prep

5 Which number has 4 as a factor?

Ⓐ 14
Ⓑ 22
Ⓒ 34
Ⓓ 48

6 Complete the table to show whether each number is divisible by 6 or 8, both 6 and 8, or neither.

Number	Divisible by 6	Divisible by 8
24	☐	☐
32	☐	☐
44	☐	☐
78	☐	☐

7 Which numbers are factors of 84? Select all the correct answers.

Ⓐ 1
Ⓑ 2
Ⓒ 3
Ⓓ 4
Ⓔ 6
Ⓕ 8

8 Tess washes grapes and puts all of them in 3 bags. She puts an equal number of grapes in each bag. Which could be the number of grapes that Tess washes?

Ⓐ 32
Ⓑ 45
Ⓒ 49
Ⓓ 53

Spiral Review

9 Choose a method. Then find the product.

$17 \times 40 =$ ______

$60 \times 34 =$ ______

10 Find the area.

9 m
3 m

______

Name ____________________

LESSON 10.3
More Practice/ Homework

ONLINE
Video Tutorials and Interactive Examples

Generate Multiples Using Factors

1 (MP) **Use Structure** There are 8 hamburger buns in a package. Which number of hamburger buns would fill a whole number of packages: 18, 32, 44, 56? Show or explain how you found your answer.

____

____

____

____

Circle the answers.

2 Which of the following are multiples of 2?

10 17 26 30

3 Which of the following are multiples of 5?

1 5 40 55

Find the first five multiples of the number. Write multiplication equations to show they are multiples.

4 4: ____________________

____

5 6: ____________________

____

Complete to show the first six multiples of the number.

6 Show multiples of 3.

3, _____ , 9, 12, _____ , _____

7 Show multiples of 7.

_____ , 14, _____, 28, _____ , _____

8 (MP) **Attend to Precision** For the tug-of-war competition at field day, students are placed on teams of 9. How many students are on 1 to 5 teams?

____

Test Prep

9 Which number is a multiple of 4?

Ⓐ 14 Ⓑ 22 Ⓒ 26 Ⓓ 28

10 Which number is ***not*** a multiple of 8?

Ⓐ 4 Ⓑ 8 Ⓒ 24 Ⓓ 40

11 Select all the multiples of 5.

Ⓐ 1 Ⓑ 15 Ⓒ 20 Ⓓ 23 Ⓔ 25 Ⓕ 30

12 Complete the table to show whether each number is a multiple of 4 or 6, both 4 and 6, or neither.

Number	Multiple of 4	Multiple of 6
22	☐	☐
36	☐	☐
40	☐	☐
54	☐	☐

13 Each remote control requires 2 batteries. How many batteries are needed for 1 to 5 remote controls?

____

Spiral Review

14 Use the area or perimeter formula to find the unknown measure.

8 in.

Area = 32 sq in. n

n = __________

15 Use compatible numbers to estimate the quotient.

$351 \div 4$

____

Name ______________________________

LESSON 10.4
More Practice/ Homework

ONLINE
Video Tutorials and Interactive Examples

Identify Prime and Composite Numbers

Construct Arguments Write *true* or *false* for the statement. Explain or give an example to support your answer.

1 All odd numbers are prime numbers.

____

2 All of the whole numbers to 1,000 are either prime numbers or composite numbers.

____

3 **Math on the Spot** A composite number cannot have three factors.

____

4 **Reason** Name the prime number between 40 and 70 where the ones digit is 5 less than the tens digit. __________

Tell whether the number is *prime* or *composite*.

5 54 __________

6 46 __________

7 37 __________

8 63 __________

9 99 __________

10 71 __________

11 **History** More than 2,200 years ago, a Greek scholar named Eratosthenes invented a system for finding prime numbers now called the Sieve of Eratosthenes. To find all the prime numbers less than a number *n*, write all the whole numbers from 1 to *n* in order. Cross out 1. The next number that is not crossed out is 2, so it is prime. Cross out all the multiples of 2. The next number that is not crossed out is 3, so it is prime. Cross out all the multiples of 3. Continue in this way until there are no multiples of primes left to cross out. All the numbers that are not crossed out are prime. Use the Sieve of Eratosthenes to find all the prime numbers less than 40.

____

Test Prep

12 Which statement about the number 91 is true?

Ⓐ It has 1 and 91 as factors, so it is prime.

Ⓑ It is only divisible by 1 and 91, so it is prime.

Ⓒ It has more than 2 factors, so it is composite.

Ⓓ It is divisible by 1, 3, 7, and 91, so it is composite.

13 Complete the table to show whether each number is prime or composite.

Number	Prime	Composite
21	☐	☐
67	☐	☐
49	☐	☐
94	☐	☐

14 What are the greatest and least prime numbers from 1 to 100?

____

Spiral Review

15 Giana runs 18 days each month. Each day, she runs for 35 minutes. About how many minutes does Giana run each month?

____

16 A kitchen has a tile floor with a counter in the center of the room. What is the area of the floor that is not covered by the counter?

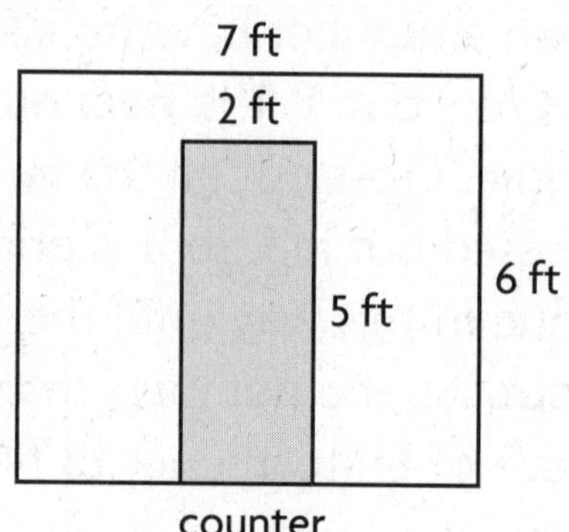

____

Name ______________________________

Generate and Analyze Number Patterns

1 (MP) **Use Structure** Workers are installing new seats in the football stadium with the team colors. Starting with the first row, every sixth row of seats is red. The other rows are blue. What color is the 35th row? Explain how you know.

____

____

____

2 **Math on the Spot** John is saving for his trip to see the Alamo. He started with $27 in his savings account. Every week he earns $20 for babysitting. Out of that, he spends $9 and saves the rest. John uses the rule *add 11* to find out how much money he has at the end of each week. What are the first 8 numbers in the pattern?

____

Use the rule to write the numbers in the pattern. Then describe another feature of the pattern.

3 Rule: Multiply by 3. First term: 3

3, ____, ____, ____, ____, ____

____

4 Rule: Add 27. First term: 27

27, ____, ____, ____, ____, ____, ____, ____

____

5 Rule: Divide by 2. First term: 768

768, ____, ____, ____, ____, ____, ____, ____

____

Test Prep

6 The first term in a pattern is 427. The pattern follows the rule *subtract 15*. Which number is a term in the pattern?

Ⓐ 417 Ⓑ 402 Ⓒ 352 Ⓓ 327

7 Lisa is knitting stars and moons in her scarf. Every fifth row has moons, starting with the first row. The other rows have stars. Which shape does the 24th row have?

____

8 The table shows the first three terms in a pattern. The rule for the pattern is *multiply by 3*. Complete the pattern.

2	6	18			

9 The first term in a pattern is 17. The pattern follows the rule *multiply by 2*. Write the first 5 terms of the pattern. Then describe another feature of the pattern.

____

____

10 The rule for a pattern is *add* 7. The first term is 9. What is the fourth term in the pattern?

Ⓐ 7 Ⓑ 12 Ⓒ 23 Ⓓ 30

Spiral Review

11 Use expanded form to find the product.

$4 \times 746 =$ ________

$5 \times 323 =$ ________

12 Draw a visual model for $19 \div 2$. What is the remainder?

____

Name ______________________________

LESSON 11.1
More Practice/ Homework

ONLINE
Video Tutorials and Interactive Examples

Compare Fractions Using Visual Models

1 (MP) **Reason** Jessa and Molly are each working on the same homework assignment. After an hour, Jessa has done $\frac{3}{4}$ of her assignment and Molly has done less.

Draw a visual model to show the part of her assignment that Molly could have done. Write the fraction it shows.

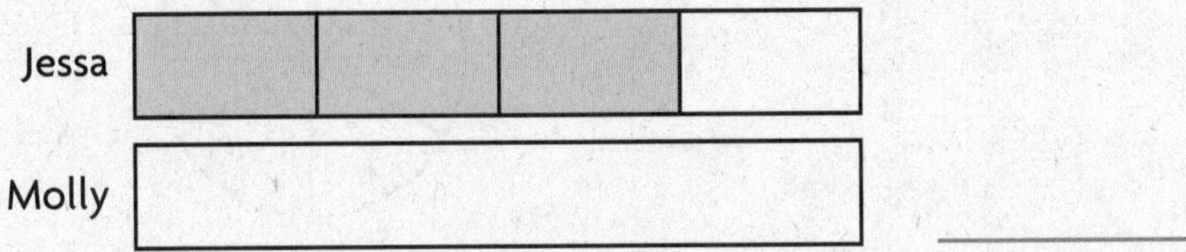

______

Explain how you know your answer is correct.

____

____

2 (MP) **Use Tools** Jorge and Shannon earn the same amount of money. Jorge spends $\frac{2}{5}$ of his money on a new game. Shannon spends $\frac{5}{6}$ of her money on a new outfit. Use fraction strips to show how much each person spends. Draw the fraction strips.

Jorge

Shannon

Who spends more money? ______________

Complete the visual model to show each fraction. Then write < or > to compare.

3 $\frac{3}{8}$ ○ $\frac{4}{6}$

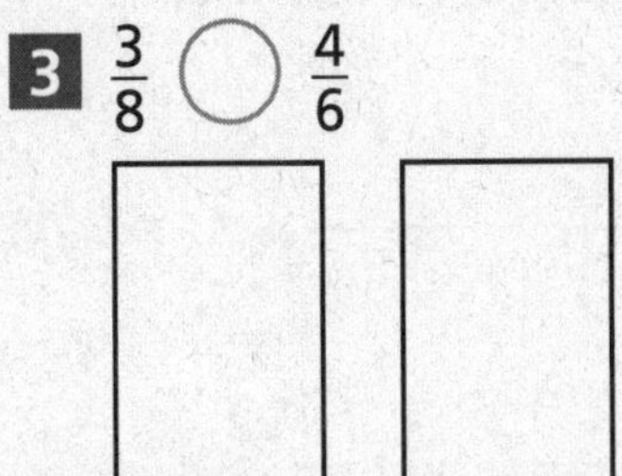

4 $\frac{3}{8}$ ○ $\frac{1}{4}$

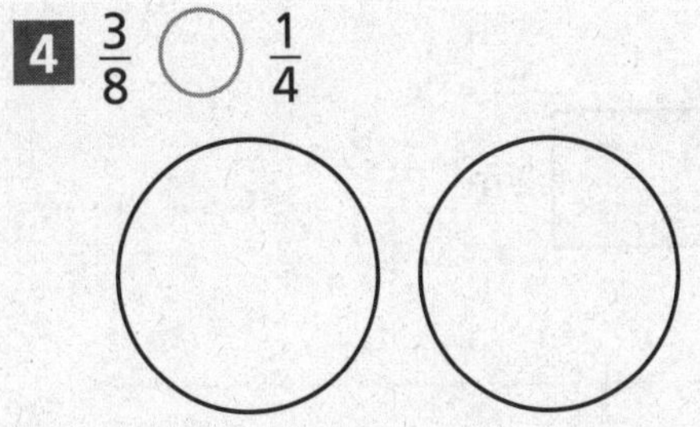

Test Prep

5 The visual models represent four fractions. Which comparisons of those fractions are true? Select all the correct answers.

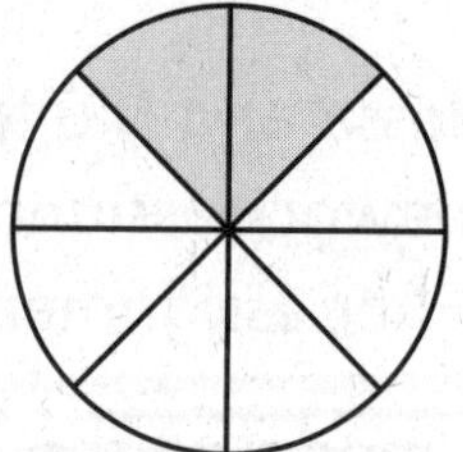
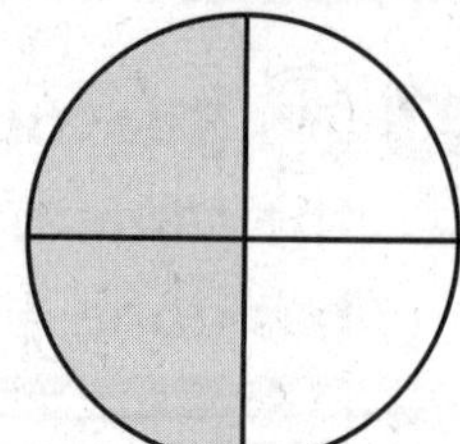

Ⓐ $\frac{2}{8} > \frac{4}{12}$

Ⓑ $\frac{1}{6} < \frac{2}{4}$

Ⓒ $\frac{1}{6} > \frac{4}{12}$

Ⓓ $\frac{4}{12} < \frac{2}{4}$

Ⓔ $\frac{2}{4} < \frac{2}{8}$

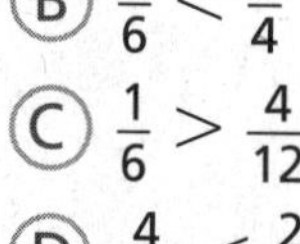

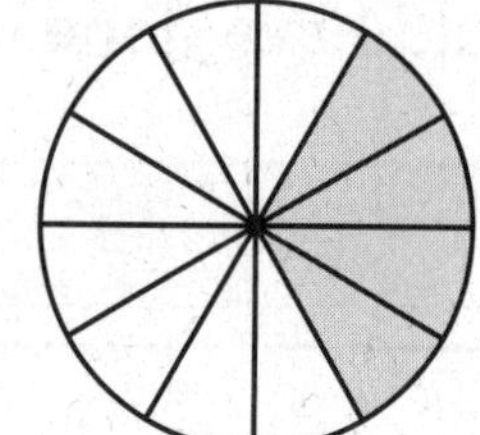
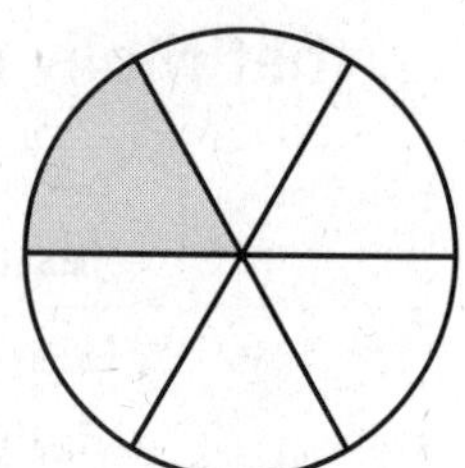

6 Write a symbol to make the comparison true.

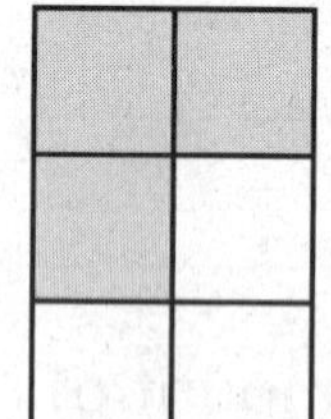

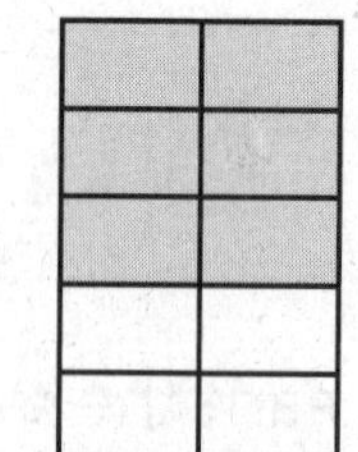

$\frac{3}{6}$ ◯ $\frac{6}{10}$

7 On Thursday, Tyler ran $\frac{8}{12}$ of the way to school and walked the rest. On Friday, he ran $\frac{4}{5}$ of the way to school and walked the rest. Complete the visual models to represent the distances he ran each day.

Thursday

Friday

Which day did Tyler run farther?

____

Spiral Review

8 Find the area.

6 m

2 m

____

9 Use expanded form to find the product.

$4 \times 862 =$ ________

$5 \times 263 =$ ________

Name ______________________

Compare Fractions Using Benchmarks

1 (MP) **Reason** Tina started a project with two 1-gallon cans of paint. One can is now $\frac{4}{10}$ full, and the other can is $\frac{5}{8}$ full. Which can is less than $\frac{1}{2}$ full?

____

2 (MP) **Model with Mathematics** Jax uses this recipe to make muffins. Does he use more baking soda or vanilla flavoring? Use comparison symbols to explain.

Muffin Recipe	
Flour	$\frac{3}{4}$ cup
Sugar	$\frac{1}{2}$ cup
Baking Soda	$\frac{7}{8}$ teaspoon
Vanilla Flavor	$\frac{1}{4}$ teaspoon
Blueberries	2 cups

____

____

____

3 **STEM** Herbivores are animals that eat only plants. Carnivores are animals that eat only meat. In general, herbivores sleep less than carnivores. For example, giraffes in the wild sleep about $\frac{1}{6}$ of the day. In contrast, lions in the wild sleep about $\frac{3}{4}$ of the day. Which animal is the herbivore? Use a benchmark fraction to explain your thinking.

____

____

4 **Open Ended** Josh helps at the school fair for $\frac{3}{8}$ of the day. Sarai helps for $\frac{8}{12}$ of the day. Write and solve a comparison question about the amount of time they help at the fair.

____

____

Write > or < for the comparison.

5 $\frac{5}{12}$ ◯ $\frac{6}{8}$

6 $\frac{4}{6}$ ◯ $\frac{2}{5}$

7 $\frac{7}{10}$ ◯ $\frac{4}{3}$

Test Prep

8 Maura is using the benchmark $\frac{1}{2}$ to compare fractions. Select $>$ or $<$ to complete a true comparison for each pair of fractions.

	$>$	$<$
$\frac{3}{5} \bigcirc \frac{2}{10}$	☐	☐
$\frac{3}{8} \bigcirc \frac{5}{6}$	☐	☐
$\frac{13}{8} \bigcirc \frac{14}{10}$	☐	☐

9 Sal makes a pizza. He puts peppers on $\frac{3}{5}$ of the pizza and mushrooms on $\frac{1}{3}$ of the pizza. Which statement about the pizza is true?

Ⓐ $\frac{3}{5} > \frac{1}{3}$, so more of the pizza is covered with peppers.

Ⓑ $\frac{1}{3} > \frac{3}{5}$, so more of the pizza is covered with mushrooms.

Ⓒ $\frac{1}{3} = \frac{3}{5}$, so the same amount of the pizza is covered with each.

Ⓓ $\frac{3}{5} < \frac{1}{3}$, so less of the pizza is covered with peppers.

10 Write $>$ or $<$ to compare.

$1\frac{4}{10} \bigcirc 1\frac{7}{12}$

Spiral Review

11 Use the area or perimeter formula to find the unknown measure of the rectangle.

6 in.

Area = 18 sq in. n

n = ____________

12 Mrs. Perdomo walks for 25 minutes each day. She walks 4 days during the first week, 6 days during the second week, and 5 days during the third week. How many minutes does she walk in the three weeks?

____

Name ______________________________

ONLINE
Video Tutorials and Interactive Examples

Explain Fraction Equivalence Using Visual Models

1 (MP) **Reason** Freida only has a $\frac{1}{4}$-cup measuring cup. She fills the measuring cup two times to get $\frac{1}{2}$ cup. Use visual models to explain why this works.

____

____

____

2 Are $\frac{2}{3}$ and $\frac{4}{6}$ equivalent fractions? Use the visual models to explain how you know.

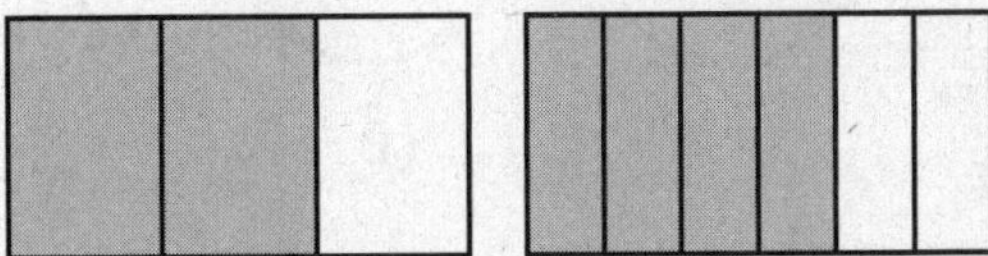

____

____

____

3 Complete the equation to show how the two fractions are equivalent.

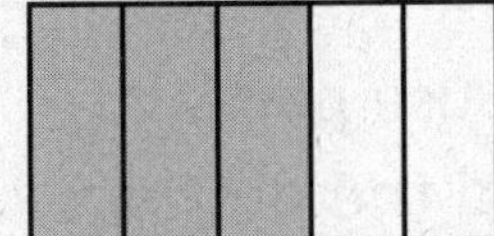

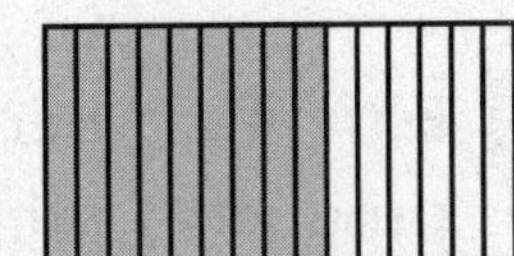

$\frac{3}{5} = \frac{\square}{\square} \times \frac{\square}{\square} = \frac{9}{15}$

4 **STEM** When an object is raised to a new height, it gains potential energy because of gravity. The amount of potential energy depends on the mass of the object and its height. Two bowling balls with the same mass start at the same height. One is raised to a height of $\frac{3}{4}$ yard, and the other is raised to a height of $\frac{9}{12}$ yard. Do the balls have the same potential energy? Use visual models to explain how you know.

____

____

Test Prep

5 Complete the visual model to show a fraction that is equivalent to $\frac{1}{3}$.

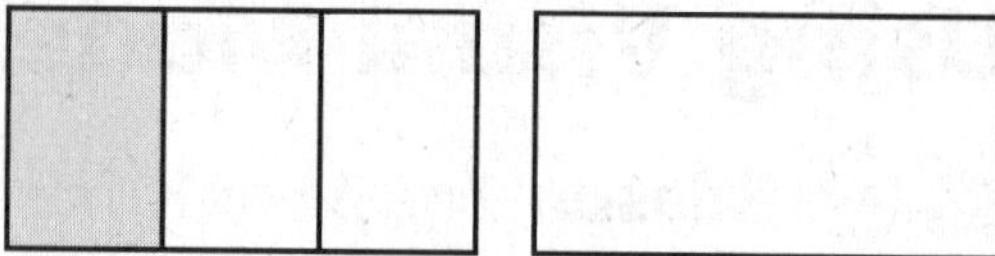

6 Serena made this visual model to represent a fraction. Which visual model represents a fraction that is equivalent to Serena's fraction?

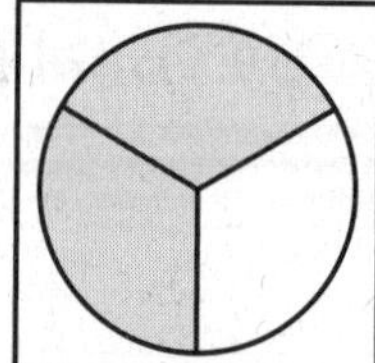

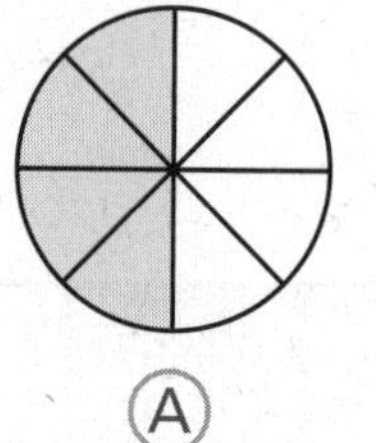
Ⓐ

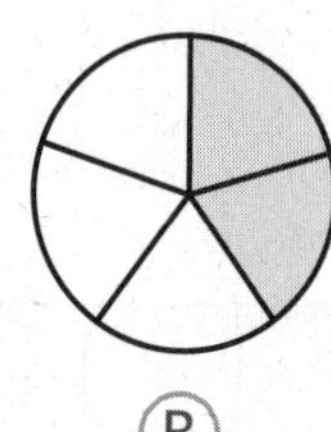
Ⓑ

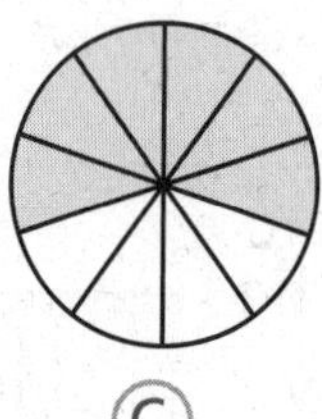
Ⓒ

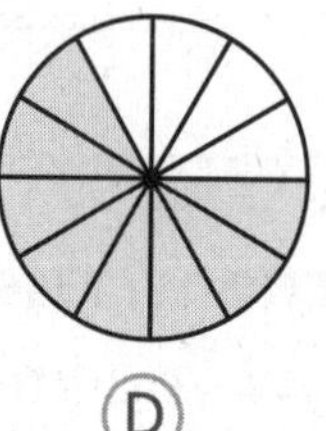
Ⓓ

7 Complete the equation to show how the two fractions are equivalent.

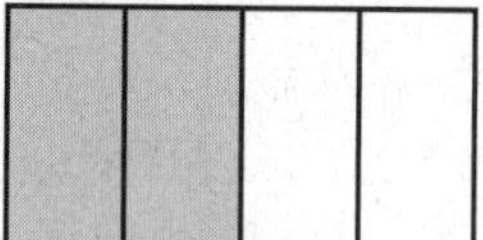

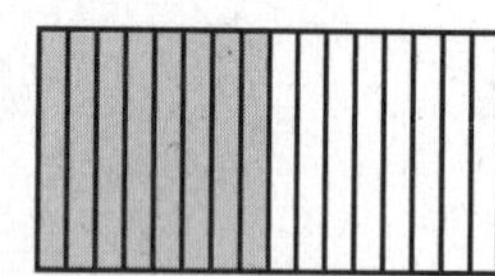

$\frac{2}{4} = \frac{\square}{\square} \times \frac{\square}{\square} = \frac{8}{16}$

Spiral Review

8 A room has a wooden floor with a rug in the center. How many square feet of the wooden floor are not covered by the rug?

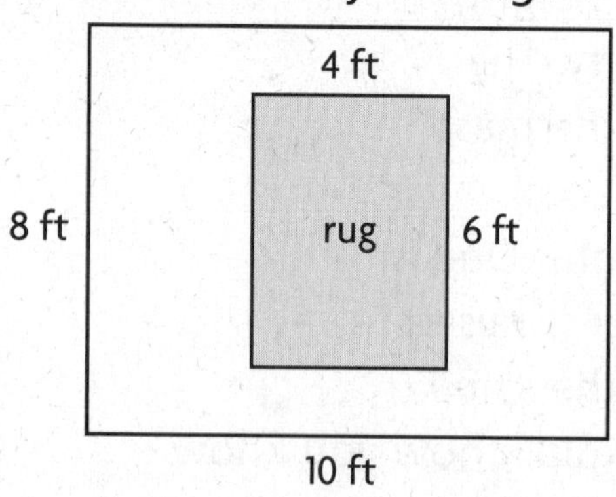

____

____

____

9 Estimate. Then use partial products to find the product.

Estimate: ______________

$$\begin{array}{r} 48 \\ \times\ 26 \\ \hline \end{array}$$

Name ______________________________

ONLINE
Ed
Video Tutorials and Interactive Examples

Generate Equivalent Fractions

1 (MP) **Reason** Jordan walks $\frac{4}{10}$ mile to school. Explain how you can use multiplication or division to write an equivalent fraction for $\frac{4}{10}$. Draw visual models to show how your fractions are equivalent.

____

____

2 (MP) **Reason** A garden is divided into 6 equal parts. Joey plants strawberries in $\frac{1}{2}$ of the garden. He plants watermelons in the other parts. How many parts of the garden have watermelons planted in them? Explain how you can use equivalent fractions to solve.

____

____

____

Use multiplication or division to generate an equivalent fraction.

3 $\frac{3}{5} = \frac{\square \times 3}{\square \times 5} = \frac{\square}{\square}$

4 $\frac{2}{3} = \frac{\square \times 2}{\square \times 3} = \frac{\square}{\square}$

5 $\frac{4}{8} = \frac{4 \div \square}{8 \div \square} = \frac{\square}{\square}$

6 $\frac{9}{12} = \frac{9 \div \square}{12 \div \square} = \frac{\square}{\square}$

Write *true* or *false* for the statement.

7 $\frac{6}{8} = \frac{3}{4}$ ______________

8 $\frac{4}{6} = \frac{8}{12}$ ______________

9 $\frac{5}{10} = \frac{1}{5}$ ______________

Test Prep

10 Which fractions are equivalent to the fraction that is represented below? Select all the correct answers.

Ⓐ $\frac{6}{16}$

Ⓑ $\frac{9}{16}$

Ⓒ $\frac{9}{24}$

Ⓓ $\frac{6}{24}$

Ⓔ $\frac{1}{4}$

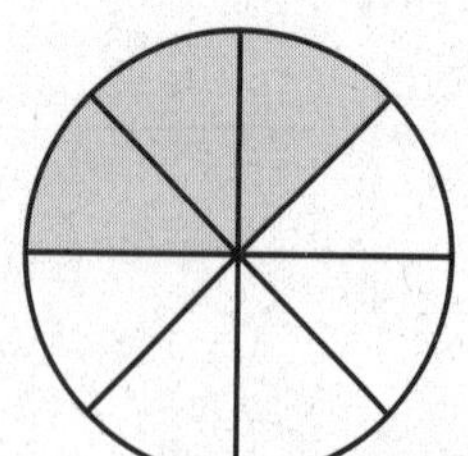

11 Carlos wants to find a fraction equivalent to $\frac{5}{6}$. His work is shown below. Which describes his error?

$\frac{5}{6} = \frac{5 \times 1}{6 \times 2} = \frac{5}{12}$

Ⓐ He multiplied the numerator and denominator by the same number.

Ⓑ He did not multiply $\frac{5}{6}$ and $\frac{1}{2}$ correctly.

Ⓒ He did not multiply the numerator by 2.

Ⓓ He multiplied $\frac{5}{6}$ by a number less than 1.

12 Generate two equivalent fractions for the fraction shown.

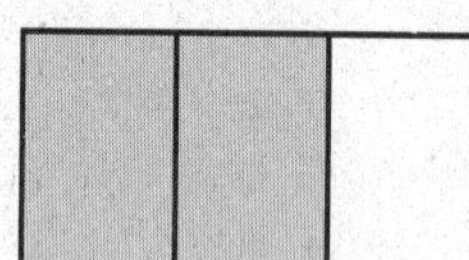

$\frac{2}{3} = \frac{\square}{\square} = \frac{\square}{\square}$

Spiral Review

13 Find all the factor pairs for the number.

30: ____________________

17: ____________________

25: ____________________

14 There are 3 baskets of apples. Each basket has 84 apples. The apples will be divided into 9 equal groups. How many apples will be in each group?

____

Name ______________________________

Use Common Multiples to Write Equivalent Fractions

1 (MP) **Attend to Precision** Nathan grates $\frac{4}{6}$ cup of cheddar cheese and $\frac{3}{4}$ cup of mozzarella cheese. Write an equivalent fraction for each fraction using a common denominator.

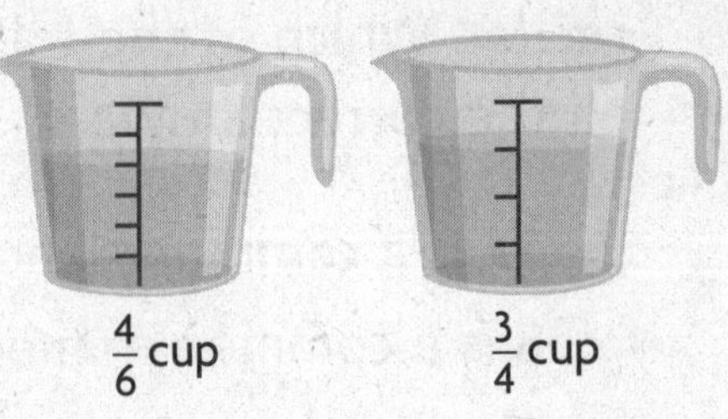

____

2 **Language Arts** Between 1590 and 1613, William Shakespeare wrote many famous plays. About $\frac{2}{5}$ of his plays are comedies, such as *The Merchant of Venice*. About $\frac{3}{10}$ are tragedies, such as *Romeo and Juliet*. Write an equivalent fraction for each fraction using a common numerator.

____

3 **Open Ended** Two fractions have a common denominator of 8. What could the two fractions be?

____

4 **Math on the Spot** Leah has two same-sized rectangles divided into the same number of equal parts. One rectangle has $\frac{1}{3}$ of the parts shaded, and the other has $\frac{2}{5}$ of the parts shaded. What is the least number of parts into which both rectangles could be divided?

____

Write the pair of fractions as a pair of fractions with a common denominator.

5 $\frac{1}{3}$ and $\frac{3}{8}$ __________

6 $\frac{2}{10}$ and $\frac{3}{5}$ __________

Write the pair of fractions as a pair of fractions with a common numerator.

7 $\frac{4}{6}$ and $\frac{2}{8}$ __________

8 $\frac{5}{12}$ and $\frac{2}{7}$ __________

Test Prep

9 Brianna is practicing the piano. She spends $\frac{2}{6}$ hour practicing scales and $\frac{3}{4}$ hour practicing the song for her recital. Which of the following statements are true? Select all the correct answers.

Ⓐ 12 is a common denominator of $\frac{2}{6}$ and $\frac{3}{4}$.
Ⓑ 8 is a common numerator of $\frac{2}{6}$ and $\frac{3}{4}$.
Ⓒ The amount of time spent practicing scales can be rewritten as $\frac{4}{12}$.
Ⓓ The amount of time spent practicing the song for the recital can be rewritten as $\frac{6}{12}$.
Ⓔ 18 is a common numerator and a common denominator of $\frac{2}{6}$ and $\frac{3}{4}$.

10 Richie swam $\frac{3}{5}$ mile. Fran swam $\frac{2}{3}$ mile. Alison swam $\frac{1}{2}$ mile.

Write an equivalent fraction for each fraction using a common numerator.

$\frac{3}{5} = \frac{\square}{\square}$ $\frac{2}{3} = \frac{\square}{\square}$ $\frac{1}{2} = \frac{\square}{\square}$

11 Which correctly shows the pair of fractions written as a pair of fractions with a common denominator?

$\frac{6}{8}$ and $\frac{2}{3}$

Ⓐ $\frac{6}{8}$ and $\frac{7}{8}$
Ⓑ $\frac{12}{16}$ and $\frac{15}{16}$
Ⓒ $\frac{18}{24}$ and $\frac{16}{24}$
Ⓓ $\frac{6}{24}$ and $\frac{2}{24}$

Spiral Review

12 Is 3 a factor of 81? Use divisibility rules to explain.

____

____

13 Find the product.

$14 \times 30 =$ _______

$80 \times 24 =$ _______

Name ______________________________

Compare Fractions Using Common Numerators and Denominators

1 **Attend to Precision** Amanda runs $\frac{2}{3}$ kilometer. Jaylan runs $\frac{3}{5}$ kilometer. Who runs farther? Use a common denominator to compare the fractions.

____

____

2 **Attend to Precision** Brian and Thiara have the same-sized water bottles. Brian's bottle is $\frac{9}{10}$ full. Thiara's bottle is $\frac{3}{4}$ full. Whose bottle has less water? Use a common numerator to compare the fractions.

____

____

____

Compare. Write >, <, or =.

3 $\frac{1}{8}$ ◯ $\frac{2}{12}$

4 $\frac{6}{4}$ ◯ $\frac{12}{8}$

5 $\frac{10}{9}$ ◯ $\frac{5}{4}$

6 **Reason** Jonah hikes $\frac{9}{10}$ mile along the Rock Ridge Trail. Jane hikes $\frac{7}{8}$ mile along the same trail. Who hikes farther? Use a fraction comparison strategy to support your reasoning.

____

____

Test Prep

7 Regina baked two same-sized quiches for a party: an onion quiche and a mushroom quiche. At the party, Regina served $\frac{8}{10}$ of the onion quiche and $\frac{6}{8}$ of the mushroom quiche. Which quiche did she serve more of, the onion or the mushroom? Explain your answer.

____

____

____

8 Write >, <, or = to make each comparison true.

$\frac{5}{3} \bigcirc \frac{9}{6}$

$\frac{2}{5} \bigcirc \frac{4}{10}$

$\frac{2}{8} \bigcirc \frac{1}{9}$

9 Use the fractions to show true comparisons.

$\frac{2}{3}$	$\frac{6}{8}$	$\frac{10}{12}$

______ $<$ $\frac{3}{4}$

$\frac{3}{4}$ $=$ ______

______ $>$ $\frac{3}{4}$

Spiral Review

10 List the first 5 multiples of the number. Write multiplication equations to show they are multiples.

6: ______________________

____

____

11 Kristen does 215 jumping jacks in 4 minutes. About how many jumping jacks does she do in 1 minute?

____

____

Name ______________________

Use Comparisons to Order Fractions

1 MP **Reason** Micah, Dara, and Chan have same-sized garden plots. Micah has corn growing in $\frac{4}{5}$ of his plot. Dara has corn growing in $\frac{2}{6}$ of her plot. Chan has corn growing in $\frac{8}{12}$ of his plot. Write the gardeners in order, from least to greatest amount of corn growing. Use fraction comparison strategies to justify your comparisons.

____

____

____

____

____

____

2 Write the fractions in order, from least to greatest: $\frac{11}{10}$, $\frac{7}{8}$, $\frac{10}{12}$.

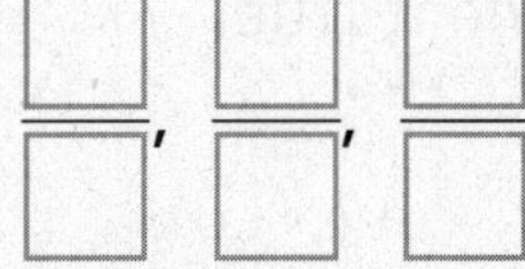

3 MP **Critique Reasoning** Ezra says that the following fractions are in order from greatest to least because the denominators are in order from greatest to least.

$\frac{7}{12}$, $\frac{9}{10}$, $\frac{10}{8}$

Is Ezra correct? Explain.

____

____

____

____

Test Prep

4 Write the fractions in order, from least to greatest.

$\frac{13}{12}$	$\frac{4}{3}$	$\frac{5}{6}$

____ < ____ < ____

5 Which shows the fractions ordered from greatest to least?

Ⓐ $\frac{5}{4}, \frac{7}{12}, \frac{11}{8}$

Ⓑ $\frac{11}{8}, \frac{5}{4}, \frac{7}{12}$

Ⓒ $\frac{5}{4}, \frac{11}{8}, \frac{7}{12}$

Ⓓ $\frac{11}{8}, \frac{7}{12}, \frac{5}{4}$

6 Wyatt, Heather, and Andy have the same size granola bars. Wyatt eats $\frac{3}{4}$ of his bar. Heather eats $\frac{5}{8}$ of her bar. Andy eats $\frac{4}{6}$ of his bar. Write the fractions in order, from least to greatest. Use fraction comparison strategies to justify your comparisons.

____

____

7 Write a numerator that makes the statement true.

$\frac{4}{10} < \frac{\square}{6} < \frac{7}{8}$

Spiral Review

8 Tell whether the number is *prime* or *composite*.

18 ____________

13 ____________

23 ____________

9 Draw a visual model for 14 ÷ 3. What is the remainder? How do you know?

____

____

____

Name ______________________________

Represent Tenths as Fractions and Decimals

1 (MP) **Use Structure** Tyler is making meatloaf for dinner. He uses $\frac{7}{10}$ pound of onions in his ground meat mixture. Use the tenths model to show the amount of onions in the meatloaf.

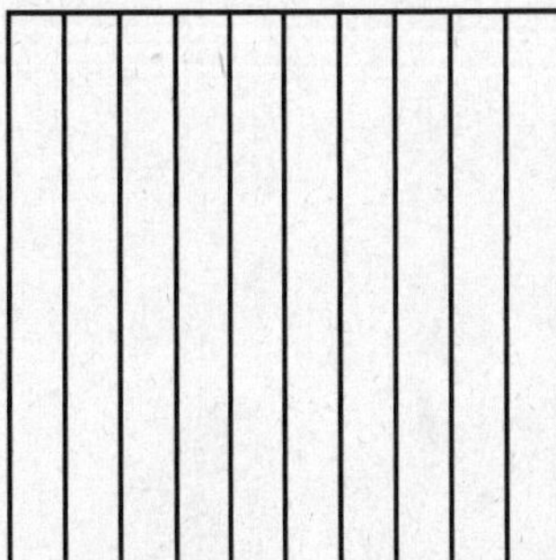

Write the weight of the onions as a decimal.

____

2 (MP) **Use Tools** Mrs. Thomas gives each student $1\frac{3}{10}$ inches of tape to write their names on and attach to their projects.

Show the length of tape that Mrs. Thomas gives each student on the number line.

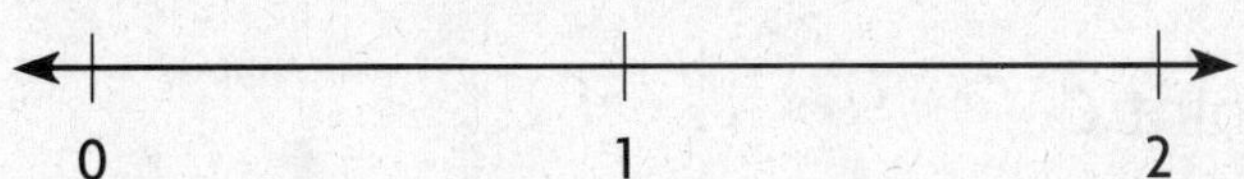

Write the length of tape that Mrs. Thomas gives each student as a decimal.

____

3 (MP) **Attend to Precision** James' dad wants to cut the grass. The tenths models show the number of gallons of gas in James' dad's lawnmower.

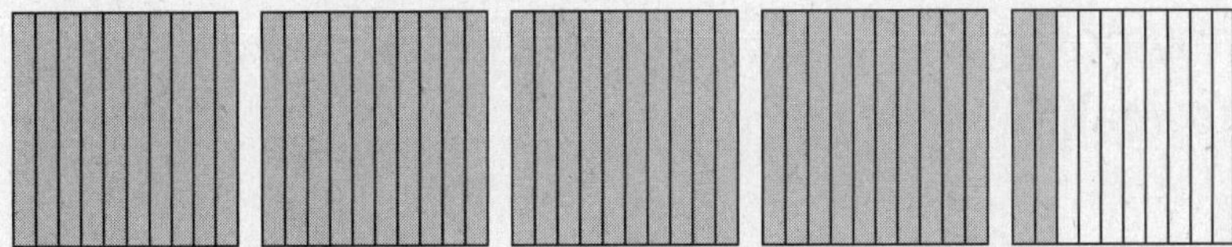

Write the number of gallons as a mixed number and as a decimal.

____

Test Prep

4 Which fraction is represented by the tenths model?

Ⓐ $\frac{4}{10}$

Ⓑ $\frac{5}{10}$

Ⓒ $\frac{6}{10}$

Ⓓ $\frac{9}{10}$

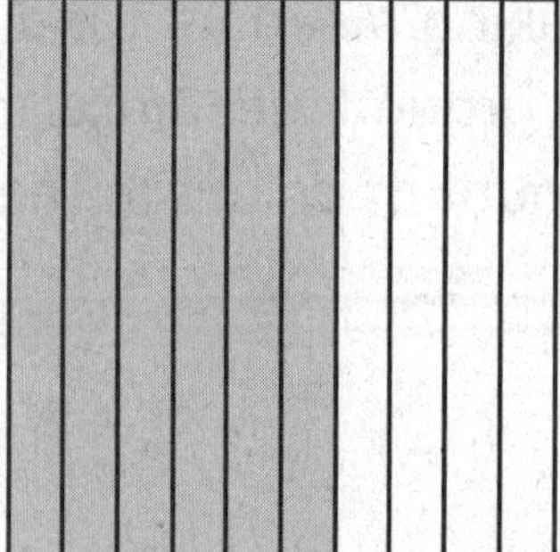

5 Billy waters a garden with $4\frac{8}{10}$ liters of water. Which shows the number of liters as a decimal?

Ⓐ 48.1 liters

Ⓑ 4.8 liters

Ⓒ 1.2 liters

Ⓓ 0.4 liter

6 Louisa runs $1\frac{6}{10}$ miles on a track. Which point on the number line shows the distance Louisa runs?

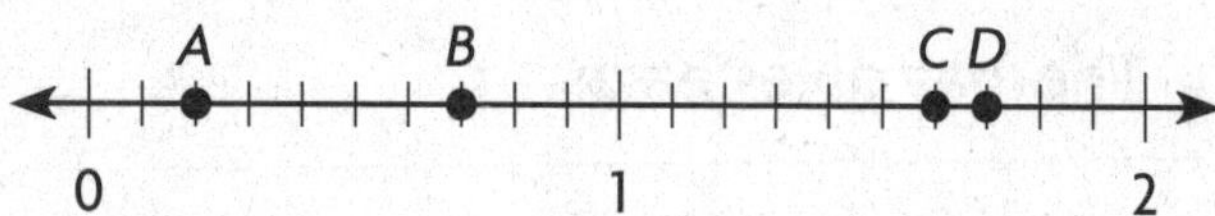

Ⓐ Point *A*

Ⓑ Point *B*

Ⓒ Point *C*

Ⓓ Point *D*

Spiral Review

7 Tina is making coffee for 18 people in a meeting. She plans for each person to get 2 cups of coffee. If each pot makes 12 cups, how many pots of coffee does Tina need to make?

____

8 Find the perimeter of a rectangular garden with a width of 49 feet and a length of 84 feet.

____

Name

Represent Hundredths as Fractions and Decimals

1 MP **Reason** Darius measures the rainfall with a rain gauge. The hundredths models show the amount of rain in centimeters that fell in one day.

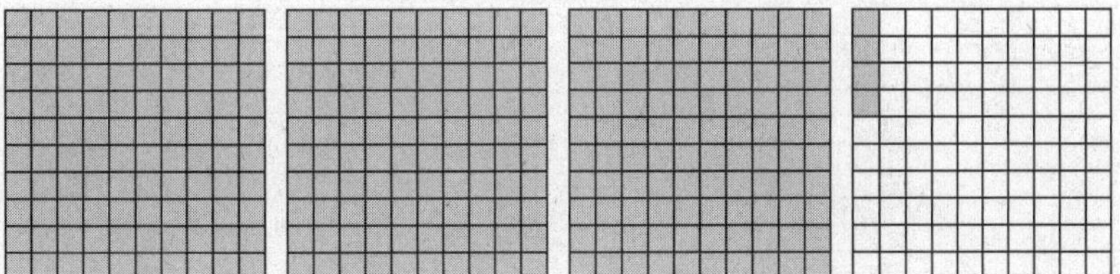

Write the amount of rain as a mixed number and as a decimal.

____

2 MP **Attend to Precision** Sherry is finding the mass of a rock in a science lab. The mass is $1\frac{74}{100}$ kilograms. Represent the mass of the rock on the hundredths models.

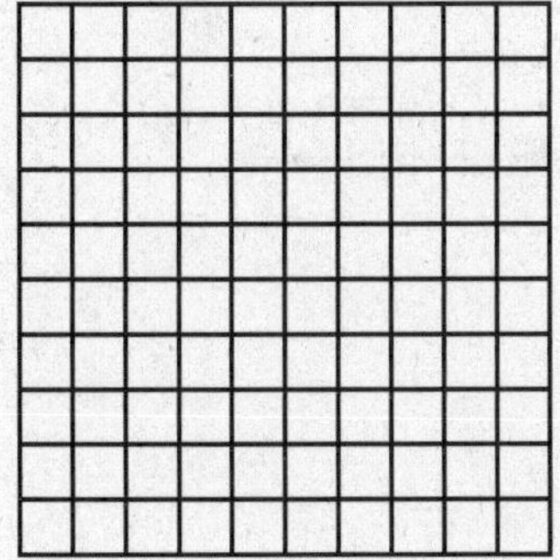

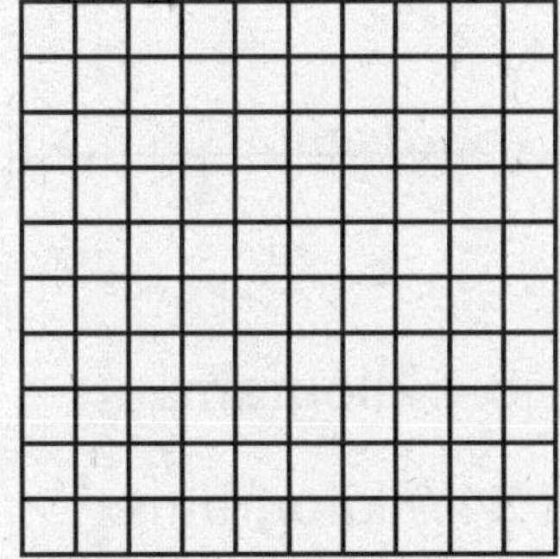

Write the mass of the rock as a decimal.

____

3 MP **Use Structure** In science class, Van uses $\frac{67}{100}$ liter of vinegar in a solution. Locate and label the number of liters of vinegar as a fraction and as a decimal on the number line.

Test Prep

4 Which shows 4.27 written as a mixed number?

Ⓐ $42\frac{7}{10}$ Ⓑ $4\frac{27}{10}$ Ⓒ $4\frac{27}{100}$ Ⓓ $4\frac{20}{100}$

5 Which hundredths model represents $\frac{19}{100}$?

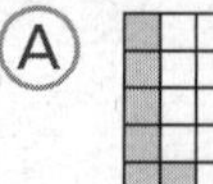

Ⓐ

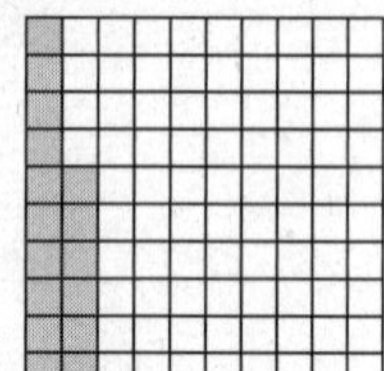

Ⓒ

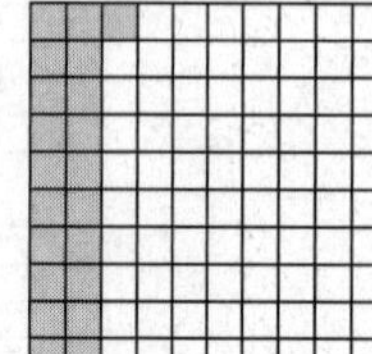

Ⓑ

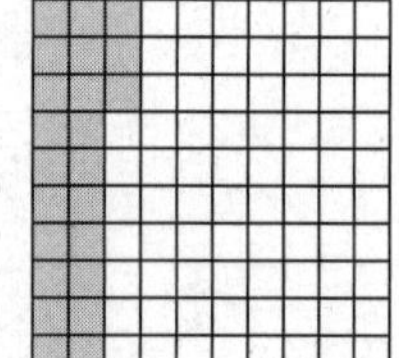

Ⓓ

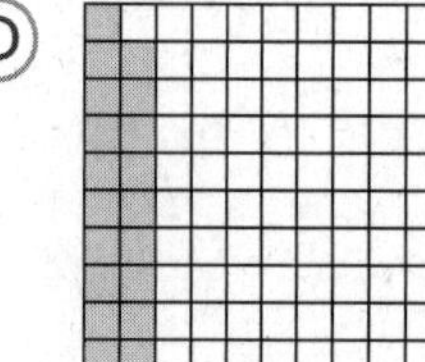

6 The number of kilograms of raisins Aria uses in her trail mix is shown on the number line. What is the mass of raisins Aria uses?

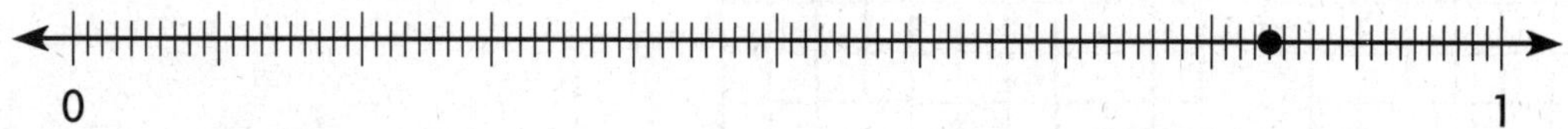

Ⓐ 0.80 kilogram

Ⓑ 0.84 kilogram

Ⓒ 8.4 kilograms

Ⓓ 84.0 kilograms

Spiral Review

7 **Divide.**

256 ÷ 8 = ______

120 ÷ 5 = ______

102 ÷ 6 = ______

8 Estimate. Then find the product.

Estimate: ____________

$$\begin{array}{r} 46 \\ \times\ 3 \\ \hline \end{array}$$

Estimate: ____________

$$\begin{array}{r} 68 \\ \times\ 5 \\ \hline \end{array}$$

Name ________________________

ONLINE
Video Tutorials and Interactive Examples

Identify Equivalent Fractions and Decimals

1 (MP) **Use Repeated Reasoning** Scott has finished $\frac{9}{10}$ of the fence he is building. Shade the hundredths model to show that amount. What is $\frac{9}{10}$ written as a decimal in hundredths?

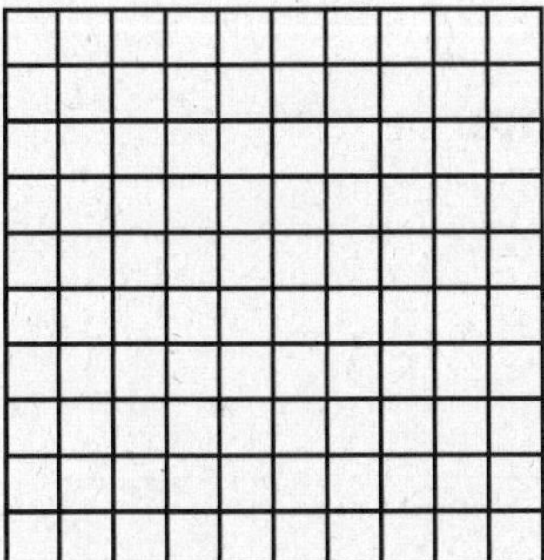

____

2 **Math on the Spot** Carter says that 0.08 is equivalent to $\frac{8}{10}$. Describe and correct Carter's error.

____

____

3 (MP) **Reason** Rachel pours 0.30 liter of juice into her sister's cup. Explain how you can rename 0.30 in tenths in fraction form and in decimal form.

____

____

____

4 Janice's jump rope is $5\frac{4}{10}$ feet long. Rename the length of the jump rope as a mixed number and as a decimal in hundredths.

____

5 There are $3\frac{60}{100}$ bags of grass seed left in the shed. Rename the amount of grass seed as a mixed number and as a decimal in tenths.

____

Test Prep

6 Which shows 0.5 as a fraction in hundredths?

Ⓐ $\frac{500}{10}$

Ⓑ $\frac{500}{100}$

Ⓒ $\frac{50}{100}$

Ⓓ $\frac{5}{100}$

7 Rename the number as a mixed number and a decimal in tenths.

$7\frac{60}{100}$

____

8 Morgan walks $2\frac{9}{10}$ miles in the park. What is $2\frac{9}{10}$ written as a decimal in hundredths?

Ⓐ 2.09 miles

Ⓑ 2.90 miles

Ⓒ 29.0 miles

Ⓓ 290.0 miles

9 Of the students in the math challenge, $\frac{70}{100}$ are fourth graders. Which decimal numbers are equivalent to the fraction of students who are in the math challenge and are in fourth grade? Select all that are correct.

Ⓐ 0.70

Ⓑ $\frac{7}{10}$

Ⓒ 7.0

Ⓓ $\frac{7}{1}$

Ⓔ 0.07

Ⓕ 0.7

Spiral Review

10 Use repeated subtraction to solve. Show your work.

23 ÷ 5 ______________

11 There are 5,280 feet in a mile. Mary runs 4 miles. How many feet does she run?

____

Name ______________________________

LESSON 12.4
More Practice/
Homework

Compare Decimals

1 (MP) **Use Structure** There are two vines growing on a tree. Vine A is 1.42 meters long. Vine B is 1.6 meters long. Which vine is longer? Shade the hundredths models for each length, and locate the lengths on the number line.

Vine A   Vine B

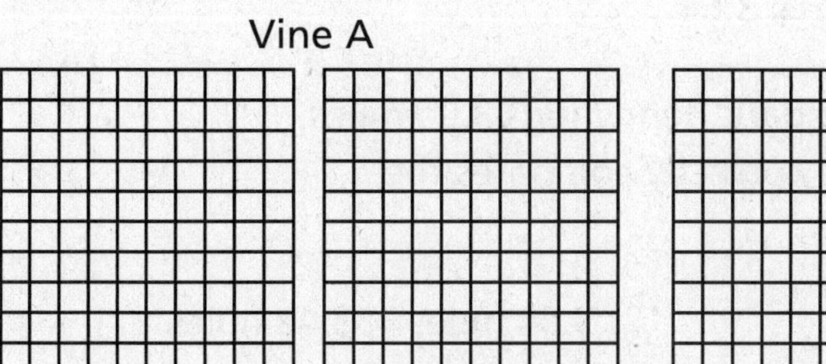

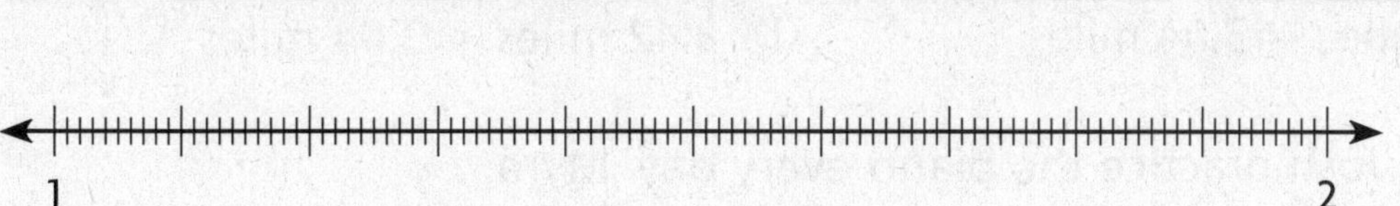

Use <, >, or = to compare the vine lengths. Then fill in the blank to state which vine is longer.

1.42 ◯ 1.6   __________ is longer.

Use the place-value chart to compare the decimals. Write <, >, or =.

2 0.26 ◯ 0.21

Ones	.	Tenths	Hundredths
	.		
	.		

3 0.63 ◯ 0.6

Ones	.	Tenths	Hundredths
	.		
	.		

Write <, >, or = to compare the decimals.

4 0.94 ◯ 0.95   **5** 0.48 ◯ 0.5   **6** 2.73 ◯ 2.06

7 2.2 ◯ 2.20   **8** 0.64 ◯ 5.21   **9** 2.11 ◯ 1.11

10 **Math on the Spot** Ricardo and Brandon ran a 1,500-meter race. Ricardo finished in 3.61 minutes. Brandon finished in 3.65 minutes. What was the time of the runner who finished last?

____

Test Prep

11 Select all the numbers that make the sentence true.

$3.46 < \blacksquare$

Ⓐ 3.5
Ⓑ 3.4
Ⓒ 3.45
Ⓓ 3.64

12 Shelia jogs 3.42 miles in the park. Jenny jogs 3.04 miles. Which comparison sentence correctly compares the distances the girls jog?

Ⓐ 3.04 miles > 3.42 miles
Ⓑ 3.42 miles = 3.04 miles
Ⓒ 3.04 miles < 3.42 miles
Ⓓ 3.42 miles < 3.04 miles

13 Myra and Josh practice the piano every day. Myra practices 4.2 hours this week. Josh practices 4.25 hours this week. Which statement is true?

Ⓐ Myra and Josh practice the same amount of time this week.
Ⓑ Myra practices more than Josh this week.
Ⓒ Josh practices less than Myra this week.
Ⓓ Josh practices more than Myra this week.

Spiral Review

14 A baker makes 75 muffins and puts them in boxes of 4. He fills as many boxes as he can. How many boxes does he need to hold all the muffins?

____

15 Miguel's goal is to read for 1,000 minutes in one month. This month he reads for 45 minutes each day for 24 days. Does Miguel reach his goal? Explain.

____

____

____

Name ______________________________

LESSON 12.5
More Practice/
Homework

ONLINE
Video Tutorials and
Interactive Examples

Relate Fractions, Decimals, and Money

1 **Use Tools** The bills and coins show how much change Steve receives at the store.

Shade the hundredths models to show the money amount.

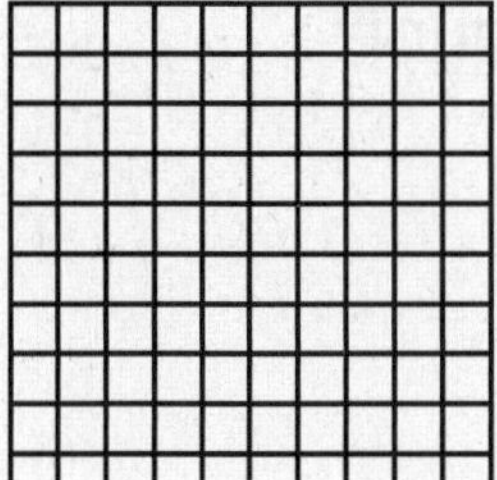
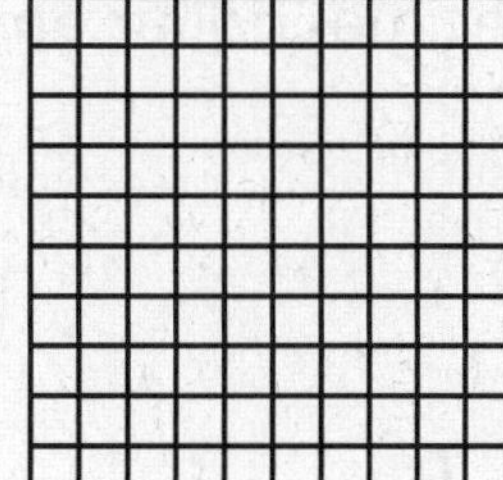
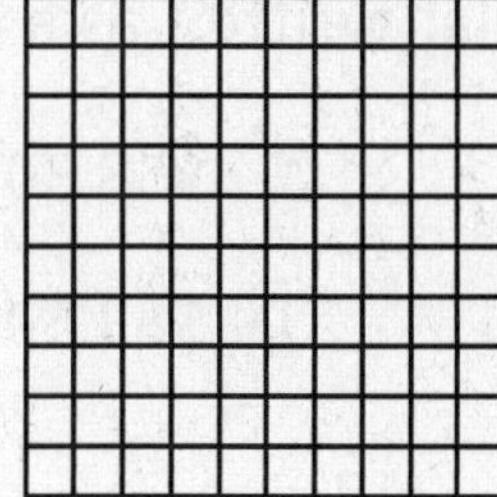

Write the amount as a mixed number, a decimal, and a decimal dollar amount.

____

2 **Math on the Spot** Kim spent $\frac{40}{100}$ of a dollar on a snack. Write as a money amount the amount she has left.

____

Pocket Change				
Name	**Quarters**	**Dimes**	**Nickels**	**Pennies**
Kim	1	3	2	3
Tony	0	6	1	6
Nick	2	4	0	2

Open Ended **Name bills and coins that could represent the fraction or mixed number. Then write the decimal dollar amount.**

3 $\frac{43}{100}$ of a dollar

____

____

4 $4\frac{94}{100}$ of a dollar

____

____

Test Prep

5 Write the amount as a mixed number, decimal, and decimal dollar amount.

______

6 Which is $5\frac{83}{100}$ of a dollar written as a decimal dollar amount?

Ⓐ $3.58
Ⓑ $5.83
Ⓒ $58.30
Ⓓ $83.50

7 Which bills and coins could show one dollar and twenty-nine cents? Select all that are correct.

Ⓐ one $1 bill, 2 dimes, 1 nickel, 4 pennies
Ⓑ one $1 bill, 1 quarter, 4 pennies
Ⓒ one $1 bill, 2 nickels, 9 pennies
Ⓓ one $1 bill, 5 nickels, 4 pennies
Ⓔ one $1 bill, 4 nickels, 4 pennies

Spiral Review

8 Divide.

$7\overline{)2,321}$

9 Find the unknown measure of the rectangle.

Area = 90 sq ft

9 ft

n

______

Name ______________________

LESSON 12.6
More Practice/ Homework

ONLINE
Video Tutorials and Interactive Examples

Solve Multistep Money Problems

1 **Open Ended** Write a decimal dollar amount that represents the value of four \$1 bills, 6 quarters, and 4 nickels. Then write two other combinations of coins and bills that have that same value.

____

2 **Math on the Spot** Four girls have \$5.00 to share equally. How much money will each girl get? Explain.

____

____

____

3 (MP) **Attend to Precision** Jack has the amount of money shown.

He buys 2 bottles of water that each cost \$0.95. How much money does he have left? Give your answer as a decimal dollar amount.

____

4 (MP) **Use Repeated Reasoning** Kerrie goes to the mall with \$8.40. She purchases a bracelet for \$3.35. Then she buys lunch for \$4.60. How much money does Kerrie have left at the end of the day? Give your answer as a decimal dollar amount.

____

5 (MP) **Construct Arguments** Wes has \$6.90 to buy supplies for his art project. He wants some paint sets that are \$2.35. Does Wes have enough money to buy 3 sets? Explain.

____

Test Prep

6 Dakota has \$3.30. She needs 4 times as much money, plus \$0.75 more, to buy the new sweater that she wants. What is the cost of the sweater?

Ⓐ \$13.75
Ⓑ \$13.85
Ⓒ \$13.95
Ⓓ \$14.90

7 Write the decimal dollar amount that represents the value of six \$1 bills, 8 quarters, 2 dimes, and 9 pennies.

____

8 Guy has \$6.00. He buys 5 packs of watermelon seeds to plant in a garden for \$0.80 each. How much money does Guy have left?

Ⓐ \$1.00
Ⓑ \$2.00
Ⓒ \$3.00
Ⓓ \$4.00

Spiral Review

9 Complete the visual model to show each fraction.
Write <, >, or = to compare.

$\frac{2}{3}$ ○ $\frac{7}{12}$

$\frac{7}{12}$ ○ $\frac{2}{3}$

10 Compare.
Write >, <, or =.

$\frac{9}{12}$ ○ $\frac{4}{5}$

$\frac{7}{8}$ ○ $\frac{4}{6}$

$\frac{11}{6}$ ○ $\frac{8}{10}$

$\frac{6}{12}$ ○ $\frac{2}{4}$

$\frac{4}{5}$ ○ $\frac{5}{6}$

Name ______________________________

Explore Lines, Rays, and Angles

1 (MP) **Model with Mathematics** Joan draws a picture of the constellation Ursa Major, or the Big Dipper. Draw and label a line segment and an angle from the picture.

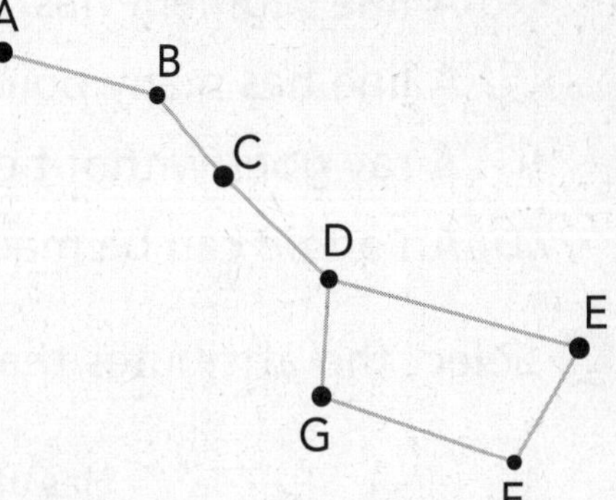

Use the figure to help you.

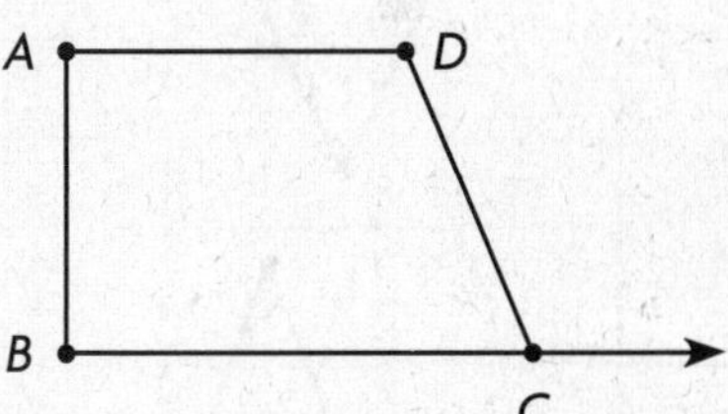

2 Name four points. ______________________________

3 Name an angle. ______________________________

Draw and label an example of each figure.

4 $\overleftrightarrow{KL}$

5 point B

6 $\overrightarrow{WV}$

7 **Math on the Spot** How many different angles are in Figure X? List them.

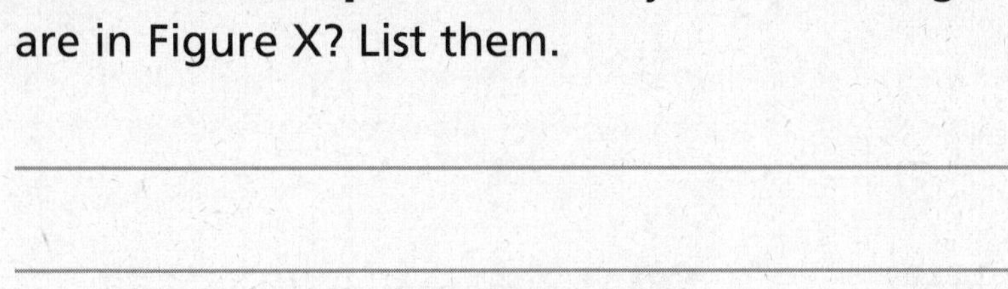

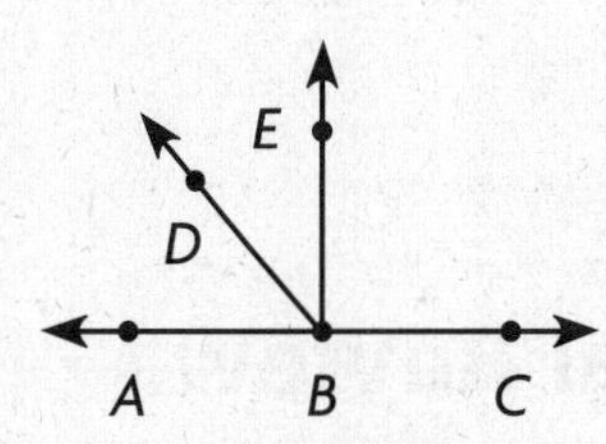

Figure X

Test Prep

8 Which statement is true?

Ⓐ A line segment has 1 endpoint.
Ⓑ A line has many points.
Ⓒ A ray goes without end in both directions.
Ⓓ An angle can be made by 2 points.

9 Select the attributes that apply to each figure.

	Has at Least One Point	Has at Least One Ray	Has at Least One Line	Has at Least One Angle
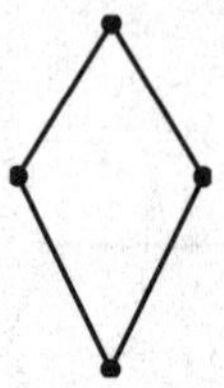	☐	☐	☐	☐
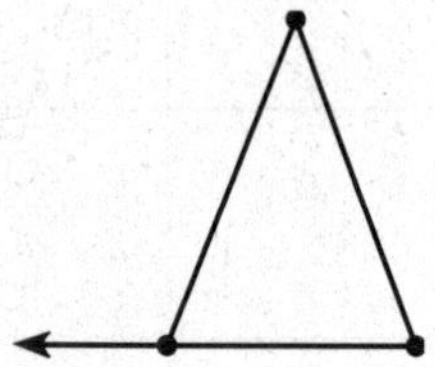	☐	☐	☐	☐

Draw and label an example of each figure.

10 $\angle STU$

11 $\overline{FG}$

Spiral Review

12 Find a common denominator for the pair of fractions.

$\frac{2}{3}$ and $\frac{3}{6}$

____

13 Use mental math to find the product.

$3 \times 5 \times 100$

____

Name ______________________________

Explore Angles

1 (MP) **Reason** Stacy draws a two-dimensional figure with 6 sides. The figure has at least 2 pairs of angles that are the same size. Draw what the figure might look like. How do you know the angle pairs are the same size?

____

____

____

2 The blade openings of the scissors form angles. Compare the angles. Then list the numbers for the scissors in order from least to greatest.

____

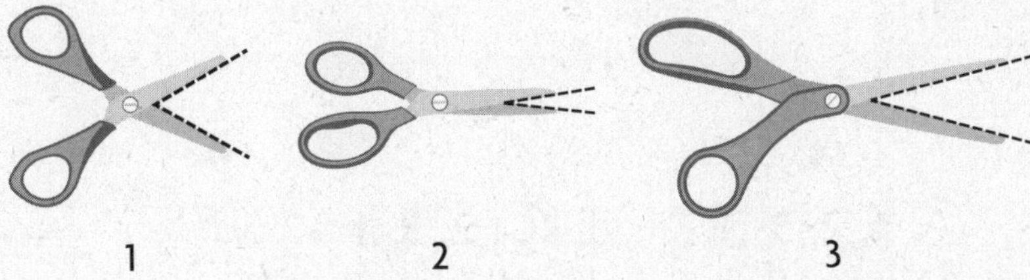

Use the unit angle shown.

3 How many unit angles come together in the center of the circle?

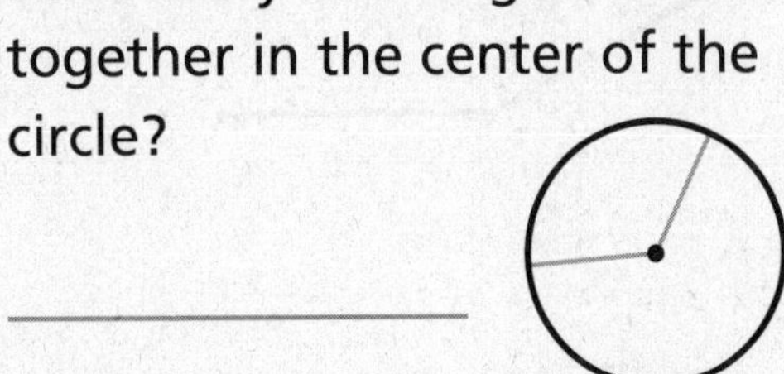

____

4 How many unit angles fill the angle?

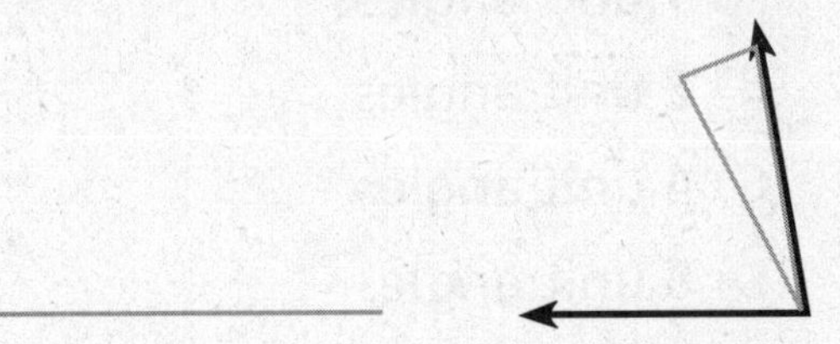

____

5 How many unit angles come together in the center of the circle?

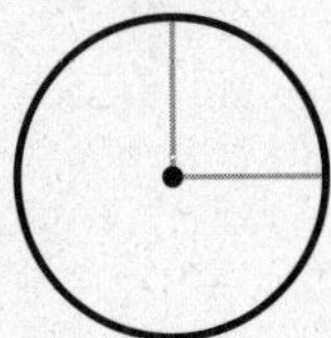

____

6 A pizza is cut into slices to form equal angles. How many slices come together in the center of the pizza?

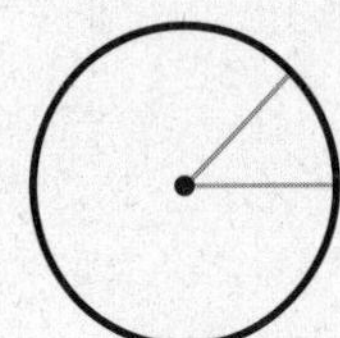

____

Test Prep

7 Select the angles that are the same size.

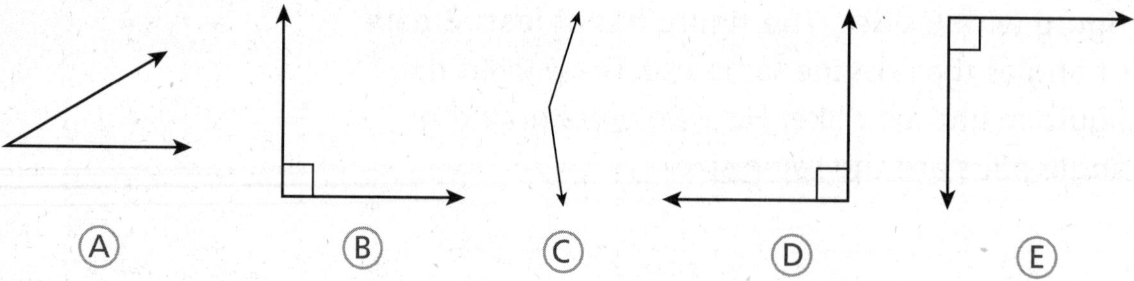

8 Compare the angles. Which shows the angles in order from least to greatest?

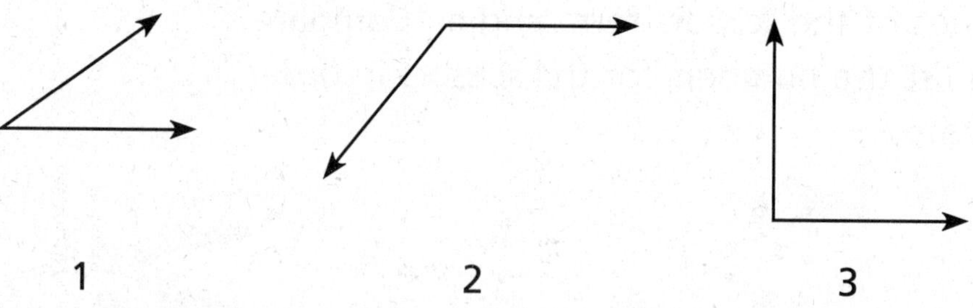

Ⓐ 1, 2, 3

Ⓑ 2, 1, 3

Ⓒ 2, 3, 1

Ⓓ 1, 3, 2

9 How many unit angles make up the angle?

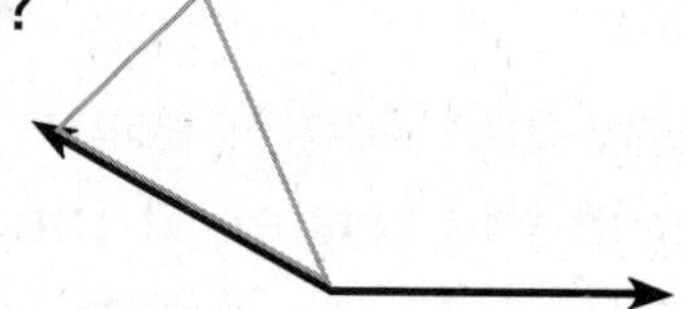

Ⓐ 1 unit angles

Ⓑ 2 unit angles

Ⓒ 4 unit angles

Ⓓ 6 unit angles

Spiral Review

10 Write the amount shown as a mixed number and as a decimal.

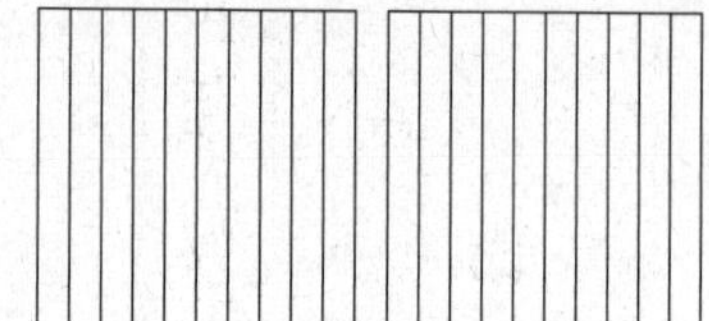

____

11 Write the fractions in order, from least to greatest: $\frac{1}{2}$, $\frac{5}{8}$, $\frac{1}{4}$.

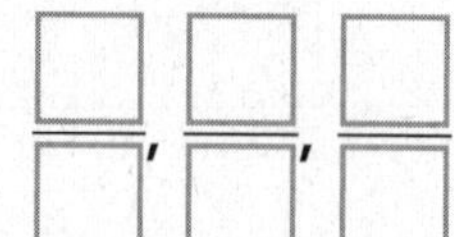

Name ______________________

Relate Angles to Fractional Parts of a Circle

1 Tatiana makes a spinner for a math game. She wants to shade $\frac{3}{8}$ of the circle gray. Is her spinner correct? Why or why not? Explain.

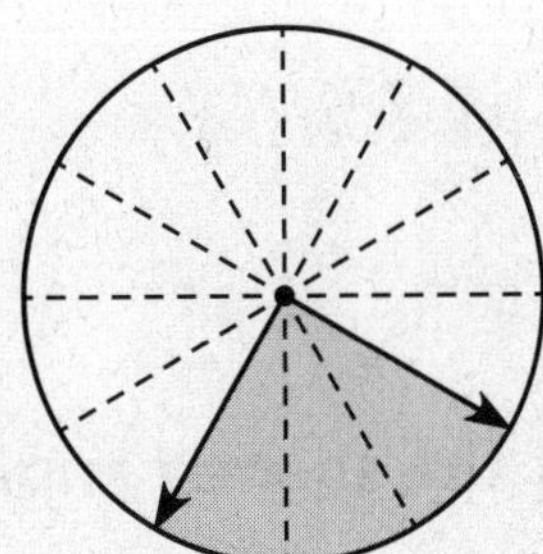

____

____

2 What is the fractional measure of the unshaded angle on Tatiana's spinner?

____

3 How can you make the fractional measure of the shaded angle $\frac{5}{12}$?

____

____

What is the fractional measure of the shaded angle?

4

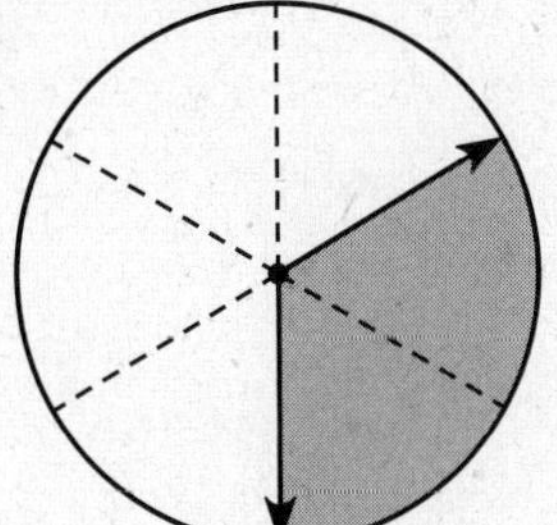

____

5

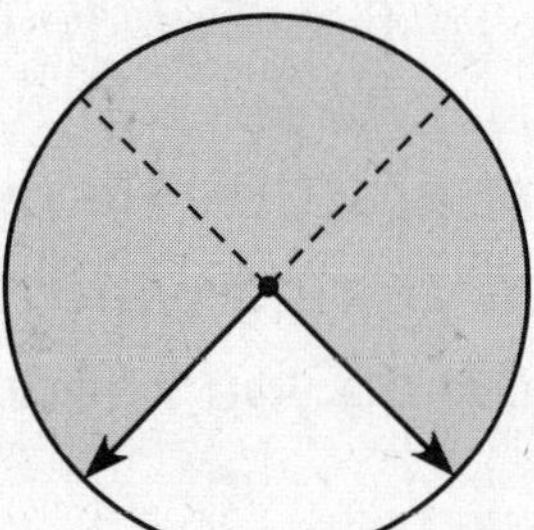

____

6

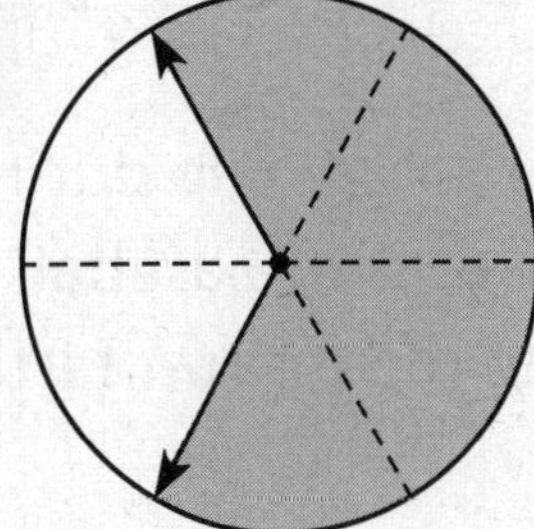

____

Test Prep

7 Gabriel divides a circle into 6 parts and shades 4 parts. Select all of the ways to show the fractional measure of the part of the circle that is shaded?

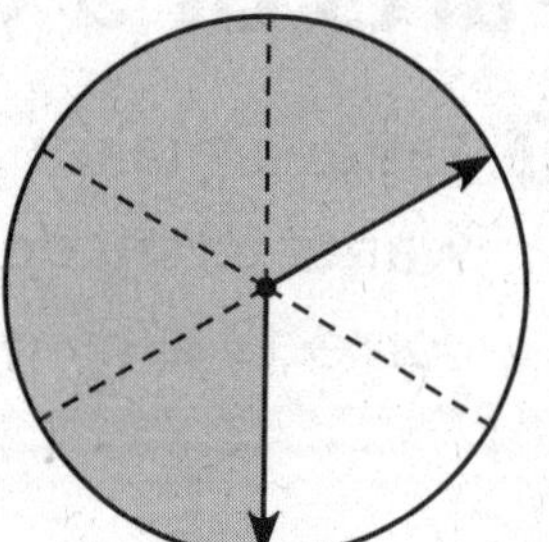

Ⓐ $\frac{1}{3}$ Ⓓ $\frac{6}{6}$

Ⓑ $\frac{4}{6}$ Ⓔ $\frac{2}{3}$

Ⓒ $\frac{2}{6}$ Ⓕ $\frac{4}{2}$

What is the fractional measure of the shaded angle?

8

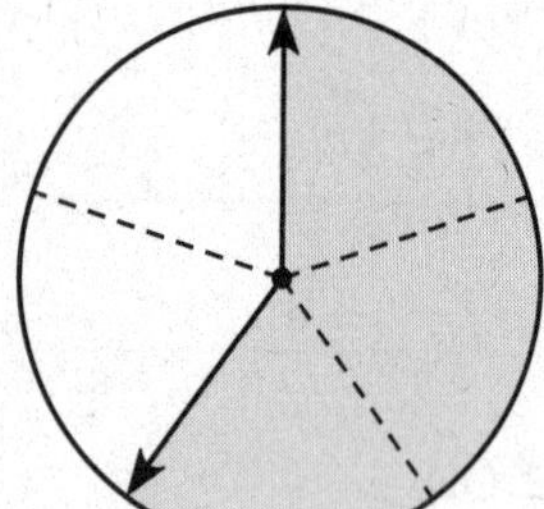

______

9

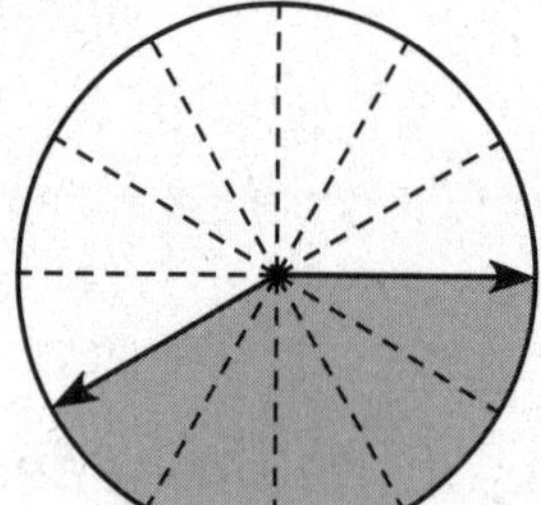

______

10

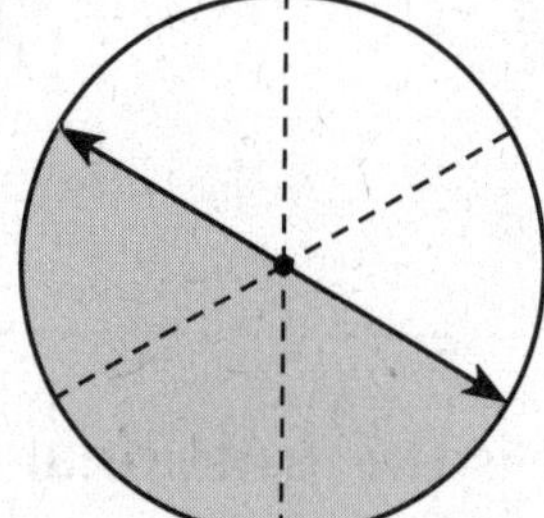

______

Spiral Review

11 Is 8 a factor of the number? Write *yes* or *no*.

23 ______

32 ______

72 ______

12 Write > or < for the comparison.

$\frac{4}{5}$ ◯ $\frac{7}{10}$

$\frac{1}{2}$ ◯ $\frac{3}{4}$

$\frac{6}{6}$ ◯ $\frac{1}{3}$

13 Cooper ran $\frac{5}{8}$ mile during soccer practice. He ran $\frac{9}{10}$ mile during baseball practice. During which practice did he run farther? How do you know?

______

Name ___

Relate Degrees to Fractional Parts of a Circle

1 Angles are used in the construction of roof trusses for homes and buildings.

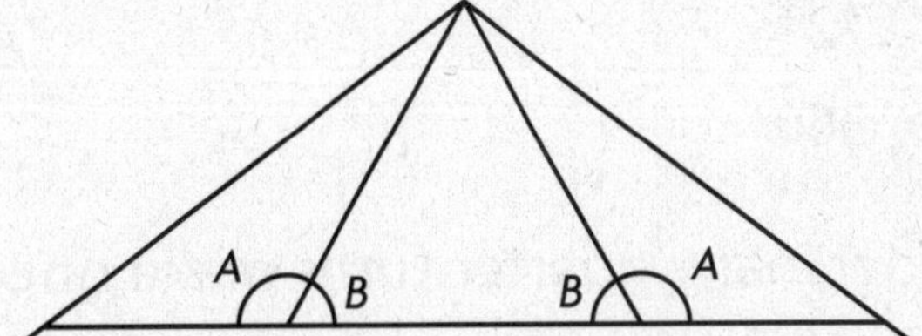

- Angle *A* turns through $\frac{1}{3}$ of a circle. What is the measure of angle *A*?

___

- Angle *B* turns through $\frac{1}{6}$ of a circle. What is the measure of angle *B*?

___

2 How many right angles turn through a circle?

___

Tell the measure of the angle in degrees.

3 ___

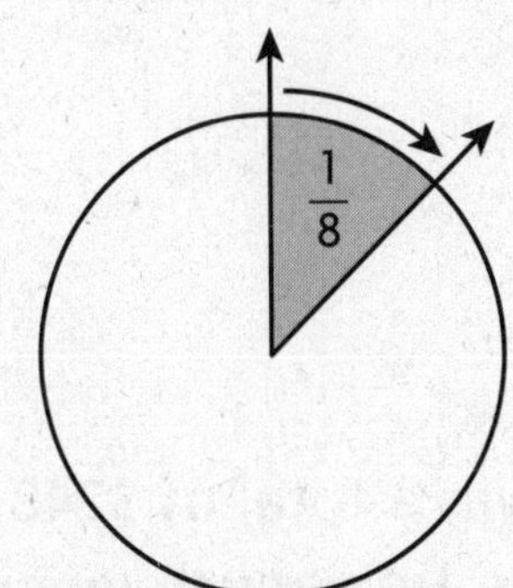

4 ___

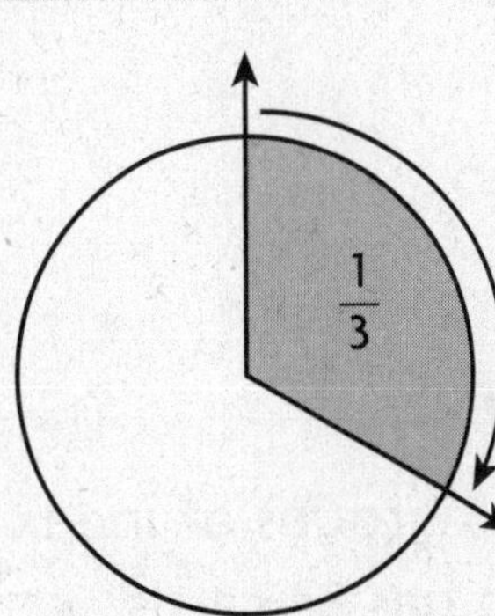

Classify the angle. Write *acute, right, obtuse, straight,* or *reflex*.

5

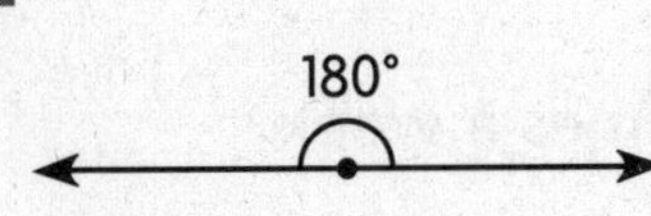

___

6

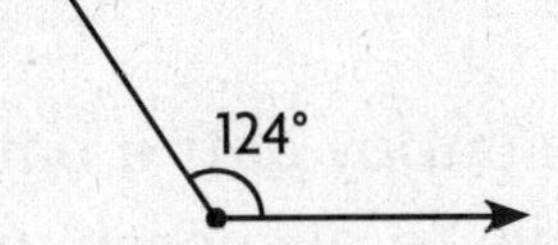

___

7

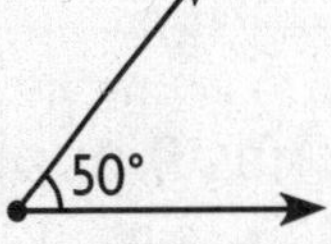

___

Test Prep

8 What is the measure of the angle in degrees?

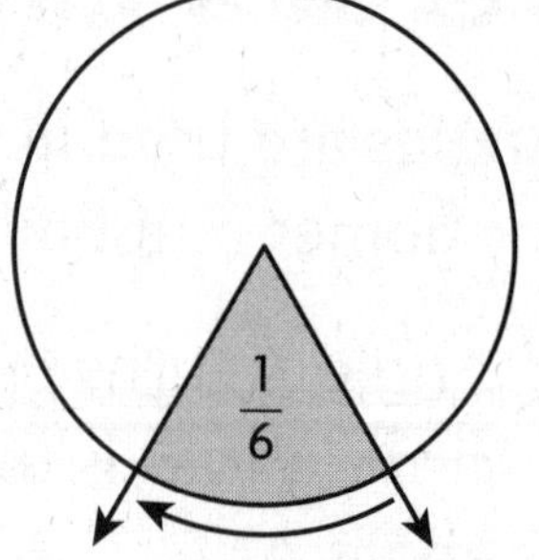

Ⓐ 60°
Ⓑ 65°
Ⓒ 72°
Ⓓ 360°

9 How many quarter turns make one full turn on a circle?

Ⓐ 2
Ⓑ 3
Ⓒ 4
Ⓓ 1

10 Classify an angle that has a measure of 174°.

Ⓐ acute angle
Ⓑ right angle
Ⓒ obtuse angle
Ⓓ reflex angle

Spiral Review

11 Mrs. Hoops has 15 groups of index cards. Each group has 64 cards. About how many index cards does Mrs. Hoops have?

____

12 Noah saves a total of $248 over 8 months. How much money does he save each month if he saves an equal amount each month?

____

13 Gia's dog has 9 puppies. Each puppy gets a bath 3 times a week. How many baths does Gia have to give each week?

____

Name ______________________________

ONLINE
Video Tutorials and Interactive Examples

Measure and Draw Angles Using a Protractor

1 (MP) **Use Tools** A seesaw is an example of a simple machine: a lever. Like a balance scale, a seesaw can be balanced and level, or one side can be higher or lower than the other side. The park department wants to order a new seesaw that has an angle of 60 degrees under it when unbalanced. Use a protractor to find the angle measure formed by the underside of the seesaw and the center support. Write each measure. Then circle the seesaw the park department should order.

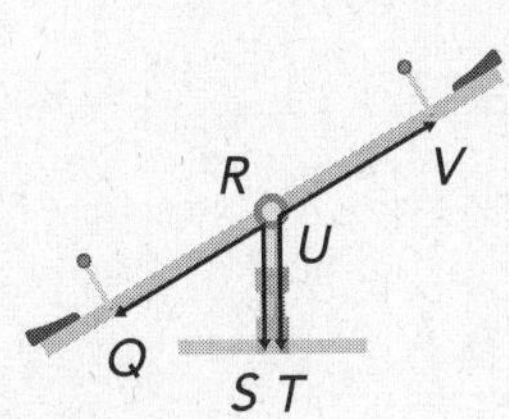

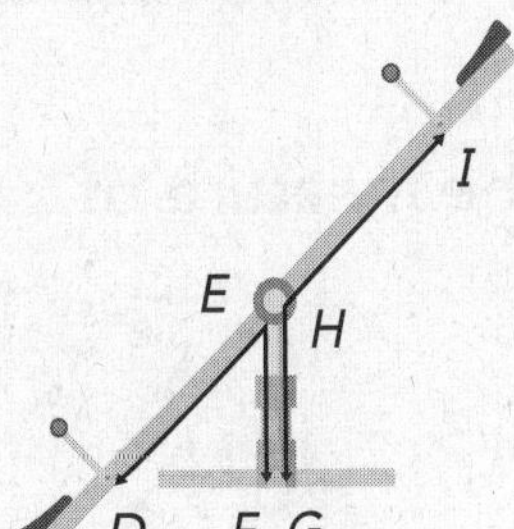

m∠QRS = __________ m∠DEF = __________

2 Use a protractor to find the angle measure.

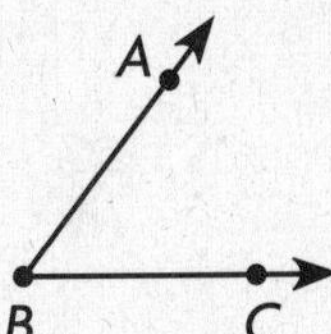

What do you need to do to each ray before you can find the measure of the angle?

____

m∠ABC = __________

Use a protractor to draw the angle.

3 82°

4 145°

5 **Math on the Spot** Draw an angle with a measure of 0°. Describe your drawing.

____

____

Test Prep

6 Use the protractor to complete ∠*RST* that measures 84°.

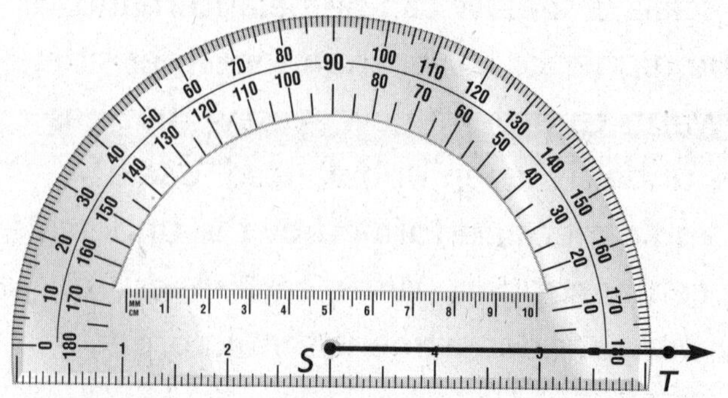

7 What is the measure of ∠*FGH*?

Ⓐ 55°
Ⓑ 65°
Ⓒ 125°
Ⓓ 135°

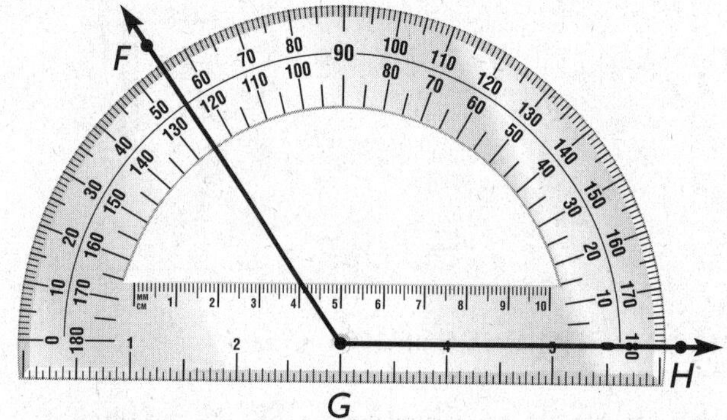

Spiral Review

8 Use the area or perimeter formula to find the unknown measure.

A fourth-grade class is painting a rectangular mural that has an area of 96 square feet. The width of the mural is 8 feet. What is the length?

9 Write the measure of the shaded angle in degrees.

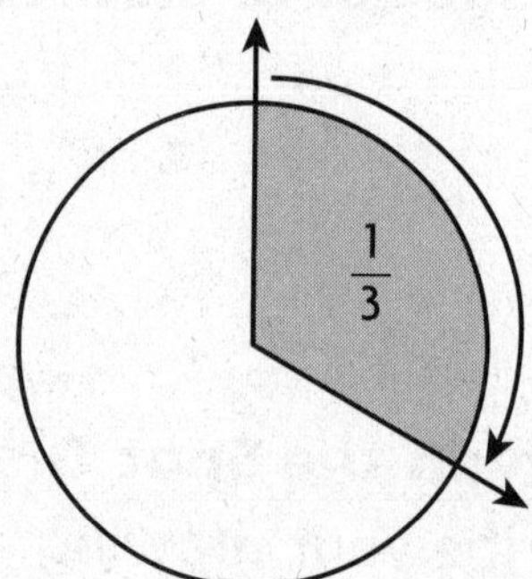

Name

Join and Separate Angles

1 Could the measures of the four angles in the circle be 75°, 105°, 80°, and 100°? Explain.

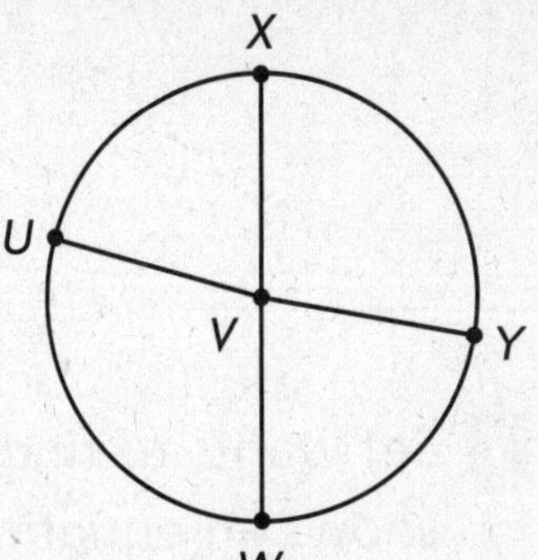

Use Tools **Use a protractor to find the measure of each angle. Label each angle with its measure. Write the sum of the angle measures as an equation.**

2

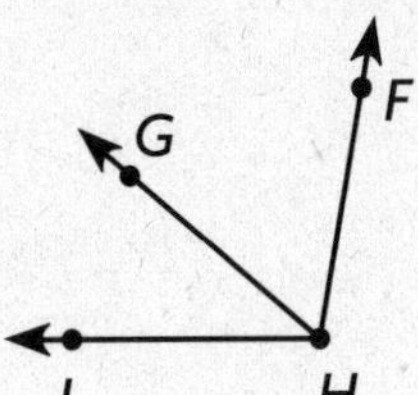

3

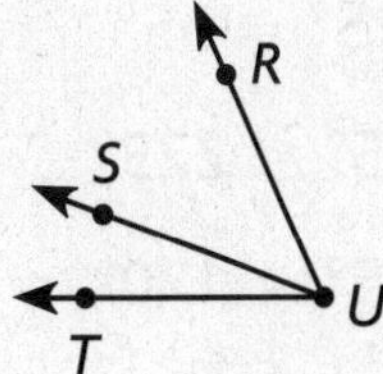

The measure of each whole angle is 170°. It is separated into two parts in two different ways. For each way, measure one part of the angle with a protractor. Then write an equation to find the measure of the second angle.

4

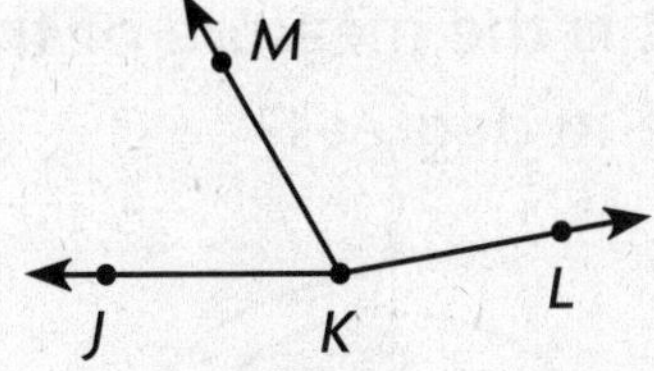

m∠ _______ = _______

5

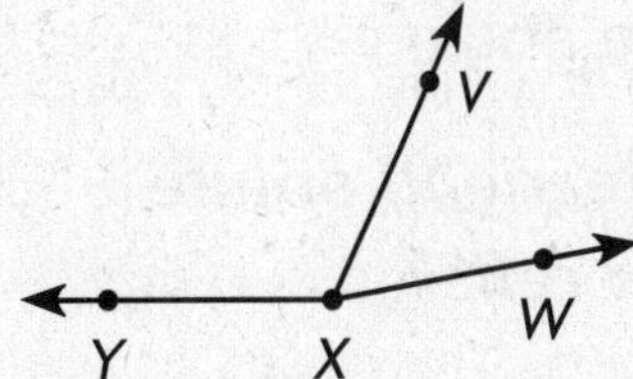

m∠ _______ = _______

Test Prep

6 Write an equation to find the measure of $\angle XYZ$.

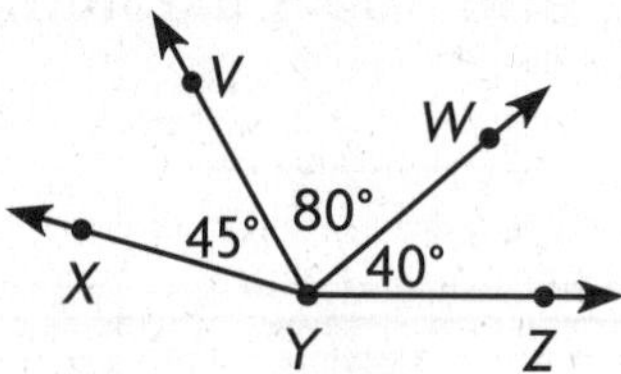

____

7 Sef wants to find the measure of $\angle ABC$. Which shows an equation he could use to find the measure of $\angle ABC$?

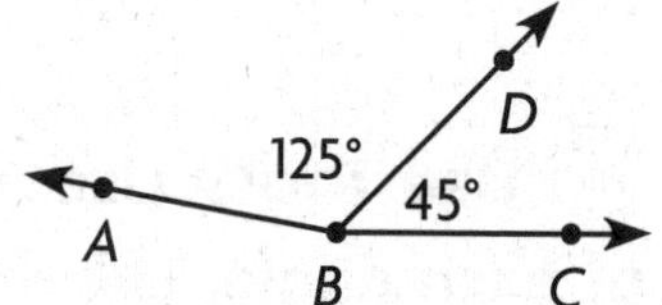

(A) $125° - 45° = 80°$

(B) $180° - 125° = 55°$

(C) $180° + 45° = 225°$

(D) $125° + 45° = 170°$

8 Use a protractor to find the measure of each angle. Label each angle with its measure. Write the sum of the angle measures as an equation.

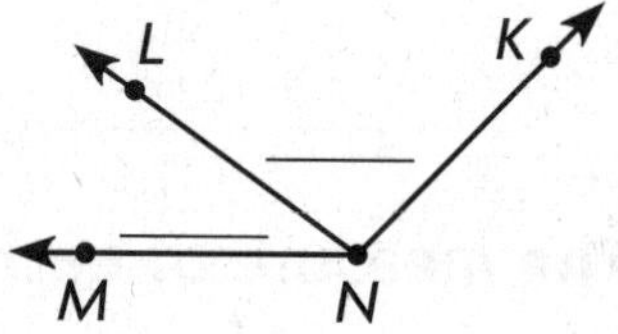

____

Spiral Review

9 Classify the angle.

Write *acute, right, obtuse, straight,* or *reflex.*

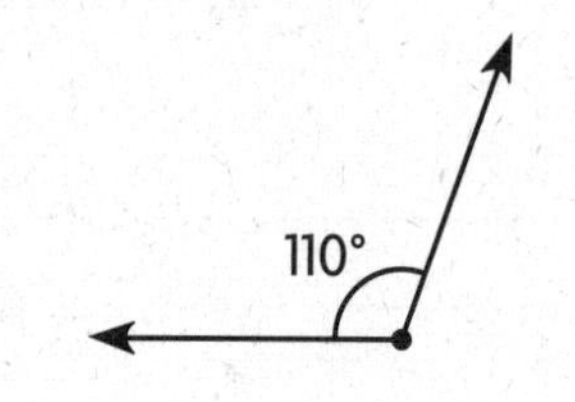

____

10 What is the measure of the angle in degrees?

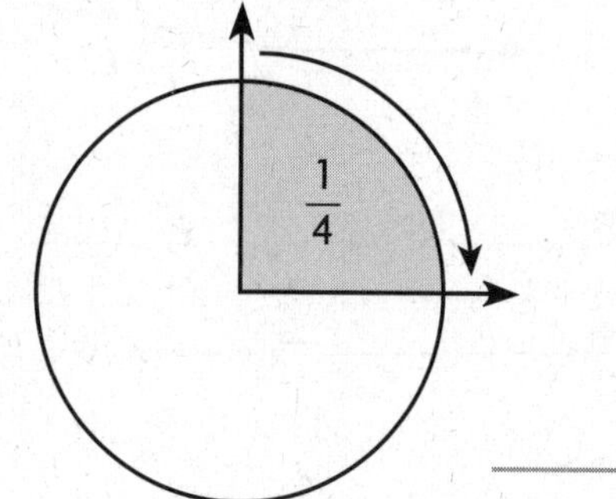

______

Name

Find Unknown Angle Measures

1 Laura cuts a square out of scrap paper as shown. What is the angle measure of the piece left over?

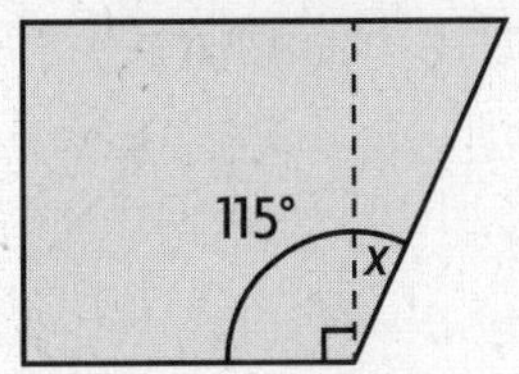

2 **Math on the Spot** What if Laura cut a smaller square as shown? Would m$\angle MNQ$ be different? Explain.

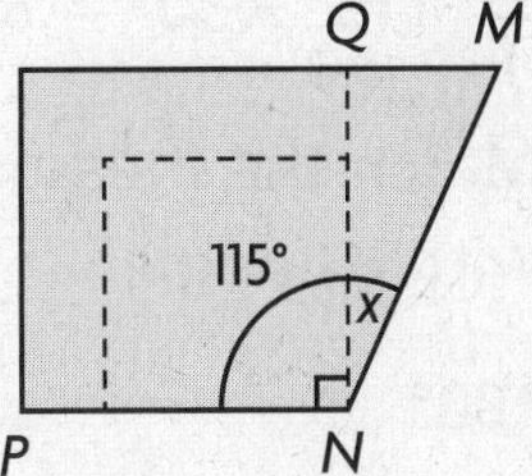

Write an equation to find the measure of the unknown angle.

3

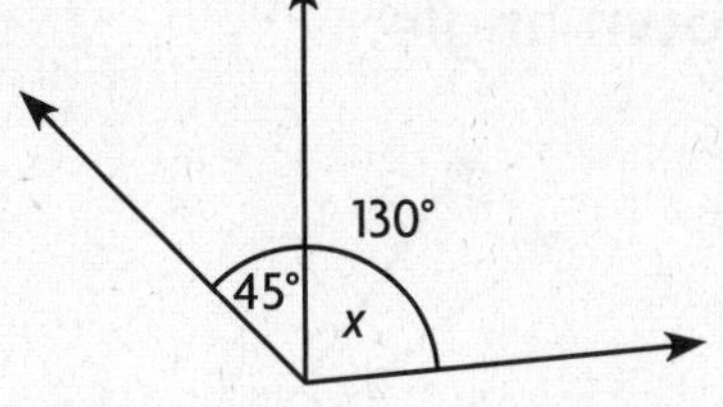

4

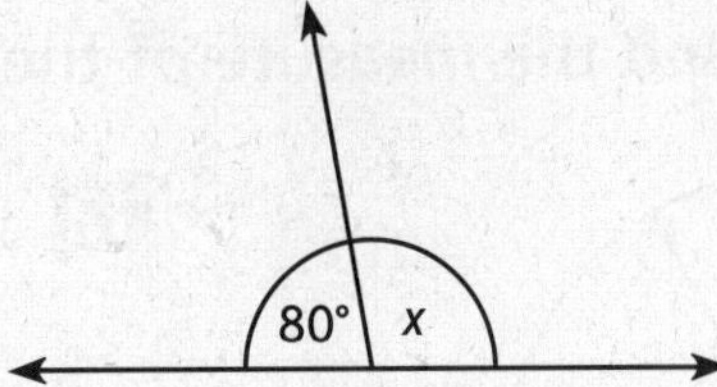

5

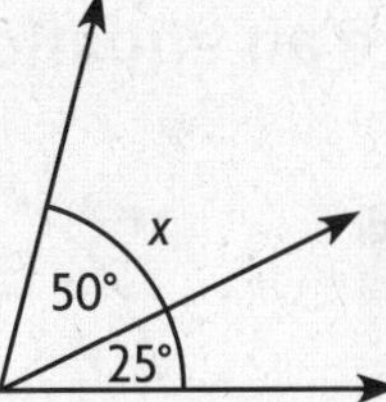

6

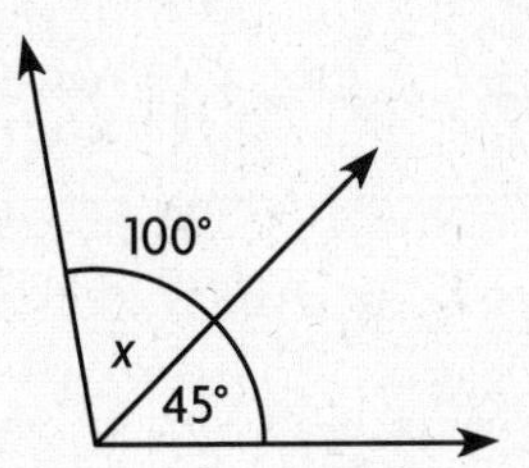

7

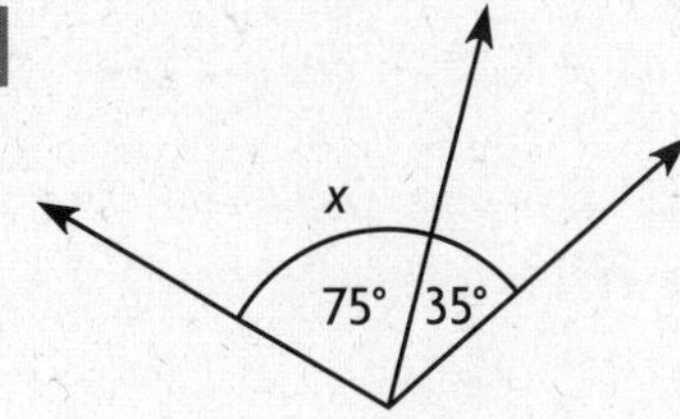

8

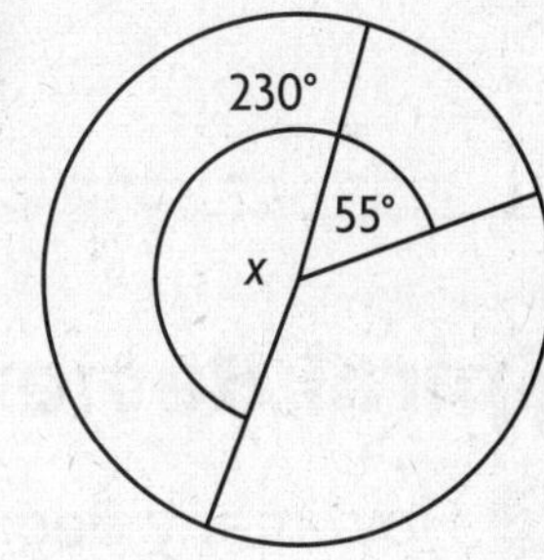

Test Prep

9 Which equation shows the measure of the unknown angle?

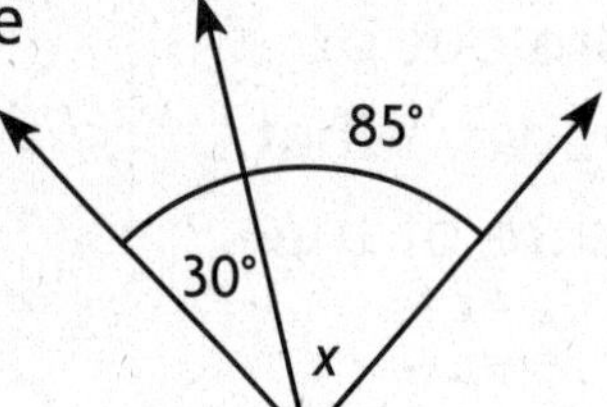

Ⓐ 85° + 30° = 115°

Ⓑ 85° − 30° = 55°

Ⓒ 115° + 30° = 145°

Ⓓ 115° − 30° = 85°

10 Match the measure of each angle with its angle.

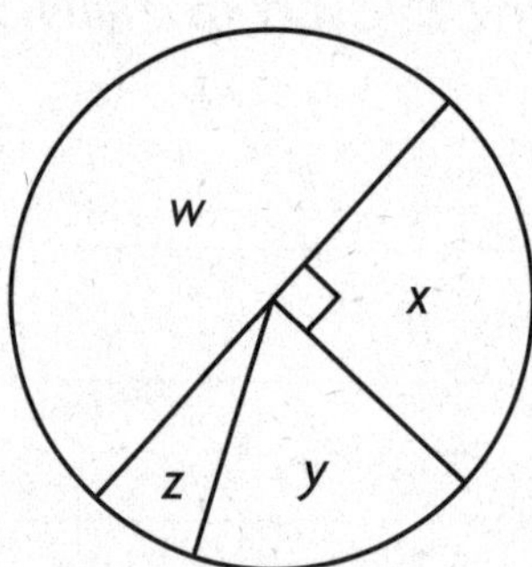

180° •	• w
65° •	• x
25° •	• y
90° •	• z

Write an equation to find the measure of the unknown angle.

11

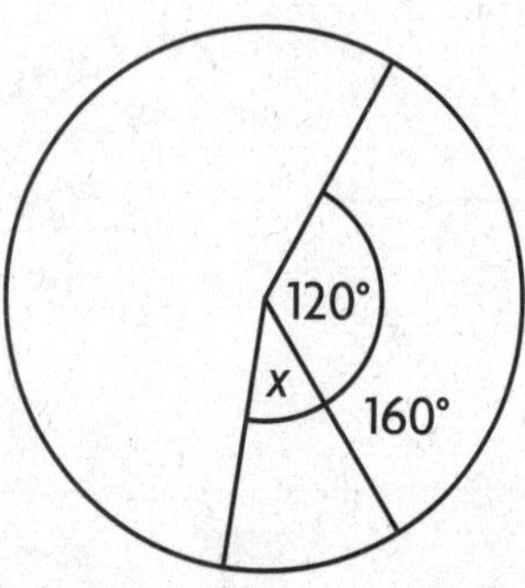

____

12

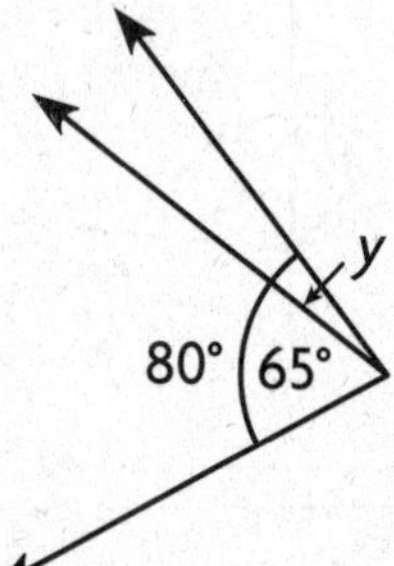

____

Spiral Review

13 How many degrees are in an angle that turns through $\frac{1}{8}$ of a circle?

____

14 Use a protractor to find the angle measure.

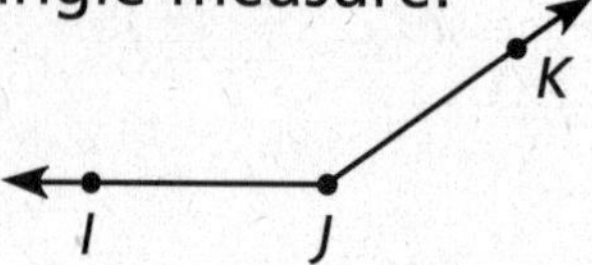

____

Name

Decompose Fractions into Sums

1 (MP) **Model with Mathematics** Look at the list of the names of the months of the year.

- Draw a visual model to show the fraction of the names of the months that contain the letter *y*.

January	July
February	August
March	September
April	October
May	November
June	December

- Write an addition equation to model the fraction as a sum of the fractions representing each month.

Write the fraction as a sum of unit fractions.

2 $\frac{2}{6} =$

3 $\frac{4}{5} =$

4 $\frac{3}{8} =$

5 (MP) **Model with Mathematics** Marlon threw a bowling ball twice and knocked down a total of 6 pins.

Shade the visual fraction models to show two ways he could have knocked down the 6 pins on the two throws. Then model each with an equation.

Write the fraction as a sum of two fractions.

6 $\frac{2}{5} =$

7 $\frac{9}{10} =$

8 $\frac{7}{8} =$

Test Prep

9 Select all the ways to represent $\frac{7}{10}$.

Ⓐ $\frac{3}{10} + \frac{2}{10} + \frac{2}{10}$

Ⓑ $\frac{1}{7} + \frac{1}{7} + \frac{1}{7} + \frac{1}{7} + \frac{1}{7} + \frac{1}{7} + \frac{1}{7}$

Ⓒ $\frac{5}{10} + \frac{2}{10}$

Ⓓ $\frac{10}{1} + \frac{10}{1} + \frac{10}{1} + \frac{10}{1} + \frac{10}{1} + \frac{10}{1} + \frac{10}{1}$

Ⓔ $\frac{1}{10} + \frac{2}{10} + \frac{3}{10} + \frac{1}{10}$

10 Lila has 12 pencils, and 6 of them are not sharpened. Which shows the fraction of the pencils that are not sharpened?

Ⓐ $\frac{1}{12} + \frac{1}{12} + \frac{1}{12} + \frac{1}{12} + \frac{1}{12}$

Ⓑ $\frac{1}{12} + \frac{1}{12} + \frac{1}{12} + \frac{1}{12} + \frac{1}{12} + \frac{1}{12}$

Ⓒ $\frac{1}{12} + \frac{1}{12} + \frac{1}{12} + \frac{1}{12} + \frac{1}{12} + \frac{1}{12} + \frac{1}{12}$

Ⓓ $\frac{1}{12} + \frac{1}{12} + \frac{1}{12} + \frac{1}{12} + \frac{1}{12} + \frac{1}{12} + \frac{1}{12} + \frac{1}{12}$

11 Gina has 10 picture frames, and 3 of them are not broken. Which shows the fraction of the picture frames that are broken?

Ⓐ $\frac{1}{10} + \frac{1}{10} + \frac{1}{10} + \frac{1}{10} + \frac{1}{10}$

Ⓑ $\frac{1}{10} + \frac{1}{10} + \frac{1}{10} + \frac{1}{10} + \frac{1}{10} + \frac{1}{10}$

Ⓒ $\frac{1}{10} + \frac{1}{10} + \frac{1}{10} + \frac{1}{10} + \frac{1}{10} + \frac{1}{10} + \frac{1}{10}$

Ⓓ $\frac{1}{10} + \frac{1}{10} + \frac{1}{10} + \frac{1}{10} + \frac{1}{10} + \frac{1}{10} + \frac{1}{10} + \frac{1}{10}$

Spiral Review

12 Is 3 a factor of the number? Write *yes* or *no*.

14 ________

54 ________

13 Which of the numbers are not multiples of 6?

6, 12, 14, 18, 24, 30, 32, 36

____

Name ______________________________

Join Parts of the Same Whole

1 **Model with Mathematics** Maria is making a smoothie. She puts vanilla yogurt in the blender and then adds strawberry yogurt.

The visual fraction model shows the fraction of 1 cup of each kind of yogurt that she adds to the blender.

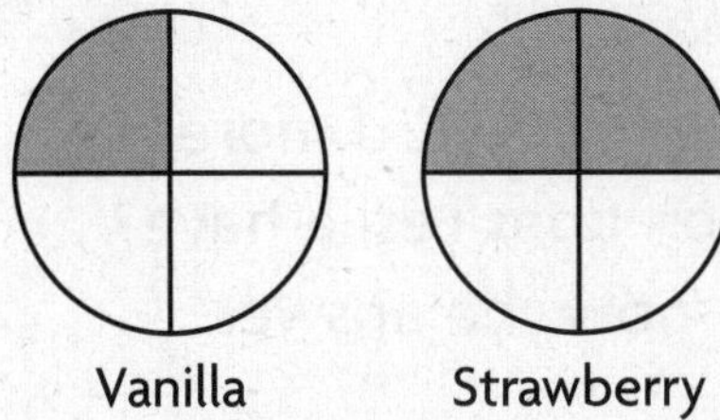

What addition equation can you write to model the total amount of yogurt Maria used?

____

2 **Construct Arguments** Clayton has two identical water bottles. One is $\frac{2}{6}$ full and the other is $\frac{3}{6}$ full. He says he has $\frac{5}{12}$ of a bottle in all.
Is Clayton's answer correct? Explain. Use visual models to support your explanation.

____

____

____

Complete the equation.

3 4 twelfths + 5 twelfths = ______________

4 2 fifths + 2 fifths = ______________

5 3 eighths + 2 eighths = ______________

Test Prep

6 Which is the sum for this visual fraction model?

Ⓐ 1 sixth
Ⓑ 3 sixths
Ⓒ 4 sixths
Ⓓ 5 sixths

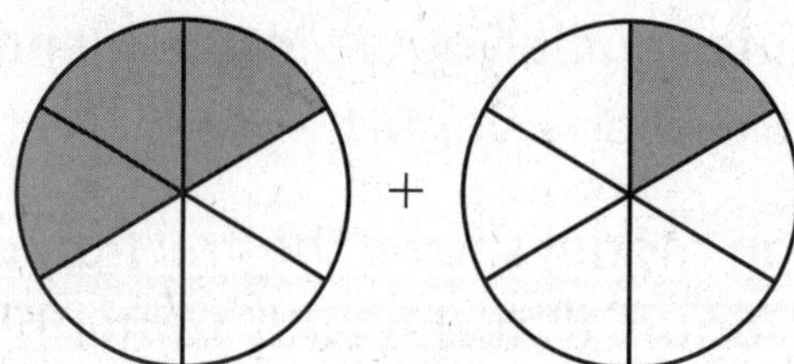

7 Courtney has $\frac{2}{8}$ yard of ribbon. Leslie has $\frac{4}{8}$ yard more than Courtney has. How much ribbon does Leslie have? Shade the visual fraction model to show the answer.

____

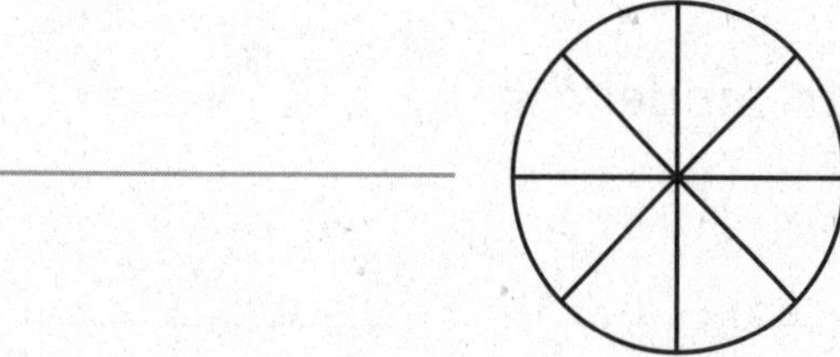

8 Taylor watches 2 tenths of a movie with his friend. He watches 6 tenths of the movie after his friend leaves. How much of the movie has Taylor watched?

Taylor has watched _______________ of the movie.

9 Match the equal amounts.

2 twelfths + 4 twelfths •	• 5 twelfths
3 twelfths + 2 twelfths •	• 6 twelfths
6 twelfths + 1 twelfth •	• 7 twelfths

Spiral Review

10 Is the number 7 prime, composite, or neither?

____

11 An artist is arranging his artwork in a gallery. Each wall has 3 fewer paintings than the wall before it. If the first wall has 30 paintings, how many are on the fifth wall?

____

Name

Represent Addition of Fractions

1 (MP) **Model with Mathematics** Kayla swims for $\frac{3}{10}$ hour in the morning and for $\frac{5}{10}$ hour in the afternoon. How long does she swim? Draw a visual fraction model and write an equation to find the answer.

2 (MP) **Use Structure** Cesar says that $\frac{2}{12} + \frac{6}{12} = \frac{4}{12} + \frac{4}{12}$. Is Cesar correct? Represent each side of the equation on the number lines to support your answer. Explain your thinking.

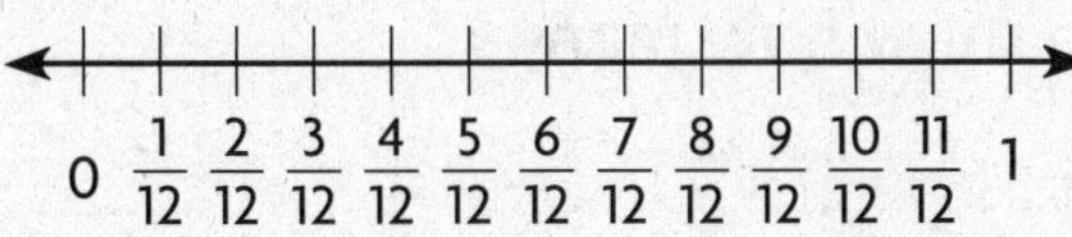

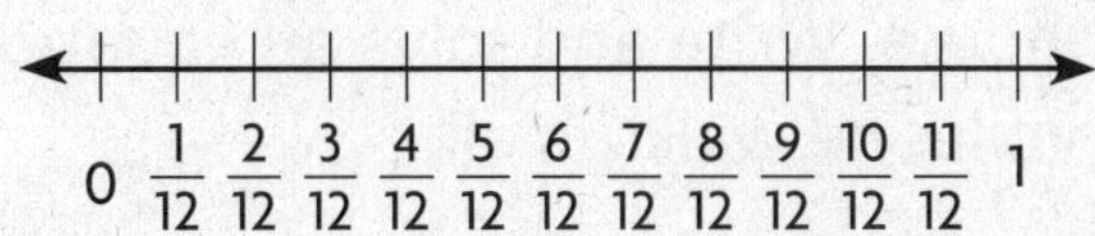

3 **Open Ended** Write a word problem to match the number line. Then write an equation and find the answer for your problem.

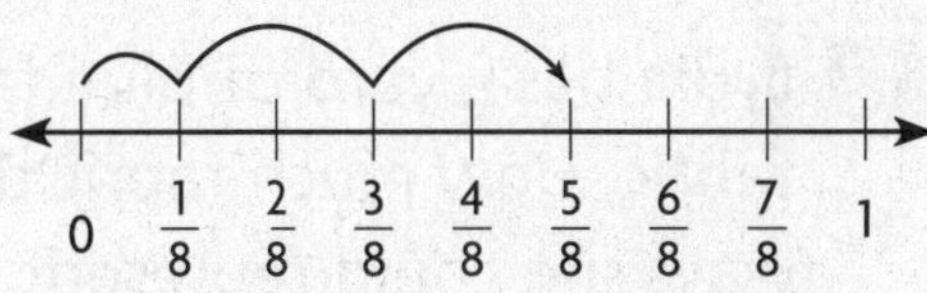

4 Brittany has $\frac{2}{6}$ yard of blue ribbon. She has $\frac{3}{6}$ yard more white ribbon than blue ribbon. How much white ribbon does Brittany have? Explain your answer.

Find the sum.

5 $\frac{3}{12} + \frac{6}{12} =$ ______

6 $\frac{65}{100} + \frac{19}{100} =$ ______

7 $\frac{4}{8} + \frac{2}{8} + \frac{1}{8} =$ ______

8 $\frac{6}{10} + \frac{2}{10} + \frac{1}{10} =$ ______

Test Prep

9 Which is the sum $\frac{3}{12} + \frac{8}{12}$?

Ⓐ $\frac{5}{12}$ Ⓒ $\frac{10}{12}$

Ⓑ $\frac{9}{12}$ Ⓓ $\frac{11}{12}$

10 Maria spends $\frac{4}{10}$ hour working on homework. She spends $\frac{2}{10}$ hour more playing outside than she spends on her homework. How long does Maria spend playing outside?

Ⓐ $\frac{2}{10}$ hour Ⓒ $\frac{6}{10}$ hour

Ⓑ $\frac{4}{10}$ hour Ⓓ $\frac{8}{10}$ hour

11 Evan walks $\frac{2}{5}$ mile to school and $\frac{1}{5}$ mile to a friend's house. Write and solve an equation to show how many miles he walks in all.

____

12 Lydia has $\frac{5}{8}$ yard of blue fabric and $\frac{2}{8}$ yard of yellow fabric. How much fabric does she have? Select all the ways she could represent the answer.

Ⓐ $\frac{3}{8}$ Ⓓ $\frac{7}{8}$

Ⓑ $\frac{5}{8} + \frac{2}{8}$ Ⓔ $\frac{2}{8} + \frac{5}{8}$

Ⓒ $\frac{5}{8} + \frac{7}{8}$

Spiral Review

13 Compare. Write $<$, $>$, or $=$.

0.62 ◯ 0.26

0.86 ◯ 0.8

14 Damien has 2 quarters, 3 dimes, and 5 pennies. How much money does Damien have?

____

Name ______________________________________

Separate Parts of the Same Whole

1 (MP) **Use Tools** Wade has $\frac{7}{12}$ pound of almonds. He uses $\frac{4}{12}$ pound to make trail mix. How many pounds of almonds are left? Use the fraction model as a tool to support your answer. __________

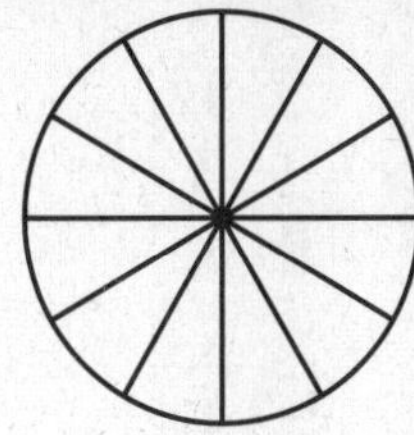

2 (MP) **Reason** Della says $\frac{7}{8}$ minus $\frac{5}{8}$ is $\frac{1}{3}$. Is Della correct? Explain. Use a visual model to support your answer.

____

____

____

____

____

____

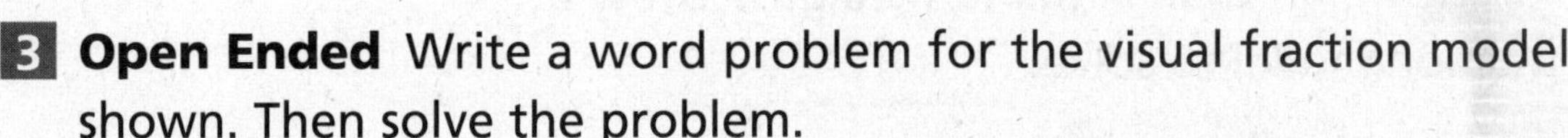

3 **Open Ended** Write a word problem for the visual fraction model shown. Then solve the problem.

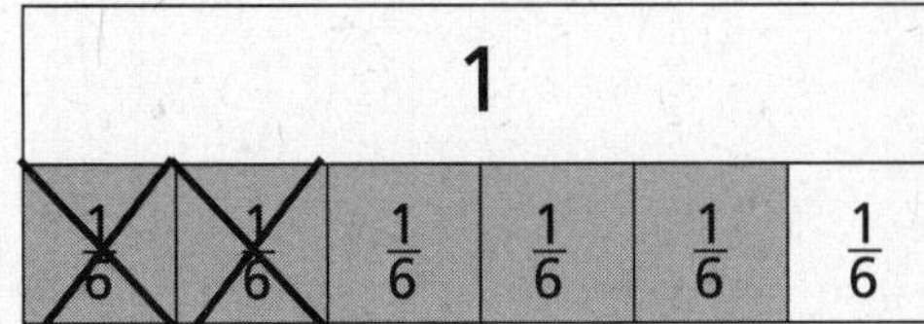

____

____

____

____

4 David exercises for $\frac{9}{12}$ hour. He spends some time lifting weights and $\frac{6}{12}$ hour running. How long does he spend lifting weights? __________

Use the visual fraction model to find the difference.

5

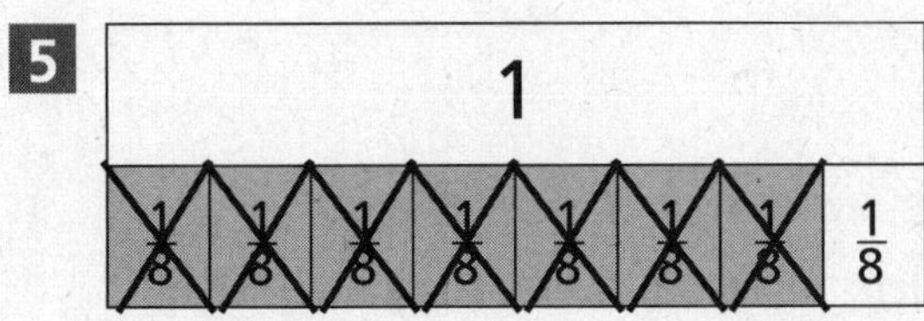

$\frac{7}{8} - \frac{7}{8} =$ ______

6

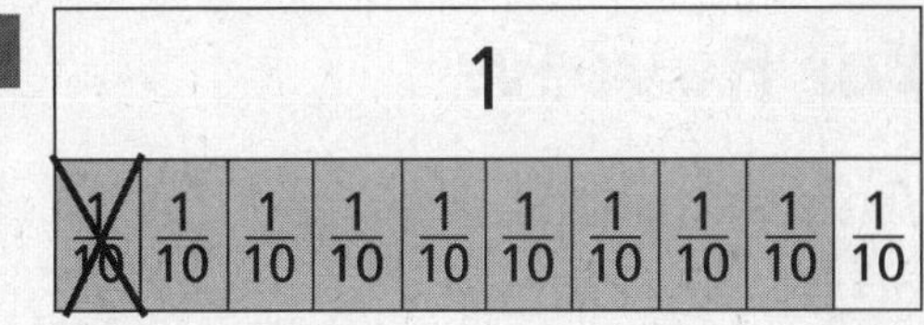

$\frac{9}{10} - \frac{1}{10} =$ ______

Test Prep

7 Which is the difference between $\frac{8}{12}$ and $\frac{4}{12}$?

Ⓐ $\frac{2}{12}$

Ⓑ $\frac{4}{12}$

Ⓒ $\frac{10}{12}$

Ⓓ $\frac{12}{12}$

8 Match the problem with the correct difference.

$\frac{9}{10} - \frac{7}{10}$ •	• $\frac{5}{10}$
$\frac{8}{10} - \frac{4}{10}$ •	• $\frac{2}{10}$
$\frac{7}{10} - \frac{2}{10}$ •	• $\frac{4}{10}$

9 Armand has a kitten that weighs $\frac{11}{12}$ pound. Julio has a kitten that weighs $\frac{10}{12}$ pound. How much less does Julio's kitten weigh than Armand's weighs? Draw a visual fraction model to solve. ________________

10 Select all that have a difference of $\frac{2}{8}$.

Ⓐ $\frac{6}{8} - \frac{4}{8}$

Ⓑ $\frac{5}{8} - \frac{3}{8}$

Ⓒ $\frac{7}{8} - \frac{6}{8}$

Ⓓ $\frac{4}{8} - \frac{1}{8}$

Spiral Review

11 Write six tenths as a fraction and as a decimal.

____

12 Write nine hundredths as a fraction and as a decimal.

____

Name ______________________________

Represent Subtraction of Fractions

1 **Model with Mathematics** Colin played $\frac{3}{6}$ of the soccer game on Friday. He played $\frac{5}{6}$ of Sunday's game. How much less did he play on Friday than on Sunday? Model the problem with an equation.

____

____

2 **Model with Mathematics** Hannah's flour jar has $\frac{6}{12}$ pound of flour in it. She adds $\frac{5}{12}$ pound to the jar. Then she uses $\frac{8}{12}$ pound in a recipe. How many pounds of flour are in Hannah's jar now? Model the problem with equations.

____

3 **Open Ended** Write a subtraction word problem with the fractions $\frac{2}{10}$ and $\frac{7}{10}$. Write an equation for your problem. Then solve the problem.

____

____

____

4 **Attend to Precision** Elijah has $\frac{4}{5}$ of a book left to read. After he reads some more of the book, he has $\frac{2}{5}$ left to read. What fraction of the book did Elijah read?

____

Find the difference.

5 $\frac{5}{6} - \frac{1}{6} =$ ______

6 $\frac{9}{10} - \frac{1}{10} =$ ______

7 $\frac{11}{12} - \frac{2}{12} =$ ______

8 $\frac{5}{6} - \frac{3}{6} =$ ______

9 $\frac{7}{8} - \frac{2}{8} =$ ______

10 $\frac{6}{8} - \frac{1}{8} =$ ______

Test Prep

11 Annie has a piece of ribbon that is $\frac{7}{12}$ yard long. She cuts $\frac{2}{12}$ yard off and gives it to her sister. Which is the length of ribbon Annie has now?

Ⓐ $\frac{3}{12}$ yard

Ⓑ $\frac{5}{12}$ yard

Ⓒ $\frac{6}{12}$ yard

Ⓓ $\frac{9}{12}$ yard

12 In a classroom, $\frac{4}{6}$ of the students are wearing sneakers. This is $\frac{3}{6}$ more than the fraction of the students wearing boots. What fraction of the students are wearing boots? Write an equation to model the problem.

____

13 A pot has $\frac{3}{10}$ pound of soil. Rex adds some soil. Now it has $\frac{9}{10}$ pound. How many pounds of soil did Rex add?

Ⓐ $\frac{2}{10}$ pound

Ⓑ $\frac{6}{10}$ pound

Ⓒ $\frac{7}{10}$ pound

Ⓓ $\frac{12}{10}$ pound

14 Match the difference with the problem.

$\frac{11}{12} - \frac{3}{12} =$ •	• $\frac{1}{12}$
$\frac{9}{12} - \frac{8}{12} =$ •	• $\frac{6}{12}$
$\frac{10}{12} - \frac{4}{12} =$ •	• $\frac{8}{12}$

Spiral Review

15 Find the sum.

$\frac{3}{12} + \frac{5}{12} =$ ______

16 Compare. Write <, >, or =.

0.73 ◯ 0.37   0.46 ◯ 0.4

Name ______________________________

ONLINE
Video Tutorials and
Interactive Examples

Add Fractional Parts of 10 and 100

1 **Attend to Precision** Charles runs $\frac{25}{100}$ kilometer. Then he walks $\frac{6}{10}$ kilometer. How far does Charles go? Model the problem with an equation. Then find the solution to the problem.

____

____

2 Erika grows two pumpkins. What is the total mass of the pumpkins, p? Model the problem with an equation. Then find the solution to the problem.

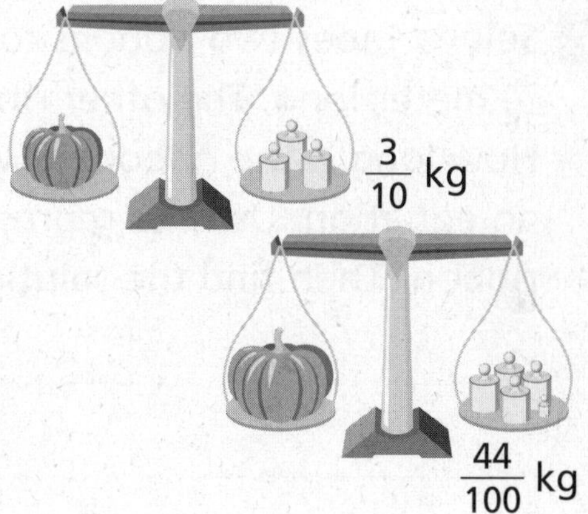

____

____

3 **Reason** Aaron wrote the following equation. Explain what Aaron did wrong.

$\frac{4}{10} + \frac{28}{100} = \frac{32}{100}$ ______________________________

____

Find the sum.

4 $\frac{1}{100} + \frac{1}{10} =$ ______

5 $\frac{7}{10} + \frac{17}{100} =$ ______

6 **Math on the Spot** Dean selects Teakwood stones and Buckskin stones to pave a path in front of his house. How many meters long will each set of one Teakwood stone and one Buckskin stone be?

Paving Stone Center	
Style	**Length (in meters)**
Rustic	$\frac{15}{100}$
Teakwood	$\frac{3}{10}$
Buckskin	$\frac{41}{100}$
Rainbow	$\frac{6}{10}$
Rose	$\frac{8}{100}$

____

Test Prep

7 A dog drinks $\frac{5}{10}$ liter of water in the morning. She drinks $\frac{45}{100}$ liter of water in the afternoon. Which is the amount of water the dog drinks during the morning and the afternoon?

Ⓐ $\frac{50}{100}$ liter
Ⓑ $\frac{50}{110}$ liter
Ⓒ $\frac{95}{100}$ liter
Ⓓ $\frac{95}{110}$ liter

8 Selena tapes two ribbons together. One ribbon is $\frac{6}{10}$ meter long. The other ribbon is $\frac{27}{100}$ meter long. How long is the ribbon now? Model the problem with an equation. Use *r* to represent the final length of the ribbon. Then find the solution to the problem.

____

____

9 Henry mixes $\frac{8}{10}$ kilogram of walnuts and $\frac{15}{100}$ kilogram of almonds in a bag. Which is the mass of the nuts?

Ⓐ $\frac{7}{100}$ kilogram
Ⓑ $\frac{23}{100}$ kilogram
Ⓒ $\frac{65}{100}$ kilograms
Ⓓ $\frac{95}{100}$ kilogram

10 Find the sum. $\frac{3}{10} + \frac{36}{100}$

Ⓐ $\frac{9}{10}$
Ⓑ $\frac{66}{100}$
Ⓒ $\frac{39}{100}$
Ⓓ $\frac{33}{100}$

Spiral Review

11 Write the fraction as a sum of unit fractions.

$\frac{5}{12} =$ ______________________________

12 Write eight hundredths as a fraction and as a decimal.

____

Name ______________________________

Add and Subtract Fractions to Solve Problems

1 MP **Reason** Wes has $\frac{7}{12}$ gallon of water in a pitcher. He pours $\frac{3}{12}$ gallon into his fish tank. Then he puts another $\frac{5}{12}$ gallon of water into the pitcher. How many gallons are in the pitcher now? Show your work.

____

____

2 **Geography** Olivia hikes the Appalachian Trail for $\frac{9}{10}$ mile on Saturday. She hikes for $\frac{3}{10}$ mile on Sunday. How much farther does Olivia hike on Saturday than on Sunday?

____

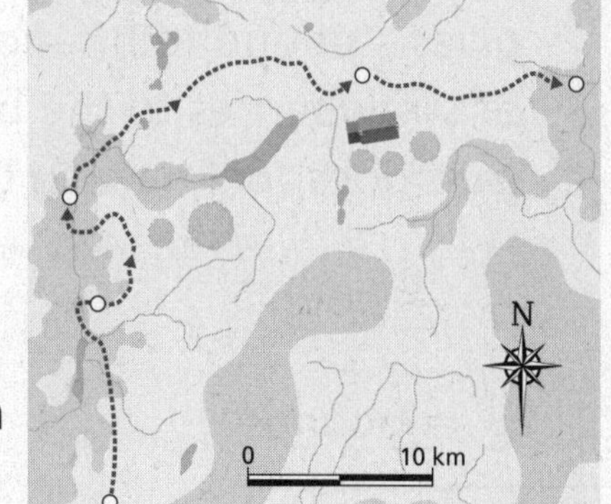

3 MP **Use Tools** Lydia spends $\frac{2}{6}$ hour on her math homework, $\frac{4}{6}$ hour on her science homework, and $\frac{3}{6}$ hour on her reading homework. How many hours does Lydia spend doing her homework? Use a visual model to explain.

____

4 Josh runs $\frac{4}{10}$ mile on Monday, $\frac{6}{10}$ mile on Tuesday, and $\frac{5}{10}$ mile on Wednesday. How many miles does Josh run this week?

____

Find the sum or difference.

5 $\frac{4}{6} + \frac{3}{6} =$ ______

6 $\frac{12}{10} - \frac{6}{10} =$ ______

7 $\frac{1}{4} + \frac{2}{4} - \frac{2}{4} =$ ______

8 $\frac{12}{8} + \frac{2}{8} + \frac{6}{8} =$ ______

Test Prep

9 Carla reads her book for $\frac{2}{8}$ hour before school, $\frac{5}{8}$ hour when she gets home from school, and $\frac{4}{8}$ hour before she goes to bed. How many hours does Carla spend reading her book?

Ⓐ $\frac{14}{8}$ hours

Ⓑ $\frac{11}{8}$ hours

Ⓒ $\frac{9}{8}$ hours

Ⓓ $\frac{7}{8}$ hour

10 Joel has $\frac{5}{6}$ pound of blueberries in a bag. He gives $\frac{3}{6}$ pound to his mom and then adds $\frac{2}{6}$ pound of strawberries to the bag. How many pounds of fruit does Joel have in his bag?

Ⓐ $\frac{10}{6}$ pounds

Ⓑ $\frac{7}{6}$ pounds

Ⓒ $\frac{4}{6}$ pound

Ⓓ $\frac{2}{6}$ pound

11 $\frac{4}{5} - \frac{3}{5} + \frac{2}{5} = ?$

Ⓐ $\frac{1}{5}$

Ⓑ $\frac{3}{5}$

Ⓒ $\frac{5}{5}$

Ⓓ $\frac{9}{5}$

Spiral Review

12 Write 6 tenths as a fraction and as a decimal.

Fraction ______

Decimal ______

13 A poster hanging on the door in the kitchen is 4 feet tall and 2 feet wide. The door is 8 feet tall and 3 feet wide. How much of the door is not covered by the poster?

____

Name ______

LESSON 15.2
More Practice/ Homework

ONLINE
Ed Video Tutorials and Interactive Examples

Rename Fractions and Mixed Numbers

1 Gina has to use $3\frac{3}{4}$ cups of flour to make enough bread for her family dinner. She only has a $\frac{1}{4}$-cup measuring cup. How many times will she fill the cup to get the flour she needs?

______

2 (MP) **Use Tools** Rename $\frac{9}{4}$ as a mixed number. Draw a visual representation to justify your answer.

______

3 Write the quantity represented by the fraction model as a fraction, as a mixed number, and as a sum of fractions that are equal to 1 or less.

1			1		
$\frac{1}{3}$	$\frac{1}{3}$	$\frac{1}{3}$	$\frac{1}{3}$	$\frac{1}{3}$	$\frac{1}{3}$

______

Write the mixed number as a fraction.

4 $3\frac{2}{3} =$ ______

5 $2\frac{7}{10} =$ ______

Write the fraction as a mixed number.

6 $\frac{15}{6} =$ ______

7 $\frac{9}{2} =$ ______

8 $\frac{25}{4} =$ ______

9 $\frac{34}{8} =$ ______

Test Prep

10 Yana wants to fill her betta fish bowl with water. The fish bowl holds $4\frac{2}{3}$ cups of water, but she only has a $\frac{1}{3}$-cup measuring cup. How many times will Yana fill her cup with water?

Ⓐ 14
Ⓑ 10
Ⓒ 9
Ⓓ 8

11 Which number does the fraction model represents? Choose all that are correct.

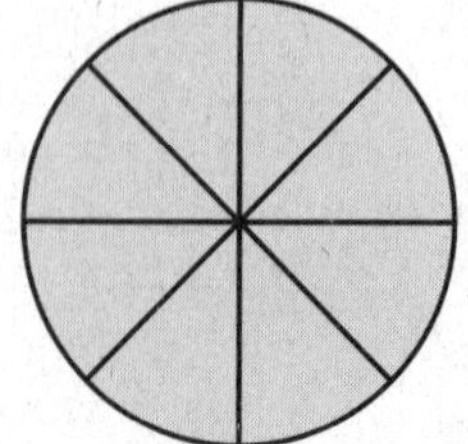 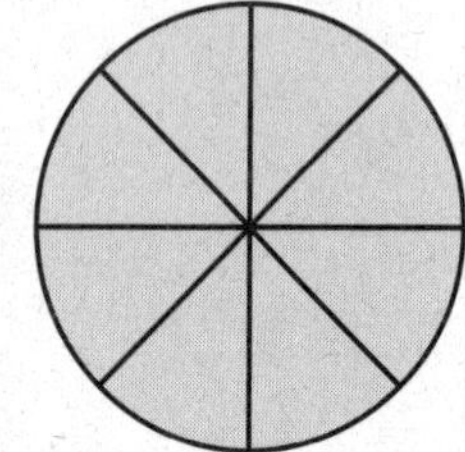 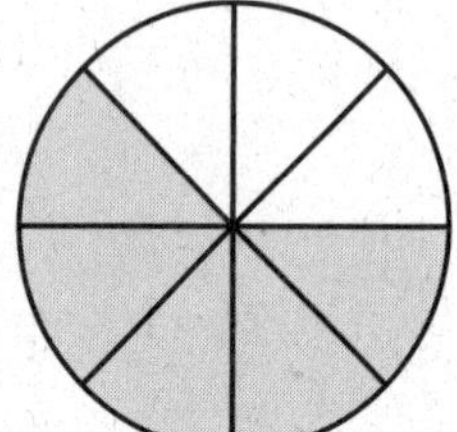

Ⓐ $2\frac{5}{8}$
Ⓑ $\frac{19}{8}$
Ⓒ $2\frac{3}{8}$
Ⓓ $\frac{21}{8}$

12 Which number completes the sentence?
$6\frac{3}{4}$ is equal to ■.

Ⓐ $\frac{9}{4}$
Ⓑ $\frac{13}{4}$
Ⓒ $\frac{18}{4}$
Ⓓ $\frac{27}{4}$

Spiral Review

13 Write 32 hundredths as a fraction and as a decimal.

Fraction ______

Decimal ______

14 A team of 4 scientists fly to Alaska to study the glaciers. Each airline ticket costs $695. What is the cost of the tickets?

____

Name

Add and Subtract Mixed Numbers to Solve Problems

1 (MP) **Use Tools** Mario plays football and basketball for $3\frac{2}{3}$ hours. If he plays football for $2\frac{1}{3}$ hours, for how long does Mario play basketball? Represent the situation with a fraction model and an equation.

2 **Math on the Spot** The driving distance from the sports arena to Kristina's house is $9\frac{7}{10}$ miles. The distance from the sports arena to Luke's house $3\frac{3}{10}$ miles. How much greater is the driving distance between the sports arena and Kristina's house than between the sports arena and Luke's house?

3 Riley has 4 mixing bowls. Each bowl has $1\frac{5}{8}$ cups of flour. How many cups of flour does Riley have? Show your work.

Find the sum. Write your answer as a mixed number.

4 $1\frac{3}{5} + 2\frac{1}{5} =$ _____

5 $\frac{4}{8} + \frac{6}{8} =$ _____

Find the difference. If possible, write your answer as a mixed number.

6 $3\frac{9}{12} - 1\frac{6}{12} =$ _____

7 $5\frac{6}{8} - 3\frac{4}{8} =$ _____

Test Prep

8 Which subtraction sentence matches the fraction model?

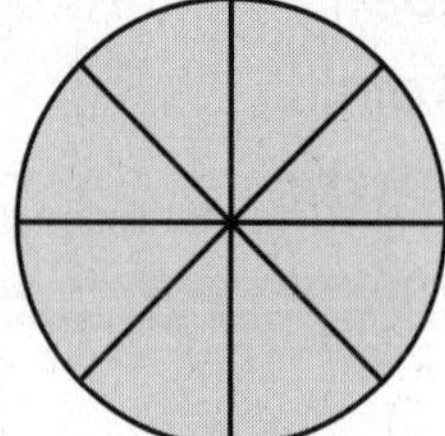 

Ⓐ $1\frac{4}{8} - \frac{3}{8}$

Ⓑ $2 - \frac{4}{8}$

Ⓒ $1\frac{3}{8} - \frac{5}{8}$

Ⓓ $1\frac{5}{8} - \frac{4}{8}$

9 Terry adds $3\frac{2}{6} + 4\frac{5}{6}$ and gets $7\frac{1}{6}$. Which could be Terry's mistake?

Ⓐ Terry added the numerators incorrectly.

Ⓑ Terry subtracted instead of adding.

Ⓒ Terry forgot to add 1 to the whole number.

Ⓓ Terry added instead of subtracting.

10 Find the difference. $8\frac{3}{4} - 6\frac{1}{4} = ?$

Ⓐ $14\frac{2}{4}$

Ⓑ $14\frac{1}{4}$

Ⓒ $2\frac{4}{4}$

Ⓓ $2\frac{2}{4}$

Spiral Review

11 Write $\frac{4}{10}$ as a fraction and as a decimal in hundredths.

Fraction ___________

Decimal ___________

12 There are 1,760 yards in a mile. Jim runs 4 miles. How many yards does he run?

____

Name ________________________________

LESSON 15.4
More Practice/ Homework

ONLINE
Ed Video Tutorials and Interactive Examples

Rename Mixed Numbers to Subtract

1 (MP) **Model with Mathematics** Jacob is helping his mother with the household chores. He spends $2\frac{1}{5}$ hours cleaning one room and $1\frac{4}{5}$ hours cleaning a second room. How many more hours does Jacob spend cleaning the first room than the second room? Write an equation to model the problem.

____

____

2 (MP) **Reason** Janet has $3\frac{2}{6}$ hours before she has to be home. She spends $1\frac{4}{6}$ hours at the park and then decides she wants to see a movie that is $2\frac{1}{6}$ hours long. Does Janet have enough time to see the movie before she has to be home? Explain.

____

____

3 **Math on the Spot** Tubas, trombones, and French horns are brass instruments. Fully stretched out, the length of a tuba is 18 feet, the length of a trombone is $9\frac{11}{12}$ feet, and the length of a French horn is $17\frac{1}{12}$ feet. The tuba is how much longer than the French horn? The French horn is how much longer than the trombone?

____

Find the difference. If possible, write your answer as a mixed number.

4 $3\frac{4}{12} - 1\frac{6}{12} =$ ______

5 $5\frac{2}{8} - 3\frac{5}{8} =$ ______

6 $4\frac{3}{5} - 2\frac{4}{5} =$ ______

7 $6\frac{1}{3} - 2\frac{2}{3} =$ ______

Test Prep

8 Stefan has $3\frac{2}{8}$ bushels of apples. If he gives $2\frac{5}{8}$ bushels to his friends, how many bushels does he have left? Select the equation that represents the solution.

Ⓐ $3\frac{2}{8} + 2\frac{5}{8} = 5\frac{7}{8}$

Ⓑ $3\frac{2}{8} - 2\frac{5}{8} = 1\frac{5}{8}$

Ⓒ $3\frac{5}{8} - 2\frac{2}{8} = 1\frac{3}{8}$

Ⓓ $3\frac{2}{8} - 2\frac{5}{8} = \frac{5}{8}$

9 The problem written on the board says $4\frac{3}{6} - 2\frac{5}{6}$. Meg rewrites the problem as $\frac{27}{6} - \frac{17}{6} = \frac{10}{6}$. Jaime rewrites the problem as $3\frac{9}{6} - 2\frac{5}{6} = 1\frac{4}{6}$. Who is correct?

Ⓐ Jaime is correct. $1\frac{4}{6}$ is the correct answer.

Ⓑ Meg is correct. $\frac{10}{6}$ is the correct answer.

Ⓒ Both answers are correct. $\frac{10}{6} = 1\frac{4}{6}$

Ⓓ Neither answer is correct.

10 Find the difference. $6\frac{1}{4} - 3\frac{3}{4} = ?$

Ⓐ $2\frac{1}{4}$

Ⓑ $2\frac{2}{4}$

Ⓒ $3\frac{2}{4}$

Ⓓ $3\frac{3}{4}$

Spiral Review

11 Compare. Write >, <, or =.

84.72 ◯ 84.27

12 Find the value of n.

$3 \times 9 + 6 \times 8 = n$ ______

Name ______________________

ONLINE
Ed Video Tutorials and Interactive Examples

Apply Properties of Addition to Add Fractions and Mixed Numbers

1 (MP) **Precision** Shari jogs $3\frac{1}{5}$ miles on Friday, $2\frac{2}{5}$ miles on Saturday, and $1\frac{4}{5}$ miles on Sunday. How many miles does Shari jog over the three days? Write an equation for this problem. Explain how you can use the Commutative and Associative Properties to solve mentally.

____

____

____

____

2 (MP) **Use Structure** Mr. Chung works on the computer for $2\frac{3}{8}$ hours in the morning. After lunch he works on the computer for $3\frac{5}{8}$ hours, and in the evening he works on the computer for $1\frac{7}{8}$ hours. For how many hours does Mr. Chung work on the computer?

____

3 **Math on the Spot** Which two expressions have the same value?

A. $\frac{1}{8} + (\frac{7}{8} + \frac{4}{8})$

B. $\frac{1}{2} + 2$

C. $\frac{3}{7} + (\frac{1}{2} + \frac{4}{7})$

D. $\frac{1}{3} + \frac{4}{3} + \frac{2}{3}$

____

Use the properties and mental math to find the sum. If possible, write the answer as a mixed number with a fractional part less than 1.

4 $1\frac{4}{10} + 3\frac{2}{10} + 5\frac{6}{10} =$ ______

5 $2\frac{4}{6} + \frac{3}{6} + 1\frac{2}{6} =$ ______

6 $5\frac{2}{8} + 3\frac{6}{8} + 7\frac{1}{8} =$ ______

7 $6\frac{1}{3} + 4\frac{1}{3} + 2\frac{2}{3} =$ ______

Test Prep

8 Ginny makes soup and adds $2\frac{6}{12}$ cups of broth, $3\frac{4}{12}$ cups of water, and $5\frac{6}{12}$ cups of vegetables to a pot. How many cups of ingredients does she add?

Ⓐ $10\frac{4}{12}$ cups

Ⓑ $11\frac{1}{12}$ cups

Ⓒ $11\frac{4}{12}$ cups

Ⓓ $11\frac{12}{12}$ cups

9 The problem written on the board is $4\frac{3}{6} + 2\frac{5}{6} + 1\frac{1}{6}$. Ryan uses the Associative Property to solve the problem. Which equation did he most likely use to solve the problem using mental math?

Ⓐ $(1\frac{1}{6} + 4\frac{3}{6} + 2\frac{5}{6}) = 8\frac{3}{6}$

Ⓑ $(1\frac{1}{6} + 4\frac{3}{6}) + 2\frac{5}{6} = 8\frac{3}{6}$

Ⓒ $(2\frac{5}{6} + 4\frac{3}{6}) + 1\frac{1}{6} = 8\frac{3}{6}$

Ⓓ $4\frac{3}{6} + (2\frac{5}{6} + 1\frac{1}{6}) = 8\frac{3}{6}$

10 Use the properties and mental math to choose which is the sum.

$6\frac{1}{4} + 3\frac{3}{4} + 8\frac{2}{4}$

Ⓐ $18\frac{3}{4}$ Ⓑ $18\frac{2}{4}$ Ⓒ $17\frac{2}{4}$ Ⓓ $16\frac{1}{4}$

Spiral Review

11 What is the amount of money? Write as a fraction and as a decimal.

3 quarters, 2 dimes, 1 penny

Fraction of a dollar: ______

Decimal: __________

12 Divide and check.

$4\overline{)828}$

Name ______________________________

ONLINE
Video Tutorials and Interactive Examples

Practice Solving Fraction Problems

1 The team was practicing shot put throws for the track meet. Murph threw $4\frac{1}{3}$ yards on his first attempt and $3\frac{2}{3}$ yards on his second attempt. How much farther did Murph throw on his first attempt than on his second attempt?

____

2 (MP) **Use Structure** Lydia wants to put a new wallpaper border in a house. She needs $7\frac{5}{8}$ feet for the bathroom. She needs $1\frac{7}{8}$ feet more border for the bedroom than for the bathroom. How much border does she need for the bedroom? How much border does she need for both rooms?

____

3 Jesse and his sister go to the pet store to buy dog food. Jesse's sister buys a bag that weighs $8\frac{4}{5}$ pounds. Jesse buys a bag that is $3\frac{2}{5}$ pounds heavier. How many pounds of dog food do the two of them buy?

____

4 Mr. Hart is working on a tool shed. He bought 25 feet of wood and has used $11\frac{5}{6}$ feet so far. How much wood does Mr. Hart have left to work on his tool shed?

____

5 (MP) **Reason** Max is building a set of shelves. He buys a board that is 4 yards long. He wants to cut as many pieces of board that are $\frac{3}{4}$ yard long as he can. How many pieces can he cut? Will he have any board left over? If so, how much? Explain your thinking.

____

____

____

Test Prep

6 Patrice makes $8\frac{7}{12}$ cups of soup with broth, water, and vegetables. She adds $3\frac{4}{12}$ cups of broth and $2\frac{5}{12}$ cups of water. Which is the amount of vegetables Patrice adds?

Ⓐ $5\frac{9}{12}$ cups
Ⓑ $5\frac{3}{12}$ cups
Ⓒ $2\frac{10}{12}$ cups
Ⓓ $\frac{11}{12}$ cups

7 Adam works $8\frac{2}{6}$ hours Monday and $7\frac{1}{6}$ hours Tuesday. How many hours can Adam work Wednesday if he cannot work more than 20 hours in a week?

Ⓐ $3\frac{3}{6}$ hours
Ⓑ $4\frac{3}{6}$ hours
Ⓒ $7\frac{3}{6}$ hours
Ⓓ $8\frac{3}{6}$ hours

8 Which is the solution to the problem below?

$8\frac{1}{4} + 3\frac{2}{4} - 4\frac{3}{4} = ■$

Ⓐ $11\frac{3}{4}$
Ⓑ 8
Ⓒ $7\frac{1}{4}$
Ⓓ 7

Spiral Review

9 Ray has $4.27. He wants to buy a game that costs $3.30. How much will Ray have left after he buys the game?

____

10 Alison buys 20 packs of cards for the holidays. There are 14 cards in each pack. How many cards does Alison buy?

____

Name ______________________

LESSON 16.1
More Practice/ Homework

ONLINE
Video Tutorials and Interactive Examples

Understand Multiples of Unit Fractions

1 **STEM** A machine that drills through rock to make tunnels can move through $\frac{1}{8}$ mile of rock per day. How far will the machine have drilled after 9 days? Show the distance on the number line. Then write an equation modeling the problem and its solution.

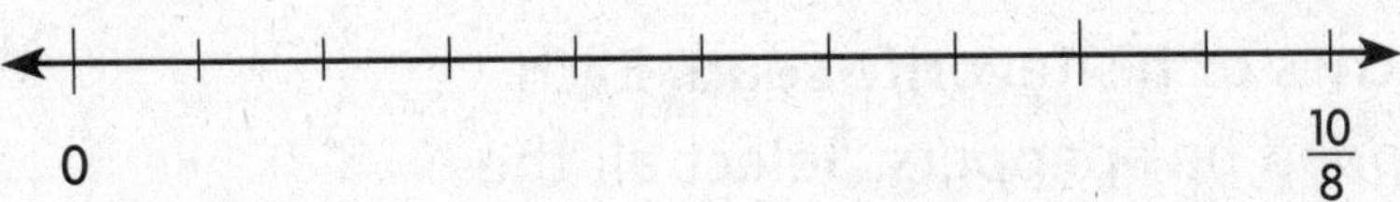

____

2 (MP) **Use Repeated Reasoning** Colin uses a small dump truck to haul gravel to pave a driveway. The truck can hold $\frac{1}{2}$ ton of gravel. He hauls 5 loads of gravel. Write an addition equation and a multiplication equation with their solutions to model how much gravel Colin hauls.

____

3 (MP) **Use Structure** A radio-controlled model airplane uses $\frac{1}{3}$ cup of fuel for each flight. Explain how to use multiples to find the total amount of fuel needed for 7 flights.

____

____

Write the fraction as a product of a whole number and a unit fraction.

4 $\frac{7}{8}$ = ______ **5** $\frac{5}{4}$ = ______ **6** $\frac{12}{5}$ = ______

7 $\frac{3}{2}$ = ______ **8** $\frac{6}{3}$ = ______ **9** $\frac{9}{10}$ = ______

10 $\frac{4}{6}$ = ______ **11** $\frac{5}{8}$ = ______ **12** $\frac{11}{3}$ = ______

Test Prep

13 Mrs. Smith uses $\frac{1}{3}$ cup of blueberries in each mixed-fruit smoothie. How many cups of blueberries does she need for 7 smoothies?

Ⓐ $\frac{1}{3}$ cup
Ⓑ $\frac{3}{7}$ cup
Ⓒ $\frac{7}{3}$ cups
Ⓓ $\frac{21}{3}$ cups

14 Alberto is making 5 batches of his favorite soup. Each batch gets $\frac{1}{8}$ cup of chopped hot peppers. Select all the equations that could be used to determine how many cups of chopped hot peppers Alberto uses.

Ⓐ $5 \div \frac{1}{8} = \blacksquare$
Ⓑ $5 \times \frac{1}{8} = \blacksquare$
Ⓒ $\frac{1}{8} + \frac{1}{8} + \frac{1}{8} + \frac{1}{8} + \frac{1}{8} = \blacksquare$
Ⓓ $5 - \frac{1}{8} = \blacksquare$

15 Elmira is adding $\frac{1}{2}$ pound of fertilizer to the soil around each of the 9 small trees she has just planted. How much fertilizer does she use?

Ⓐ $\frac{18}{2}$ pounds
Ⓑ $\frac{9}{2}$ pounds
Ⓒ $\frac{9}{18}$ pound
Ⓓ $\frac{2}{9}$ pound

Spiral Review

16 Use the visual models to show each fraction. Write <, >, or = to compare.

$\frac{2}{3}$ ◯ $\frac{7}{12}$

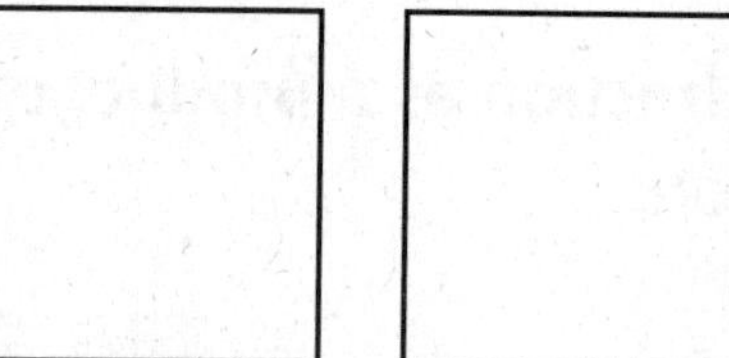

Write <, >, or = to compare.

17 $\frac{11}{12}$ ◯ $\frac{6}{5}$

18 $\frac{5}{8}$ ◯ $\frac{2}{6}$

19 $\frac{11}{6}$ ◯ $\frac{12}{10}$

20 $\frac{9}{10}$ ◯ $\frac{6}{4}$

21 $\frac{9}{4}$ ◯ $\frac{12}{6}$

22 $\frac{15}{5}$ ◯ $\frac{12}{4}$

Name ______________________

Find Multiples of Fractions

1 Adam is restoring old wagon wheels and needs to cut 3 wooden spokes that are each $\frac{5}{8}$ yard long. What is the total length of wood that he needs to cut? Write an equation using unit fractions that models the problem and the solution.

____

2 **Health and Fitness** Every week from Monday to Friday, Charles rides his bicycle for $\frac{3}{4}$ hour after school. How long does Charles ride his bicycle in a week? Use the number line to show how many hours Charles rides by finding multiples of $\frac{3}{4}$, then answer the question.

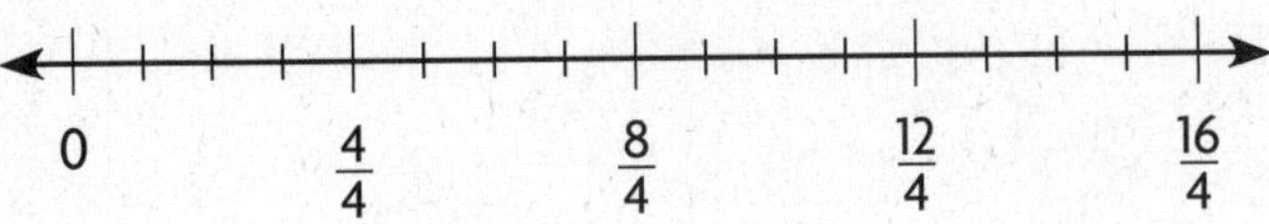

____

3 (MP) **Critique Reasoning** Alexa claims she can use counting by 8 to find the fifth multiple of $\frac{8}{9}$. Is Alexa correct? Explain.

____

____

____

Complete the equation to find the product.

4 $5 \times \frac{5}{12} =$ ______ $\times \frac{1}{12} =$ ______

5 $8 \times \frac{3}{4} =$ ______ $\times \frac{1}{4} =$ ______

6 $9 \times \frac{2}{3} =$ ______

7 $3 \times \frac{7}{8} =$ ______

8 $2 \times \frac{8}{10} =$ ______

Write the first 6 multiples of the fraction.

9 $\frac{4}{5}$: ______________________

10 $\frac{6}{8}$: ______________________

Test Prep

11 Fill in the first 5 multiples of $\frac{2}{3}$ on the number line. Write your answers as fractions greater than 1.

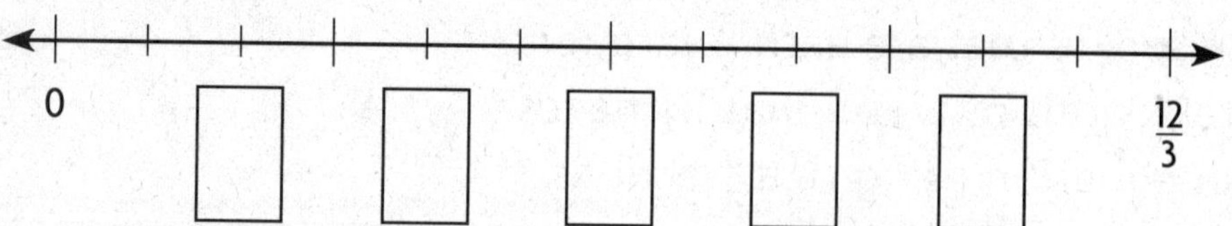

12 Fill in the table to show the fifth multiple of each fraction. Write your answers as fractions greater than 1.

Fraction	Fifth Multiple
$\frac{2}{6}$	
$\frac{7}{10}$	
$\frac{3}{8}$	
$\frac{5}{12}$	
$\frac{7}{6}$	

13 Chef Joseph mixes $\frac{5}{8}$ gallon of sanitizer with water in a large sink to sanitize pots and pans. He changes the water each day. How much sanitizer does he use in 5 days?

Ⓐ $\frac{5}{8}$ gallon
Ⓑ $\frac{10}{8}$ gallons
Ⓒ $\frac{20}{8}$ gallons
Ⓓ $\frac{25}{8}$ gallons

Spiral Review

14 Marcia times herself climbing a rope. Her first climb takes $\frac{4}{12}$ minute. Her second climb takes $\frac{5}{10}$ minute. Which climb took her the least amount of time?

$\frac{4}{12}$ ◯ $\frac{5}{10}$

____

____

15 Jace makes a $\frac{5}{6}$ turn on his skateboard. Keira makes a $\frac{4}{12}$ turn, and Alec makes a $\frac{10}{12}$ turn. Which two skaters make the same-size turn? Explain.

____

____

____

Name ______________________

LESSON 16.3
More Practice/ Homework

ONLINE
Video Tutorials and Interactive Examples

Represent Multiplication of a Fraction by a Whole Number

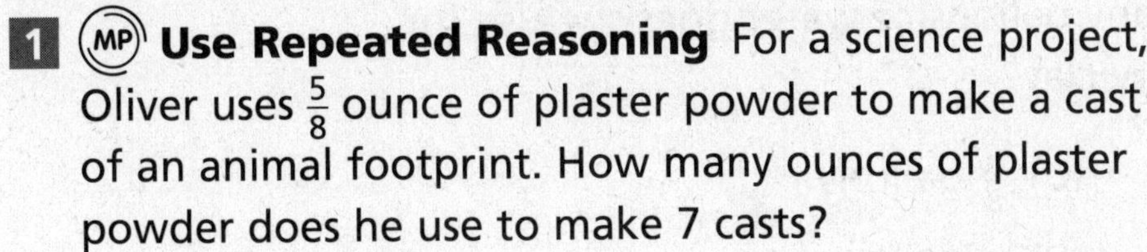

1 **(MP) Use Repeated Reasoning** For a science project, Oliver uses $\frac{5}{8}$ ounce of plaster powder to make a cast of an animal footprint. How many ounces of plaster powder does he use to make 7 casts?

____

2 **Open Ended** Write and solve a story problem that can be modeled by the equation $11 \times \frac{2}{5} = n$.

____

3 **STEM** When first born, a wolf pup weighs about $\frac{3}{4}$ pound. One mother wolf has 5 pups and another has 6 pups. About how many pounds do all the pups weigh? Explain how you know.

____

____

4 **Math on the Spot** Patty has 2 cups of warm water. Is that enough water to make 4 batches of sidewalk chalk? Explain how you know without finding the exact product.

____

____

Sidewalk Chalk Recipe

$\frac{3}{4}$ cup warm water

$1\frac{1}{2}$ cups plaster of Paris

$2\frac{2}{3}$ tablespoons powdered paint

Find the product. Write your answer as a fraction.

5 $8 \times \frac{7}{10} =$ ______

6 $7 \times \frac{3}{5} =$ ______

7 $6 \times \frac{2}{3} =$ ______

8 $3 \times \frac{7}{8} =$ ______

9 $4 \times \frac{3}{10} =$ ______

10 $5 \times \frac{3}{2} =$ ______

Test Prep

11 Alicia uses $\frac{7}{8}$ gallon of water for each batch of pottery clay she mixes. How many gallons of water does she use for 9 batches of pottery clay?

Ⓐ $\frac{79}{8}$ gallons
Ⓑ $\frac{63}{8}$ gallons
Ⓒ $\frac{16}{8}$ gallons
Ⓓ $\frac{63}{72}$ gallon

12 Frank cuts a board into equal-sized pieces that are $\frac{3}{4}$ foot long. If he was able to cut exactly 8 pieces from the board with nothing left over, how long was the board?

Ⓐ $\frac{24}{32}$ foot
Ⓑ $\frac{11}{4}$ feet
Ⓒ $\frac{24}{4}$ feet
Ⓓ $\frac{32}{4}$ feet

13 Charlene collects rainwater to water her indoor plants. Each of her collection containers holds $\frac{11}{12}$ gallon of water. How much water can she collect with 8 containers?

Ⓐ $\frac{3}{12}$ gallon
Ⓑ $\frac{88}{96}$ gallon
Ⓒ $\frac{19}{12}$ gallons
Ⓓ $\frac{88}{12}$ gallons

Spiral Review

14 Are the fractions $\frac{3}{4}$ and $\frac{6}{8}$ equivalent? How do you know?

____

____

____

____

15 Generate two equivalent fractions for the given fraction.

$\frac{10}{12} = \frac{\square}{\square} = \frac{\square}{\square}$

Name ______________________________

ONLINE
Video Tutorials and Interactive Examples

Solve Problems Using Multiplication of a Fraction or Mixed Number by a Whole Number

1 **Art** An artist uses $2\frac{7}{10}$ liters of water for each batch of pottery clay that she makes. How many liters of water does she use for 7 batches of pottery clay?

____

2 **Open Ended** Write a story problem that could be modeled by the multiplication equation $4 \times 2\frac{3}{5} = n$. Then solve it.

____

____

____

3 (MP) **Reason** William has 5 books in his backpack and 3 books in a book bag. If each book weighs $1\frac{1}{4}$ pounds, how many pounds do the books weigh? Explain how you know.

____

____

Find the product. If possible, write your answer as a mixed number.

4 $3 \times 2\frac{3}{10} =$ ______

5 $5 \times 3\frac{5}{12} =$ ______

6 $4 \times 1\frac{1}{3} =$ ______

7 $2 \times 5\frac{3}{4} =$ ______

8 $7 \times 3\frac{3}{8} =$ ______

9 $9 \times 2\frac{1}{2} =$ ______

Test Prep

10 Dell cares for 3 flowerbeds in one yard and 2 flowerbeds in another yard. He uses $2\frac{2}{3}$ gallons of plant food in each flowerbed. How much plant food does he use in the flowerbeds?

Ⓐ $1\frac{1}{3}$ gallons
Ⓑ $4\frac{1}{3}$ gallons
Ⓒ $10\frac{1}{3}$ gallons
Ⓓ $13\frac{1}{3}$ gallons

11 Frieda gives each sheep $1\frac{3}{4}$ scoops of feed each day. How many scoops does she use for 4 sheep? Select all the equations that could be used to determine how many scoops.

Ⓐ $4 \times 1\frac{3}{4} = \blacksquare$
Ⓑ $\frac{7}{4} + \frac{7}{4} + \frac{7}{4} + \frac{7}{4} = \blacksquare$
Ⓒ $4 \div 1\frac{3}{4} = \blacksquare$
Ⓓ $4 \times \frac{7}{4} = \blacksquare$

12 Kai uses $2\frac{1}{12}$ feet of string to make a bead necklace. How much string does Kai need for 5 necklaces?

Ⓐ $2\frac{5}{12}$ feet
Ⓑ $5\frac{1}{12}$ feet
Ⓒ $10\frac{5}{12}$ feet
Ⓓ $12\frac{5}{12}$ feet

Spiral Review

13 Rename each fraction so the pair of fractions have a common numerator.

$\frac{3}{5}$ and $\frac{5}{8}$: ____________

14 Find a number that makes the statement true.

$\frac{1}{4} > \frac{\square}{6}$

Name ______________________________

Identify and Draw Perpendicular and Parallel Lines

Use the figure for Problems 1–3.

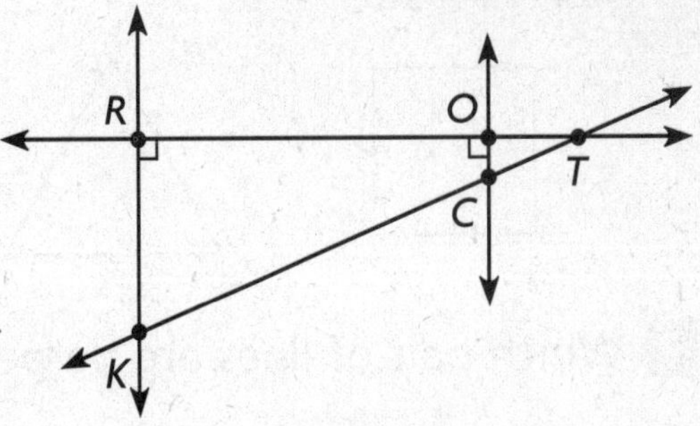

1 Which two pairs of lines are perpendicular?

____

2 Which pair of lines appears to be parallel?

____

3 Lines $\overleftrightarrow{RO}$ and $\overleftrightarrow{KC}$ intersect at what point?

____

Draw and label the figure described.

4 $\overleftrightarrow{CA}$ intersecting $\overleftrightarrow{DO}$ at point T

5 $\overleftrightarrow{HO} \parallel \overleftrightarrow{US}$ and $\overleftrightarrow{SN} \perp \overleftrightarrow{US}$

6 **Math on the Spot** Name a pair of line segments that appears to be parallel.

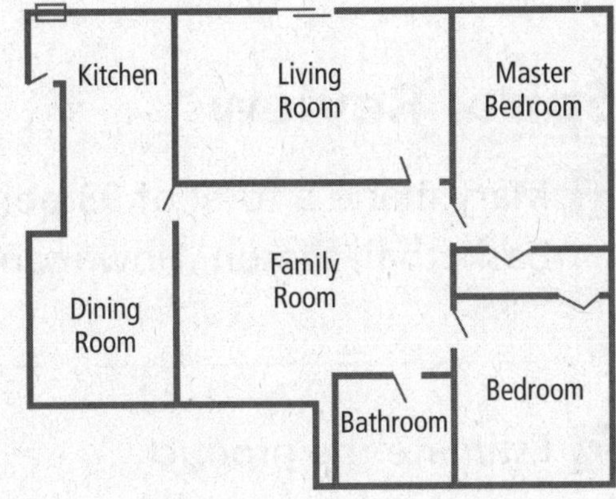

____

____

7 (MP) **Reason** Cindy walks on James Street and then turns at a right angle to walk on Hallowell Street. What can you say about James Street and Hallowell Street?

____

Test Prep

8 **Which shapes appear to have parallel sides? Select all that apply.**

Ⓐ 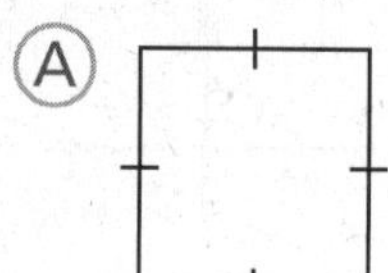 Ⓑ 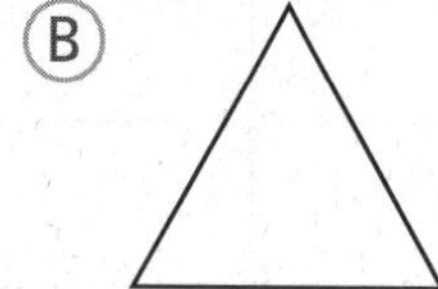 Ⓒ 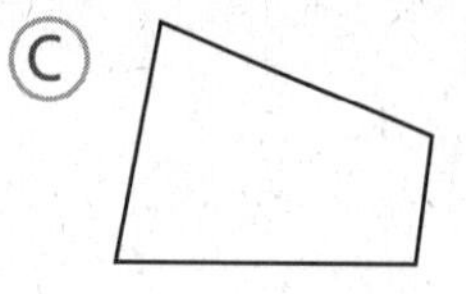 Ⓓ 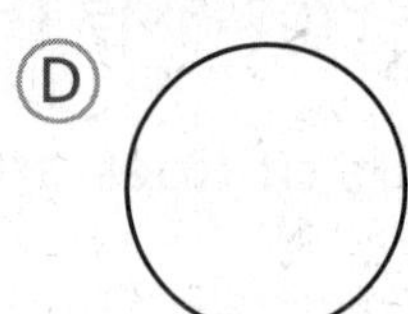 Ⓔ 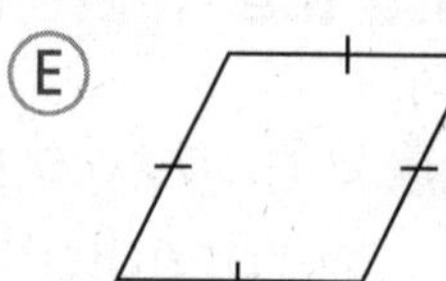

9 Which pair of lines are perpendicular?

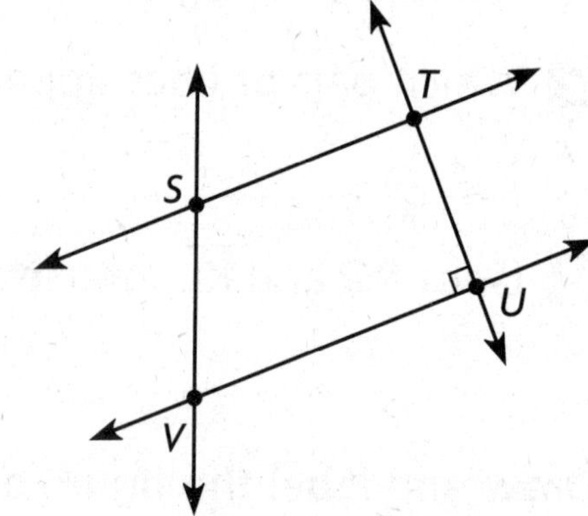

Ⓐ $\overleftrightarrow{ST}$ and $\overleftrightarrow{VU}$

Ⓑ $\overleftrightarrow{SV}$ and $\overleftrightarrow{ST}$

Ⓒ $\overleftrightarrow{TU}$ and $\overleftrightarrow{VU}$

Ⓓ $\overleftrightarrow{VS}$ and $\overleftrightarrow{UT}$

10 A piano keyboard has a total of 88 keys. Which best describes the relationship the black keys have with each other?

Ⓐ The black keys intersect each other.

Ⓑ The black keys are parallel to each other.

Ⓒ The black keys are perpendicular to each other.

Ⓓ The black keys are neither parallel nor perpendicular to each other.

Spiral Review

11 Mary made a total of 93 points from 3-point shots during the basketball season. How many 3-point shots did Mary make?

---

12 Estimate the product.

4×361

ONLINE
Video Tutorials and
Interactive Examples

Name ______________________

Identify and Classify Triangles by Angles

Classify the triangle. Write *acute*, *right*, or *obtuse*.

1 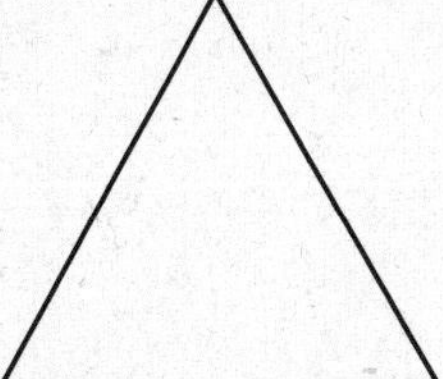

____

2 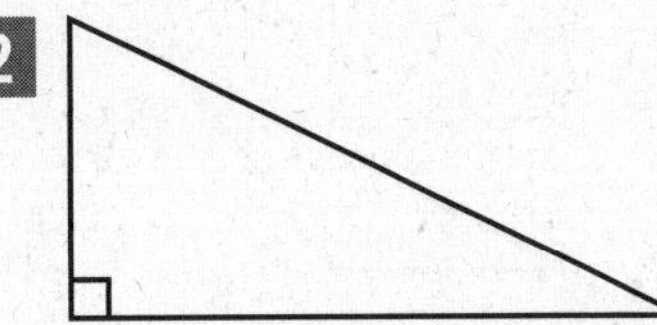

____

3 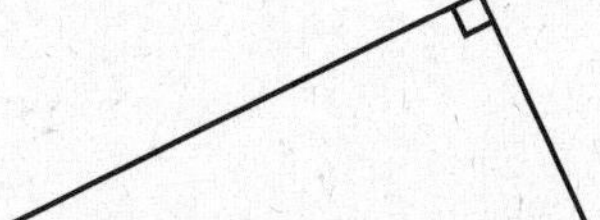

____

4 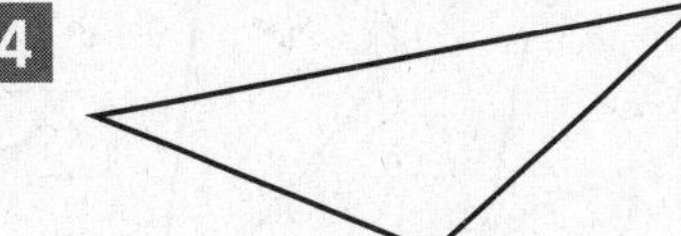

____

5 

____

6 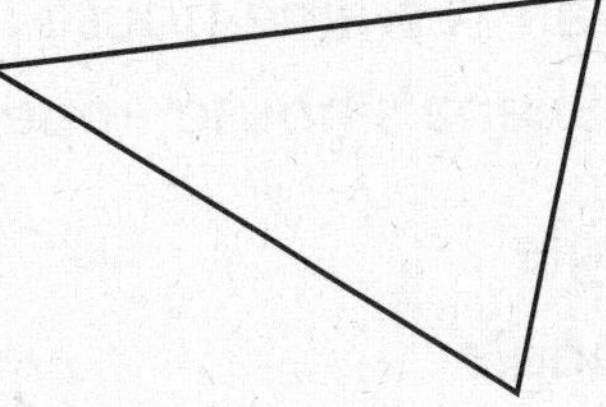

____

7 On the triangle, draw a line segment from point X to point Z. Identify and classify the triangles formed.

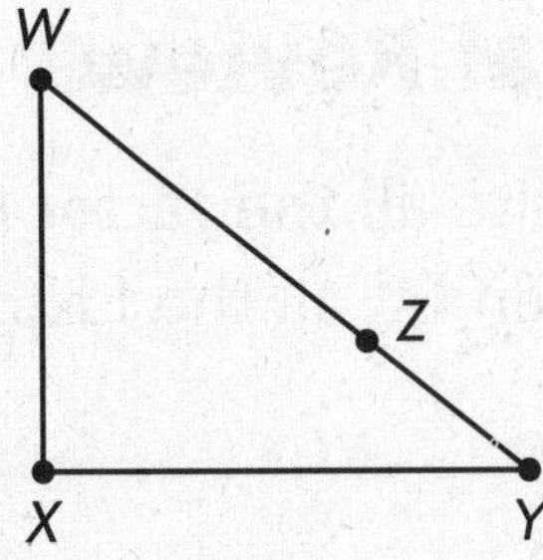

____

____

Test Prep

For Problems 8 and 9, cross out the figure that does not belong. Explain why.

8

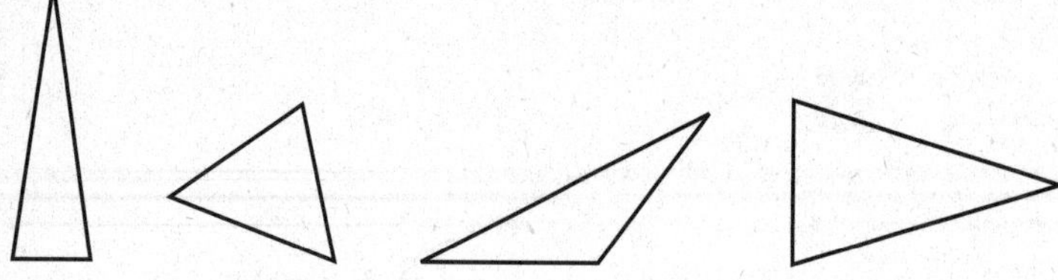

____

____

9

____

____

10 Shana lives in an A-frame house. What kind of triangle does Shana's house appear to be?

Ⓐ right triangle
Ⓑ obtuse triangle
Ⓒ acute triangle
Ⓓ equilateral triangle

Spiral Review

11 Write all the factor pairs of 20. Then list all the factors of 20.

____

____

____

12 Use divisibility rules to solve and explain. Is 6 a factor of 24?

____

____

____

Name ____________________

LESSON 17.3
More Practice/ Homework

ONLINE Ed
Video Tutorials and Interactive Examples

Identify and Classify Triangles by Sides

Identify and classify the triangle. Write *equilateral, isosceles,* or *scalene*. Use a centimeter ruler if needed.

1

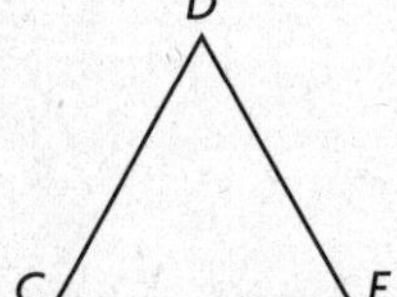

____

2

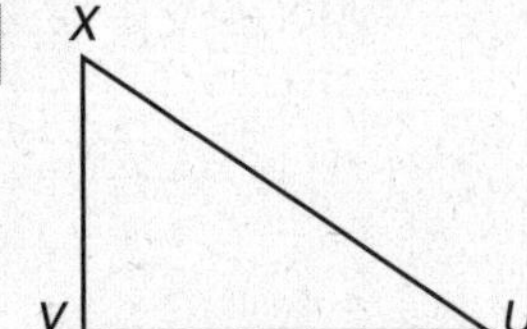

____

3

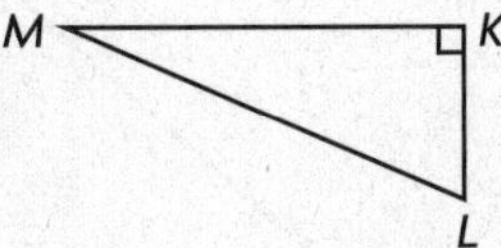

____

4

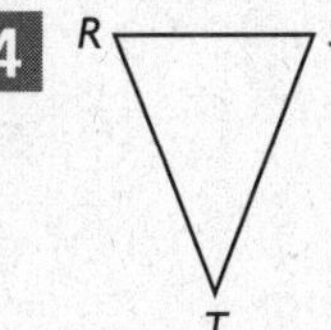

____

5 (MP) **Attend to Precision** Mike uses straws to make a figure shaped like a triangle. What type of triangle does Mike make? Explain how you know.

____

____

____

6 (MP) **Construct Arguments** Jolene has a square sheet of construction paper. She draws a diagonal line from point *A* to point *C*, so that she can cut it into two triangles.

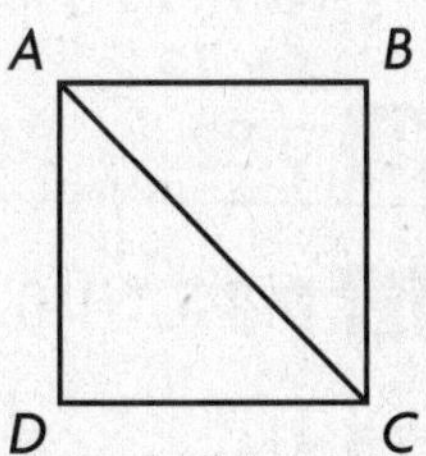

- How can you classify each triangle?

____

- Can you classify both triangles the same way? Explain how you know.

____

____

Test Prep

7 Joan draws a triangle. Each side measures 6 inches. What type of triangle does Joan draw? Select all that apply.

Ⓐ obtuse
Ⓑ equilateral
Ⓒ isosceles
Ⓓ right
Ⓔ scalene

8 How can you identify and classify the triangle?

Ⓐ equilateral
Ⓑ isosceles
Ⓒ scalene
Ⓓ obtuse

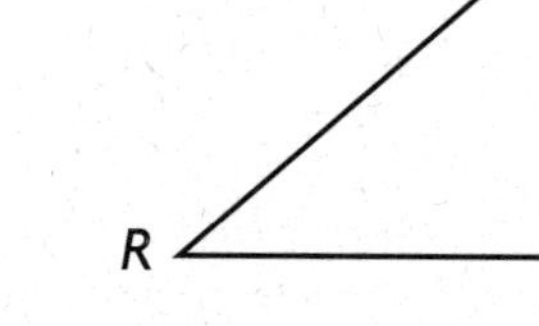

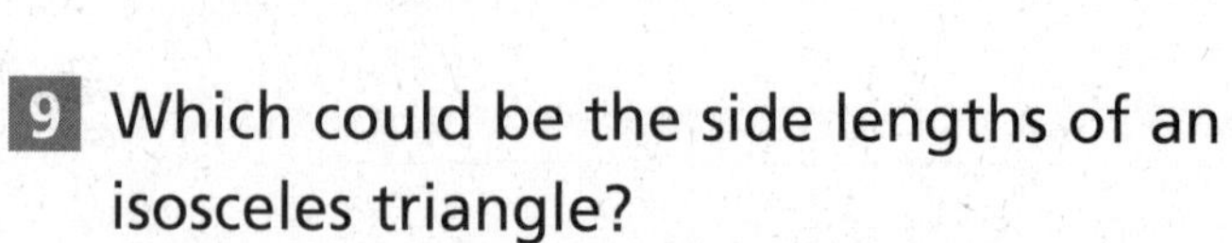

9 Which could be the side lengths of an isosceles triangle?

Ⓐ 6 inches, 8 inches, 10 inches
Ⓑ 8 feet, 5 feet, 8 feet
Ⓒ 5 centimeters, 12 centimeters, 13 centimeters
Ⓓ 8 meters, 15 meters, 17 meters

Spiral Review

Write <, >, or = to compare the decimals.

10 0.82 ◯ 0.28

11 0.4 ◯ 0.23

12 Name the bills and coins that could represent the mixed number. Then write the decimal dollar amount.

$2\frac{63}{100}$

____

Name

ONLINE
Video Tutorials and Interactive Examples

Identify and Classify Quadrilaterals

Identify and classify the quadrilateral. Explain why you chose that category.

1

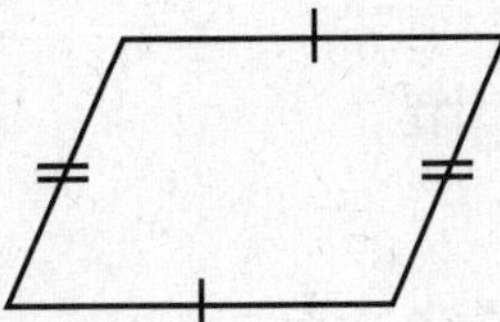

2

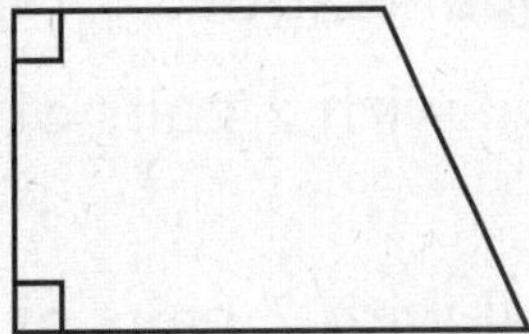

Classify the figure in as many ways as possible. Write *quadrilateral, rectangle, square, parallelogram, rhombus, or trapezoid*. Define a trapezoid as having *at least* 1 pair of parallel sides.

3

4

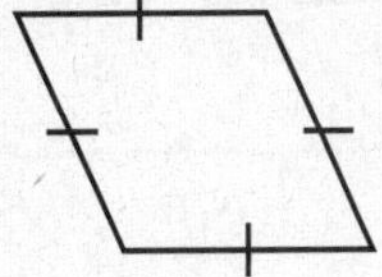

5 (MP) **Reason** Explain how a rhombus and square are alike and how they are different.

Test Prep

6 Which best describes a rhombus?

Ⓐ a quadrilateral with 2 pairs of parallel sides

Ⓑ a quadrilateral with 2 pairs of parallel sides and 2 pairs of sides of equal length

Ⓒ a quadrilateral with 2 pairs of parallel sides and 4 right angles

Ⓓ a quadrilateral with 2 pairs of parallel sides and 4 sides of equal length

7 Classify the figure. Select all that apply.

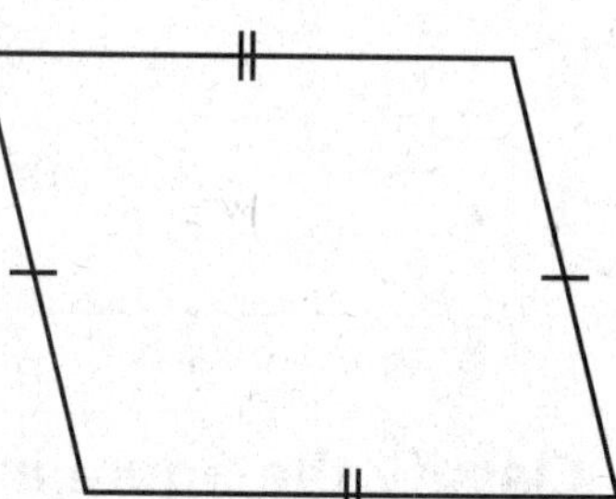

Ⓐ quadrilateral

Ⓑ trapezoid

Ⓒ rectangle

Ⓓ parallelogram

Ⓔ rhombus

Ⓕ square

8 Is it possible to draw a quadrilateral that is both a square and a rectangle? Explain.

____

____

____

Spiral Review

9 Josh hikes every day. On Monday, he hikes $\frac{5}{8}$ of a mile. On Tuesday, he hikes $\frac{7}{12}$ of a mile. On which day does he hike a shorter distance? Explain.

____

____

10 Tina scores 52 points in a game of bowling. In the same game, Jen scores twice as many points. How many points does Jen score in the game?

____

Name ______________________________

Measure and Draw Angles of Two-Dimensional Figures

Use a protractor to find the measure of the angle.

1

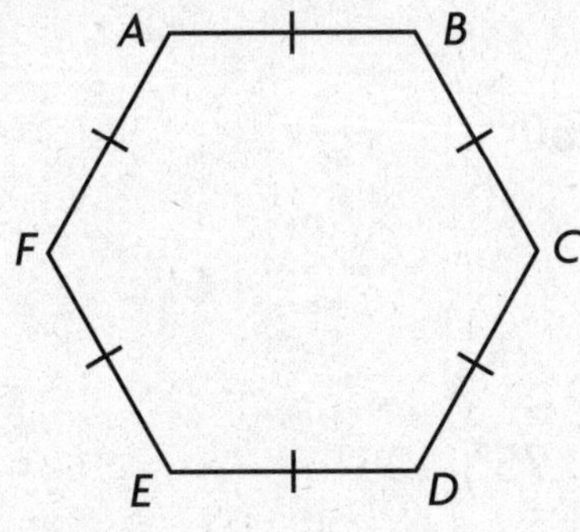

m∠*ABC* = ___________

2

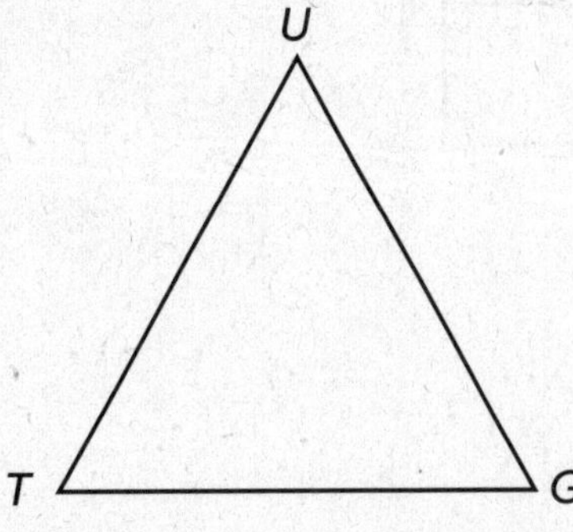

m∠*GTU* = ___________

3

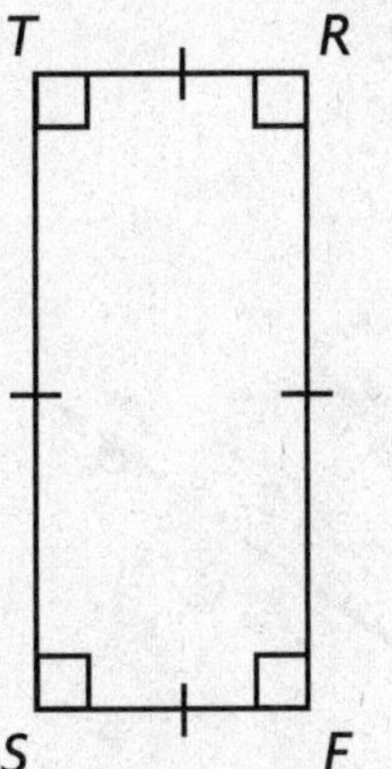

m∠*RFS* = ___________

4

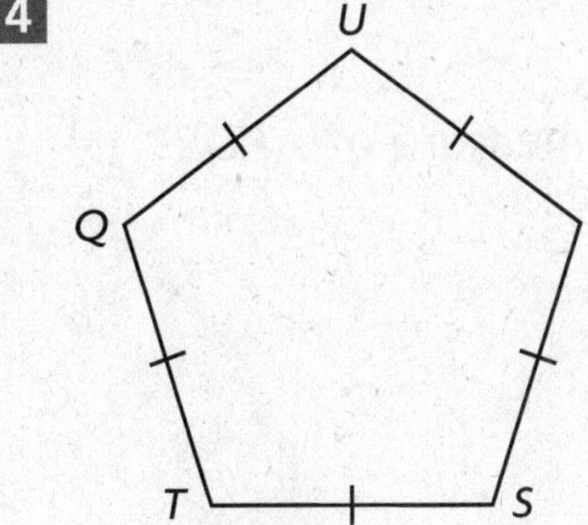

m∠*QUE* = ___________

5 (MP) **Attend to Precision** Moesha is designing a triangular tray to display her homemade breads. The measures of two angles are 120° and 30°. Use a protractor to draw what could be the shape of Moesha's triangular tray.

Test Prep

6 Use a protractor to measure the angles. Then match each figure with its angle measures.

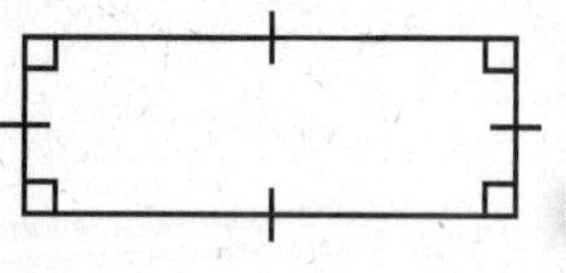

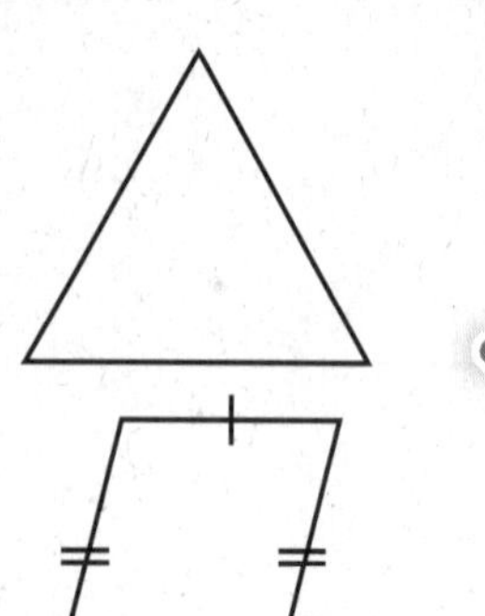

•	• 60°, 60°, 60°
•	• 75°, 105°, 75°, 105°
•	• 90°, 90°, 90°, 90°

7 Which is the measure of $\angle PQR$?

Ⓐ 155°
Ⓑ 35°
Ⓒ 145°
Ⓓ 45°

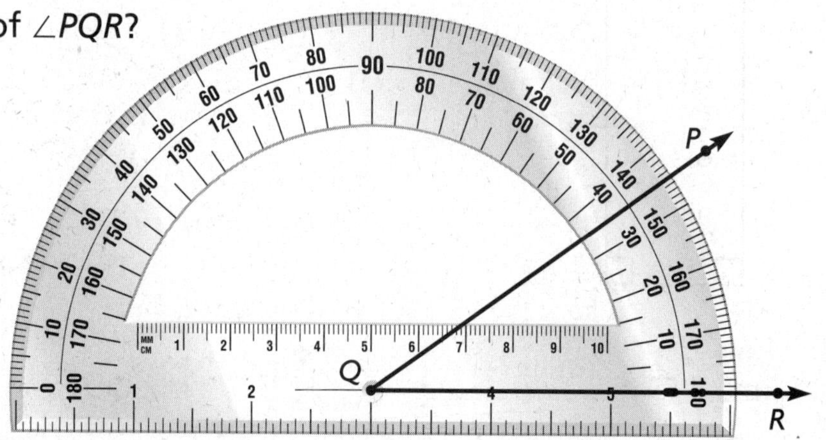

Spiral Review

8 Write the amount shown as a fraction and as a decimal.

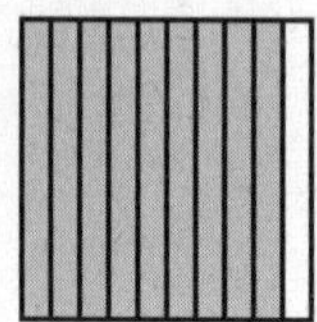

____

9 Use the fraction model to find the difference.

1				
$\frac{1}{5}$	$\frac{1}{5}$	$\frac{1}{5}$	$\frac{1}{5}$	$\frac{1}{5}$

$\frac{4}{5} - \frac{1}{5} =$ ____________

Name

Recognize Lines of Symmetry

1 **Open Ended** The construction team is building a new seating area at a restaurant. The seating area has at least 5 sides. Draw a design that has 2 lines of symmetry. Show the lines of symmetry.

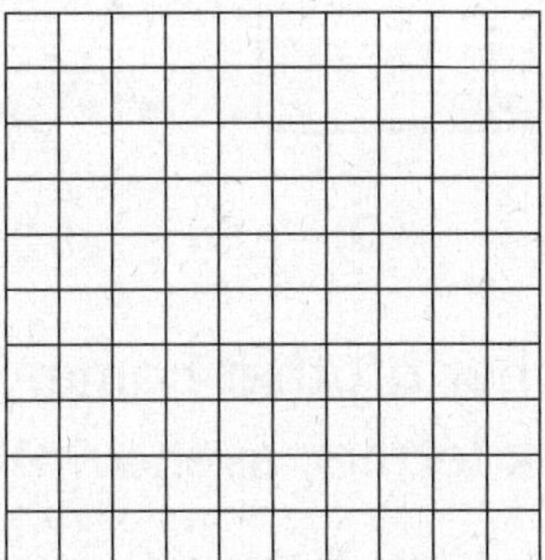

2 **Math on the Spot** The letter C has horizontal symmetry. The letter A has vertical symmetry. Which letters appear to have both horizontal and vertical symmetry?

A	H	S
B	I	T
C	J	U
D	L	V
E	N	W

Tell if the line appears to be a line of symmetry. Write *yes* or *no*.

3

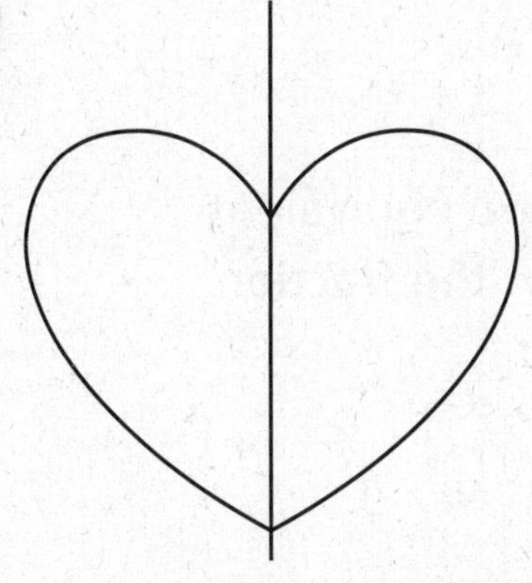

4

5

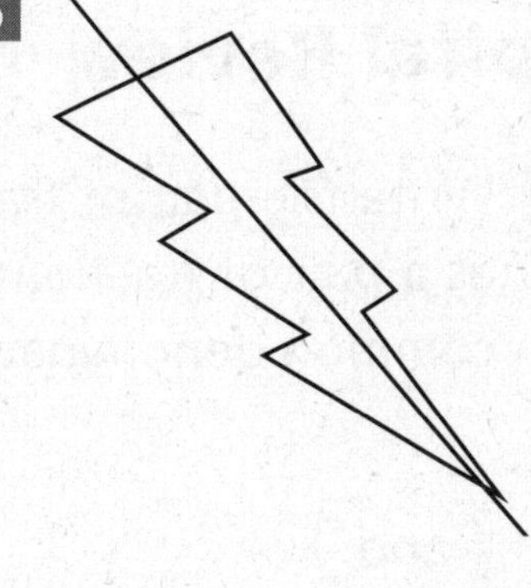

Test Prep

6 Which figures have at least 1 line of symmetry? Select all that are correct.

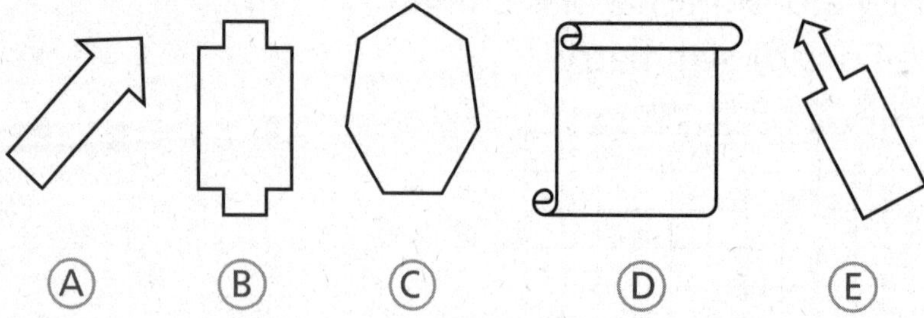

Ⓐ Ⓑ Ⓒ Ⓓ Ⓔ

7 Joy makes a sign welcoming her brother home. She draws the word "Welcome" in block letters, as shown. Which letters have line symmetry?

W E L C O M E

____

8 You are asked to draw a quadrilateral with exactly 2 lines of symmetry. What quadrilateral will you draw? Explain.

____

____

Spiral Review

9 Write the pair of fractions as a pair of fractions with a common denominator.

$\frac{2}{5}$ and $\frac{4}{6}$ __________

10 Generate two equivalent fractions for the fraction.

$\frac{8}{16} = \frac{\square}{\square} = \frac{\square}{\square}$

Name

Identify and Draw Lines of Symmetry

1 Circle any triangle that has line symmetry. Draw all the lines of symmetry.

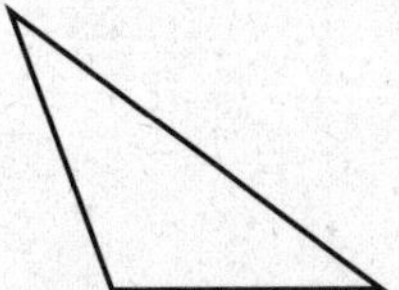
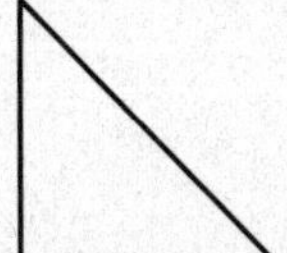
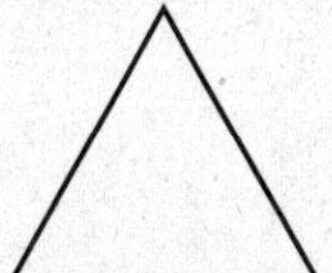
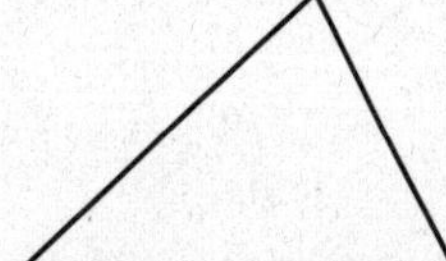

Does the design have line symmetry? Write *yes* or *no*. If your answer is yes, draw all the lines of symmetry.

2

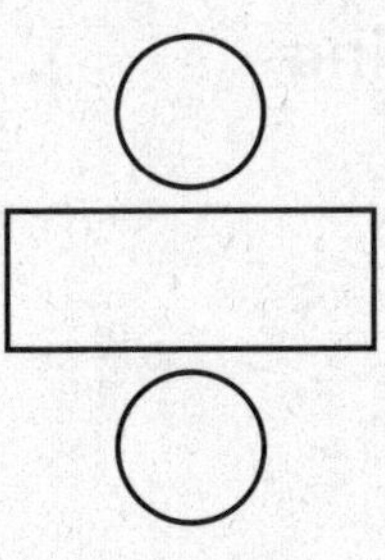

3

4

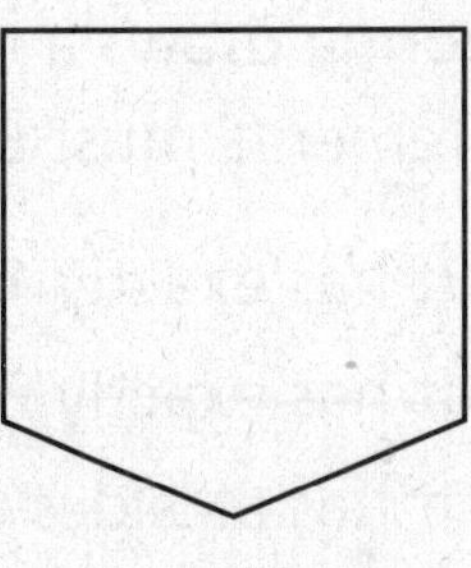

MP Attend to Precision Complete the drawing to show a symmetrical design.

5

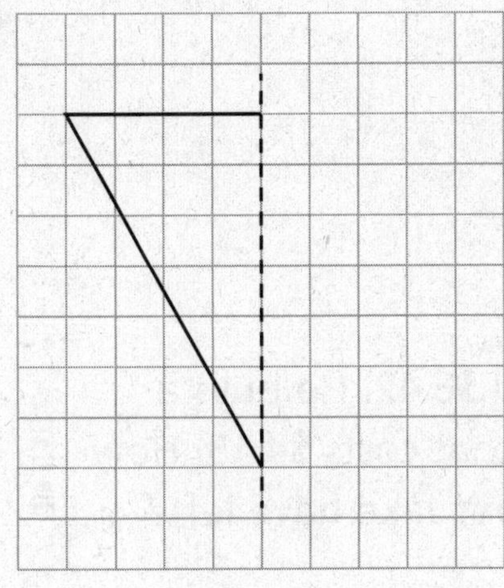

6

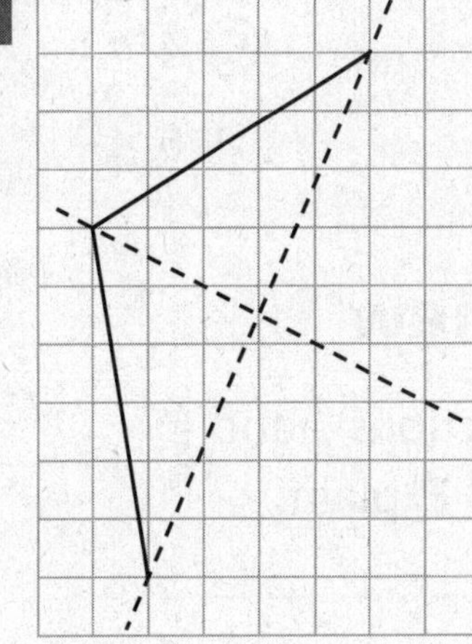

Test Prep

7 Draw a square and a rectangle. Next, draw all the lines of symmetry. Which figure has more lines of symmetry?
Explain why one figure has more lines of symmetry than the other.

____

____

____

8 Myonna draws a regular polygon. Which of the following statements must be true about Myonna's polygon?

(A) It has exactly 1 line of symmetry.

(B) It has exactly 2 lines of symmetry.

(C) It has all sides equal in length, but it has different angle measures.

(D) The number of lines of symmetry equals the number of sides of the polygon.

9 A regular hexagon has 6 sides. Which is the number of lines of symmetry a regular hexagon has?

(A) 0

(B) 2

(C) 4

(D) 6

Spiral Review

10 Are the fractions $\frac{4}{8}$ and $\frac{2}{3}$ equivalent? Explain.

____

____

11 Jake had $6.42. He buys a marker that costs $4.15. How much does Jake have left?

____

Name ______________________________

Generate and Identify Shape Patterns

1 Craig uses rubber stamps to make the following pattern. What might be the next five figures in his pattern?

____

2 (MP) **Attend to Precision** Sara sews this pattern on placemats she is making. Describe a possible pattern. Use precise geometric terms.

____

____

3 Describe a pattern and predict the missing figure in the pattern.

____

____

4 Use the figures to write a number pattern. Then describe your number pattern. How many small squares will be in the seventh figure in your pattern?

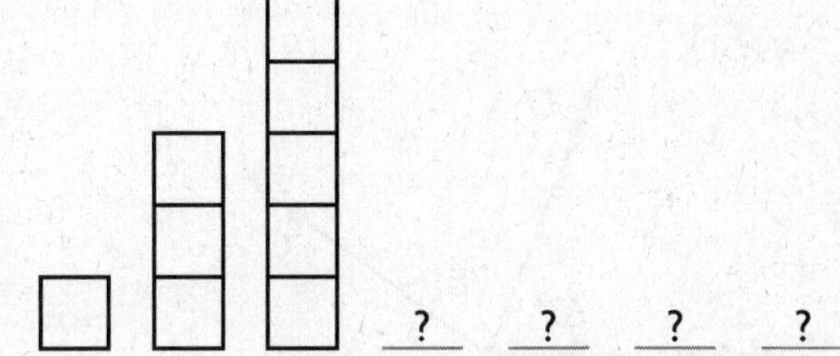

____

____

Test Prep

5 Evan makes the following pattern on a poster. The pattern starts with 2 triangles and 1 pentagon. This repeats using the rule *add 1 pentagon* to continue the pattern. What are the next six figures in the pattern?

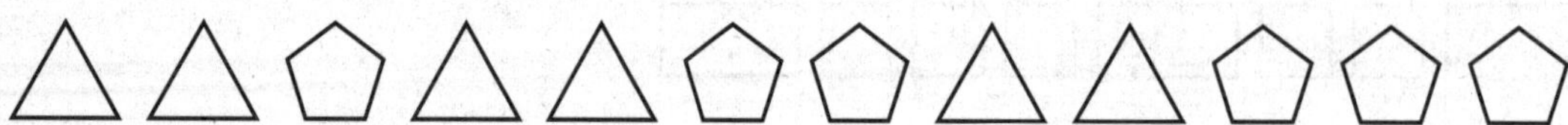

____

6 Naomi makes the following pattern: *triangle, quadrilateral, pentagon, hexagon. She uses the rule increase the number of sides of the polygon by 1.* How many sides will the next figure in her pattern have?

Ⓐ 6　　Ⓒ 8

Ⓑ 7　　Ⓓ 9

7 Marco is drawing a shape pattern. His pattern follows the rule *add 1 square to the top and 1 square to the right.* These are the first three figures in his pattern.

Which will be the number of squares in the fifth figure in Marco's pattern?

Ⓐ 5　　Ⓑ 7　　Ⓒ 9　　Ⓓ 11

Spiral Review

8 Add to find the measure of ∠ABC. Write an equation to record your work.

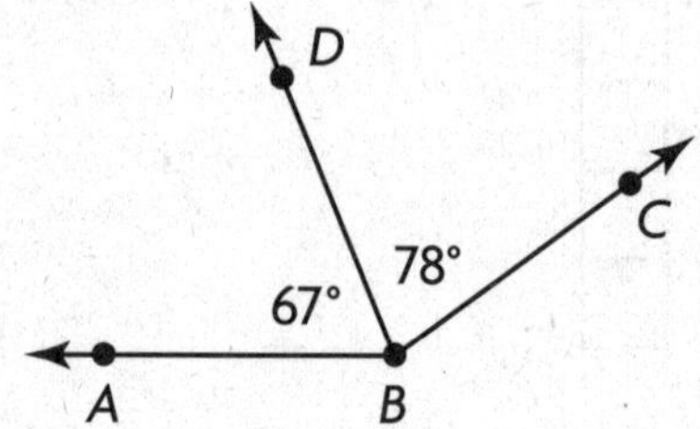

____

____

9 Marley makes $24.50 washing cars. He wants to buy a shirt that costs $16.85. Can he also buy the matching hat for $7.95? Explain.

____

____

____

Name ____________________

Identify Customary Measurement Benchmarks

1 What objects in your home weigh more than an ounce?

____

2 (MP) **Critique Reasoning** Carla says that the best unit to measure her dad's height would be inches. Is she correct? Why or why not? What would be a better unit to use?

____

____

____

____

3 Which image represents a possible benchmark for a pound? Circle the answer.

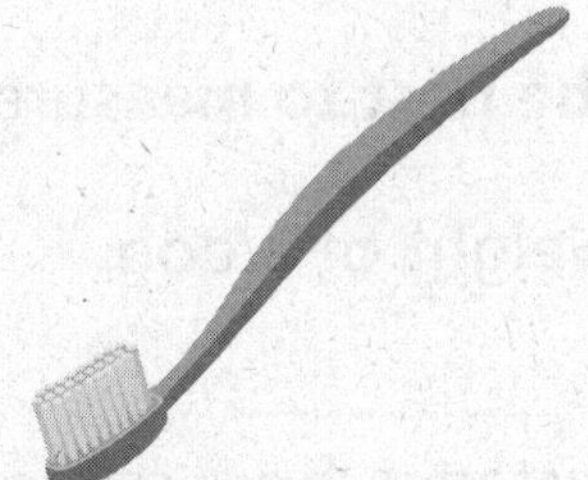

4 **Math on the Spot** Cristina makes macaroni and cheese for her family. Would Cristina use 1 pound of macaroni or 1 ounce of macaroni?

____

____

(MP) **Attend to Precision Use benchmarks for liquid volume to choose the customary unit you would use to measure each.**

5 a drinking glass __________

6 a bathtub __________

7 a water bottle __________

8 a saucepan __________

Test Prep

9 For which measurement unit could you use a small coffee mug as a benchmark?

Ⓐ cup
Ⓑ gallon
Ⓒ pint
Ⓓ quart

10 Select all the measurements that are about 1 yard long.

Ⓐ the length of a student's desk
Ⓑ the height of a classroom
Ⓒ the width of a classroom door
Ⓓ the length of a movie ticket
Ⓔ the height of a building

Which unit from the given list would be best to measure each object?

cups
gallons
ounces
pounds
feet
miles

11 liquid volume of a mug

____

12 weight of a dog

____

13 height of a building

____

14 distance from school to home

____

Spiral Review

15 Write the fraction as a sum of unit fractions.

$\frac{3}{8} =$ ______________

16 Manny does not eat $\frac{4}{9}$ of his orange at lunch. Josh does not eat $\frac{5}{9}$ of his orange at lunch. How much orange do Manny and Josh have left over?

____

Name ______________________________

LESSON 19.2
More Practice/ Homework

ONLINE
Video Tutorials and Interactive Examples

Compare Customary Units of Length

1 (MP) **Use Structure** Darren has a rectangular space that is 3 feet 9 inches wide and 4 feet long. Does he have enough space for a trampoline that has a length and width of 46 inches? Explain your answer.

____

____

____

2 **Math on the Spot** Joanna has 3 yards of fabric. She needs 120 inches of fabric to make curtains. Does she have enough fabric to make curtains? Explain. Make a table to help.

____

____

Complete.

3 4 feet = _____ inches

4 1 yard = _____ inches

5 4 yards = _____ feet

6 7 feet 2 inches = _____ inches

7 5 yards = _____ feet

8 6 yards = _____ feet

Compare. Write >, <, or =.

9 9 inches ◯ 1 foot

10 6 feet ◯ 66 inches

11 6 yards ◯ 18 feet

12 4 yards ◯ 11 feet 6 inches

13 58 inches ◯ 5 feet

14 2 yards ◯ 76 inches

Test Prep

15 Shannon has a piece of ribbon that is 6 yards long. She needs to know if she has enough ribbon for the costumes she is making. How many feet of ribbon does Shannon have?

Ⓐ 6 feet
Ⓑ 12 feet
Ⓒ 18 feet
Ⓓ 24 feet

16 Write the correct letter to match the equivalent lengths.

_____ 2 yards　　**A.** 60 inches
_____ 36 inches　　**B.** 6 feet
_____ 5 feet　　**C.** 1 yard

17 Jordan is the quarterback for the football team. On his first pass, he throws the ball 5 yards. How many feet did he throw the ball on his first pass? Complete the table to find the answer.

_____ feet

Yards	Feet
1	3
2	
3	
4	
5	

Spiral Review

18 Gabriela goes to dance class for $\frac{4}{4}$ hour on Monday and $\frac{2}{4}$ hour on Wednesday. How much longer is Gabriela's dance class on Monday than on Wednesday?

____

____

19 Eric makes a fishing rod. He has 5 yards of fishing line, but he only uses $3\frac{1}{4}$ yards. How many yards of fishing line will Eric have left when he is finished?

____

____

Name

LESSON 19.3
More Practice/ Homework

ONLINE
Video Tutorials and Interactive Examples

Compare Customary Units of Weight

1 (MP) **Use Structure** An adult orca weighs about 8,000 pounds. Does it weigh more than 4 tons? Draw a representation to show how these weights compare. Explain your answer.

Complete.

2 3 pounds = ________ ounces

3 ________ ounces = 1 pound

Compare. Write >, <, or =.

4 52 ounces ◯ 3 pounds

5 13,250 pounds ◯ 6 tons

6 8 pounds ◯ 143 ounces

7 88 ounces ◯ 6 pounds

8 (MP) **Use Repeated Reasoning** Sophia has 6 pounds of tomatoes. How many ounces of tomatoes does she have? Make a table to find the answer.

________ ounces

9 **Math on the Spot** If you could draw a number line that shows the relationship between tons and pounds, what would it look like?

Test Prep

10 Ethan uses a table to find the number of ounces in 5 pounds. Which describes his error?

Pounds	Ounces
1	12
2	24
3	36
4	48
5	60

Ⓐ Ethan thinks there are 12 ounces in a pound instead of 16.

Ⓑ Ethan thinks there are 12 ounces in a pound instead of 2,000.

Ⓒ Ethan adds the same amount instead of multiplying.

Ⓓ Ethan multiplies by the same amount instead of adding.

11 Draw lines to match the equivalent weights.

5 tons •	• 4 pounds
8 pounds •	• 1 ton
2,000 pounds •	• 10,000 pounds
64 ounces •	• 128 ounces

Spiral Review

12 Draw all the lines of symmetry on the figure. How many lines of symmetry does the figure have?

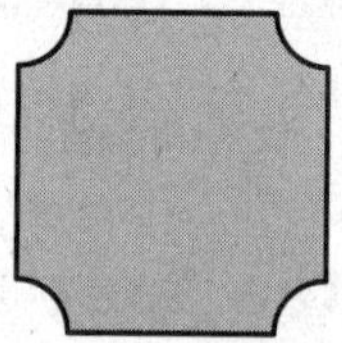

____

13 Elena trains for a marathon. She runs 15.3 miles on Monday, 15.35 miles on Wednesday, 15.05 miles on Friday, and 15.2 miles on Saturday. On which day does she run the farthest?

____

Name ______________________________

LESSON 19.4
More Practice/ Homework

ONLINE
Video Tutorials and Interactive Examples

Compare Customary Units of Liquid Volume

1 (MP) **Model with Mathematics** How do 1 fluid ounce and 1 gallon compare? Explain your thinking. Use comparison symbols.

____

____

Complete the table.

2

Quarts	Pints
1	2
2	
3	
4	
5	

3

Gallons	Quarts
1	4
2	
3	
4	
5	

Complete.

4 4 cups = _____ fluid ounces

5 2 gallons = _____ quarts

Compare. Write >, <, or =.

6 125 fluid ounces ◯ 1 gallon

7 10 cups ◯ 4 pints

8 **Math on the Spot** A soccer team has 11 players. The team's thermos holds 2 gallons of water. If the thermos is full, is there enough water for each player to have 3 cups? Explain. Make a table to help.

____

____

____

Test Prep

9 Sam fills a glass that holds 20 fluid ounces of liquid. Jesse fills a glass that holds 2 pints of liquid. Does Sam's or Jesse's glass hold more liquid? Show your thinking.

________________ glass holds more liquid.

10 Which number completes the statement? Fill in the bubble that makes the statement true.

3 quarts = ■ cups

Ⓐ 4
Ⓑ 6
Ⓒ 8
Ⓓ 12

11 Compare. Write >, <, or = to make the statement true.

30 fluid ounces ◯ 2 pints

Spiral Review

12 Marc and his 5 friends go on a hike. Each hiker eats $\frac{3}{4}$ pound of trail mix. How much trail mix do they eat?

____

13 Caroline fills $\frac{3}{4}$-pint glasses with grape juice. The grape juice container is too heavy, so she uses a smaller $\frac{1}{4}$-pint pitcher to pour the juice. How many times does she have to fill the smaller pitcher in order to fill 3 of the glasses with grape juice?

____

Name ______________________________

Represent and Interpret Measurement Data in Line Plots

1 (MP) **Attend to Precision** Mr. Smith measures how much his baby grows each month for six months. Make a line plot to display the data. Include a title and label the units.

Baby's Growth (in inches)
$\frac{5}{8}$, $\frac{1}{2}$, $\frac{3}{4}$, $\frac{7}{8}$, $\frac{3}{4}$, $\frac{1}{2}$

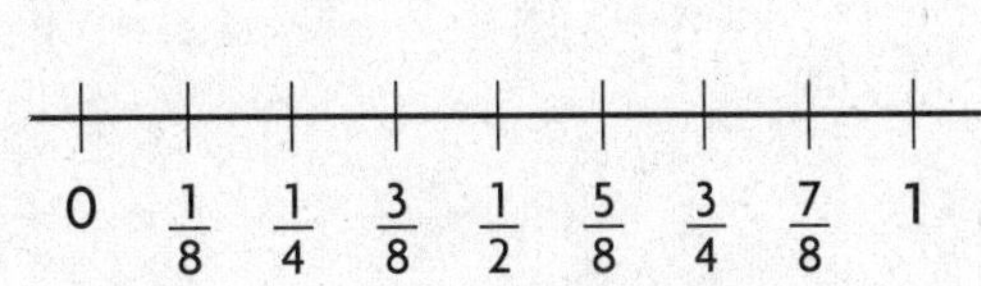

2 (MP) **Model with Mathematics** The weights of six tablets are shown. Complete the tally table, and make a line plot to represent the data.

$\frac{5}{4}$, $\frac{4}{4}$, $\frac{5}{4}$, $\frac{3}{4}$, $\frac{5}{4}$, $\frac{3}{4}$

Tablet Weights	
Pounds	**Tally**
$\frac{3}{4}$	
$\frac{4}{4}$	
$\frac{5}{4}$	

3 (MP) **Use Tools** The line plot shows the distances a delivery drone travels for five deliveries.

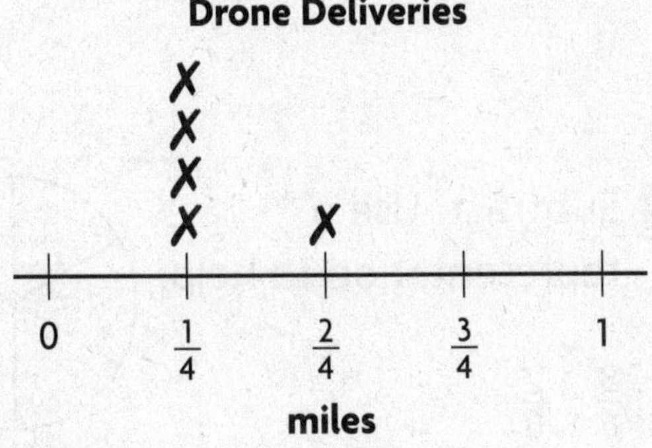

What distance does the drone travel for the five deliveries?

______________ miles

Test Prep

4 The line plot shows the distances Ricky runs each day for five days.

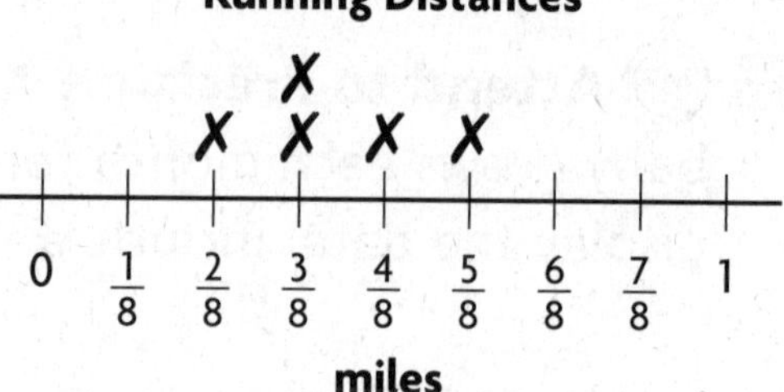

What distance does Ricky run over the five days? Show your thinking.

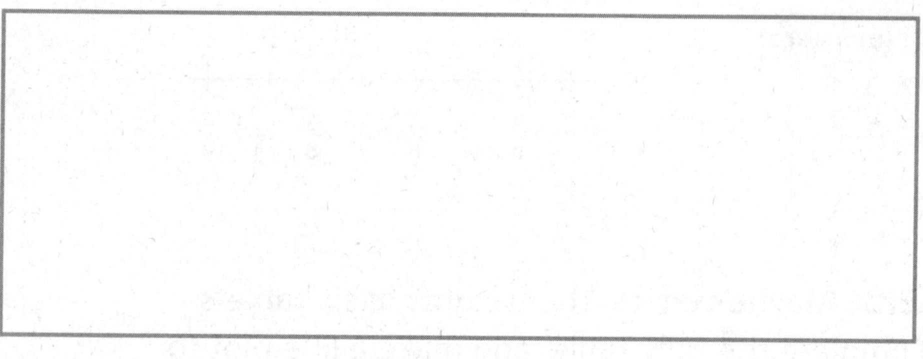

______________ miles

5 Select the line plot that represents the data.

$\frac{1}{8}, \frac{1}{2}, \frac{3}{4}, \frac{7}{8}, \frac{1}{2}, \frac{3}{8}$

Ⓐ 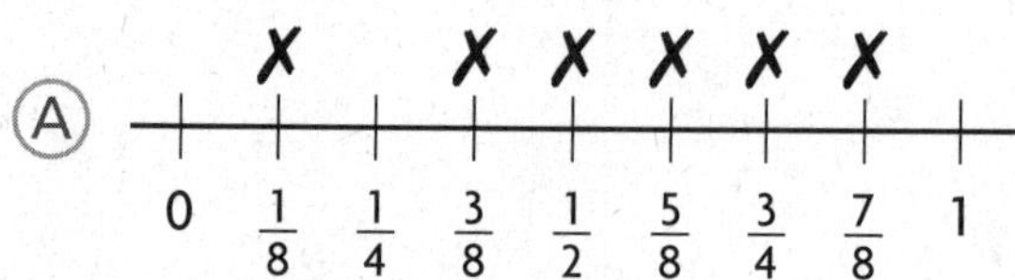

Ⓑ 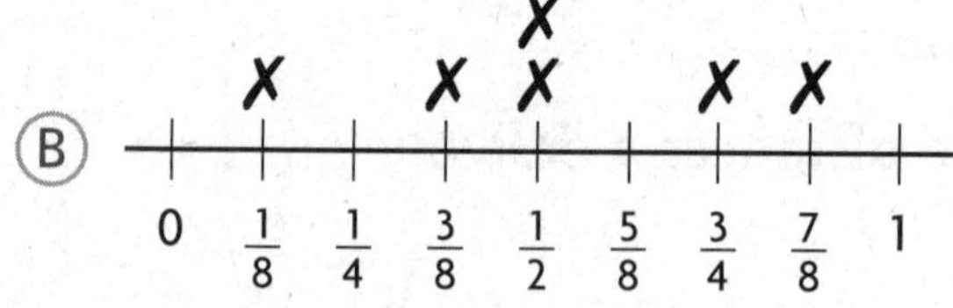

Ⓒ 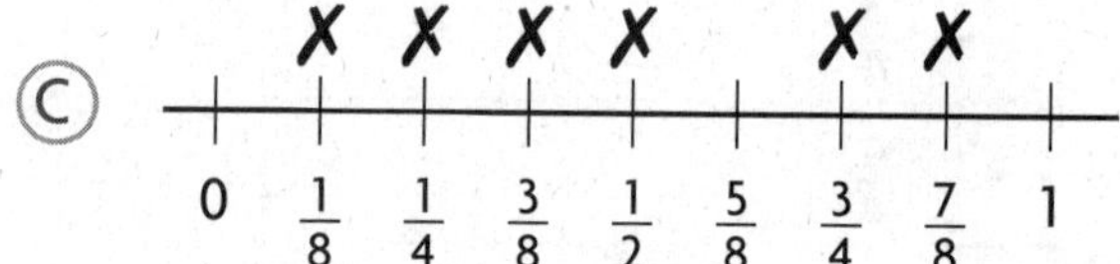

Ⓓ 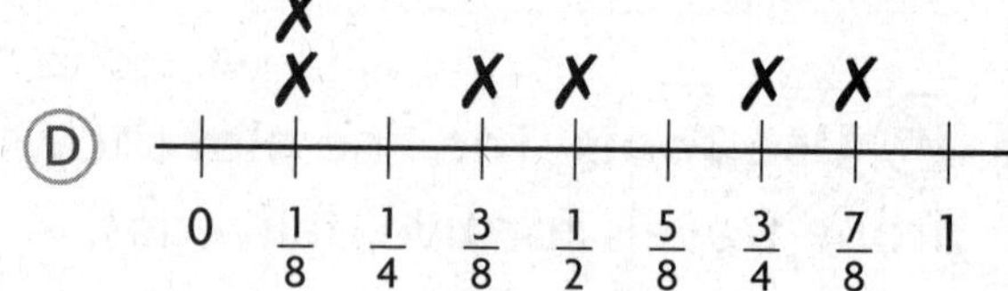

Spiral Review

6 Use a protractor to find the angle measure of $\angle ABC$.

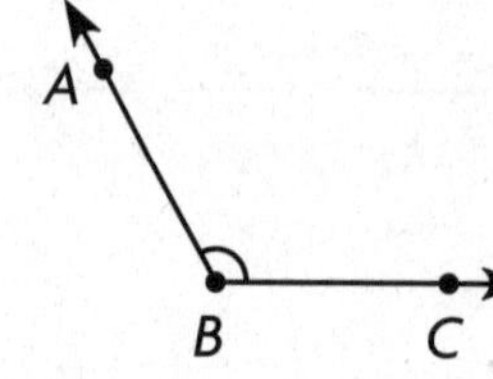

____

7 Subtract. Use a representation to help.

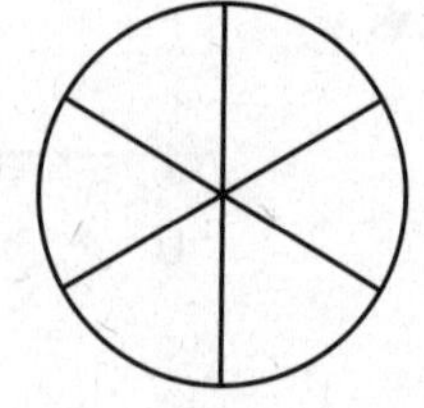

$\frac{3}{6} - \frac{2}{6} =$ ______________

Name ______________________________

Identify Metric Measurement Benchmarks

1 Which amount is a reasonable mass for a banana?

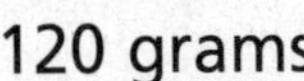

120 grams   12 kilograms

2 (MP) **Reason** Charlie says that a small mug holds about 1 liter. Is he correct? Why or why not?

____

____

____

3 Taryn wants to measure the height of her 4-year-old brother. Which could she use?

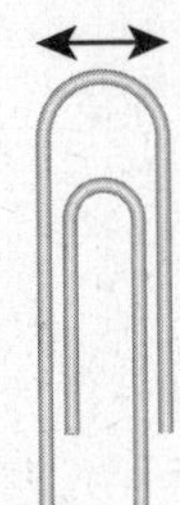

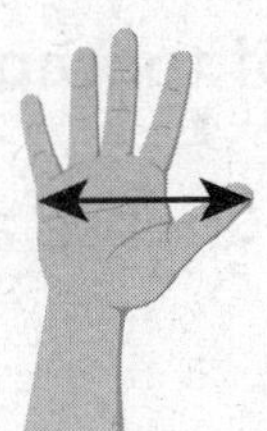

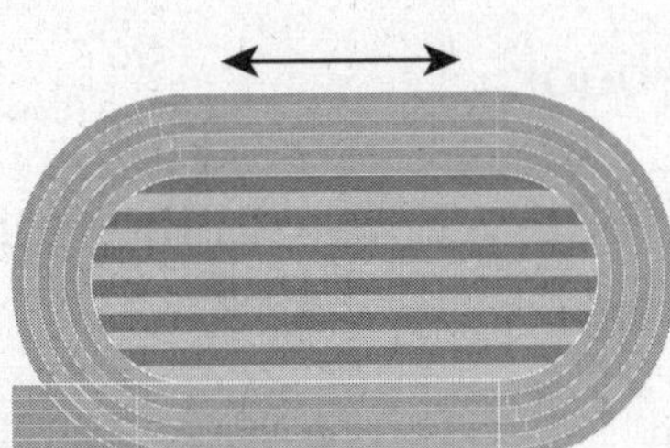

(MP) **Attend to Precision For each item, tell what metric unit you would use to measure.**

4 mass of a dog ______________

5 length of a road trip ______________

6 amount of water in a pool ______________

7 mass of a feather ______________

8 Record an object whose mass you could measure in grams.

____

9 Record an object whose liquid volume you could measure in liters.

____

Test Prep

10 Kip measures the length of his shoe. Which measurement could be correct?

Ⓐ 19 centimeters
Ⓑ 19 kilometers
Ⓒ 19 meters
Ⓓ 19 millimeters

11 Which could you use to measure liquid volume? Choose all that are correct.

Ⓐ gram
Ⓑ kilogram
Ⓒ liter
Ⓓ meter
Ⓔ milliliter
Ⓕ millimeter

12 Shenika finds that an object has about the same mass as 25 paper clips. Which could be Shenika's object?

Ⓐ boot
Ⓑ notebook
Ⓒ paper plate
Ⓓ tube of toothpaste

13 Which could you use to measure mass? Choose all that are correct.

Ⓐ gram
Ⓑ kilogram
Ⓒ liter
Ⓓ meter
Ⓔ milliliter
Ⓕ millimeter

Spiral Review

14 Classify the figure.

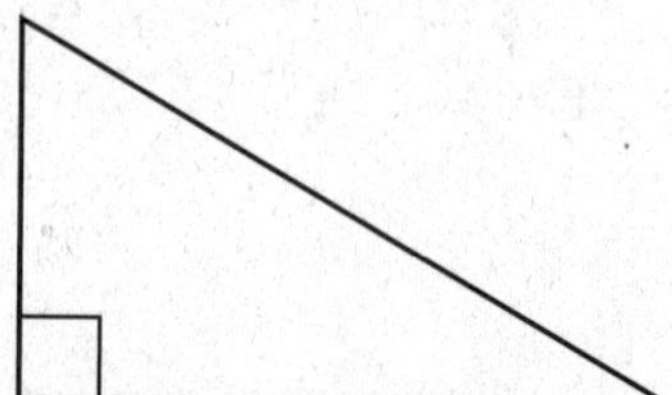

____

15 Draw and label an angle. Use the labels to identify the points, line segments, and rays that are shown on the drawing.

____

Name ______________________________

ONLINE
Video Tutorials and Interactive Examples

Compare Metric Units of Length

1 (MP) **Use Structure** John has 6 meters of wire. He needs at least 500 centimeters to finish a project. Will he have enough wire?

- Use a table to compare the lengths.

Meters	Centimeters
1	
2	
3	
4	
5	
6	

- John __________ have enough wire because __________________________
____.

Complete.

2 7 cm = _____ mm

3 40 decimeters = _____ meters

4 1 kilometer = _____ meters

5 32 m = _____ cm

6 (MP) **Construct Arguments** A plot of land is 7 kilometers long. Jacob says the land is 700 meters long. Is Jacob's statement correct? Describe how you know.

____

____

Compare. Use <, >, or =.

7 2 decimeters ◯ 10 centimeters

8 30 centimeters ◯ 3 decimeters

9 6 kilometers ◯ 5,000 meters

10 8 meters ◯ 90 decimeters

Test Prep

11 Which is greater than 500 centimeters? Choose all that are correct.

Ⓐ 5 kilometers
Ⓑ 6 meters
Ⓒ 500 decimeters
Ⓓ 500 millimeters

12 Complete the table and compare the measurements.

27 millimeters ◯ 3 centimeters

Centimeters	Millimeters
1	
2	
3	

13 Which measurement is equal to 5 decimeters? Choose all that are correct.

Ⓐ 5 centimeters
Ⓑ 50 centimeters
Ⓒ 500 millimeters
Ⓓ 5,000 millimeters

14 Write the correct letter to match the equivalent lengths.

_____ 9 meters — **A** 90 centimeters

_____ 9 decimeters — **B** 9 kilometers

_____ 9,000 meters — **C** 900 centimeters

Spiral Review

15 Compare. Use >, <, or =.

2 feet ◯ 2 yards

3 inches ◯ 2 feet

6 pounds ◯ 12 ounces

16 Mike cuts a rope into 8 equal pieces, and each piece of rope is $5\frac{1}{2}$ feet long. How long was the original piece of rope?

____

Name ______________________________

LESSON 20.3
More Practice/ Homework

ONLINE
Ed Video Tutorials and Interactive Examples

Compare Metric Units of Mass and Liquid Volume

1 (MP) **Attend to Precision** Bethany has two glasses of water. One glass has 400 milliliters of water. The other has 500 milliliters of water. She pours all the water into an empty pitcher that can hold 1 liter. Is the pitcher full? How do you know?

____

2 Grant uses 3 grams of ginger in a recipe. How many milligrams of ginger does he use?

____

Compare. Write >, <, or =.

3 2,900 mL ◯ 3 L   **4** 14 g ◯ 1,400 mg   **5** 7 kg ◯ 7,000 g

Complete.

6

Liters	Milliliters
1	1,000
4	
9	

7

Grams	Milligrams
1	1,000
6	
11	

8

Kilograms	Grams
1	1,000
5	
17	

9 (MP) **Use Structure** Kelli has two pitchers of water. The blue pitcher holds 3 liters of water. The red pitcher holds 2,800 milliliters. Which pitcher has the greater liquid volume? How do you know?

____

____

____

____

Test Prep

10 Melinda's dog crate can hold a dog with a mass up to 12 kilograms. Which mass for a dog would the crate safely hold? Choose all that are correct.

Ⓐ 30,000 grams
Ⓑ 11,000 grams
Ⓒ 10,000 grams
Ⓓ 5,000 grams
Ⓔ 12,500 grams
Ⓕ 21,000 grams

11 Mahesh fills a walkway with 7 kilograms of pebbles. How many grams of pebbles does Mahesh use?

__________ grams

12 **Compare. Select $>$, $<$, or $=$.**

	$<$	$>$	$=$
3,000 mL ◯ 2 L	☐	☐	☐
5 kg ◯ 5,200 g	☐	☐	☐
9,000 mg ◯ 9 g	☐	☐	☐

13 David puts 2 liters of water into a cooler that holds 10 liters. How many more milliliters can he add to the cooler until it is full?

__________ mL

Spiral Review

14 Use benchmarks to decide which customary unit you would use to measure the liquid volume of a swimming pool.

____

15 Janine records the following data about the growth of each plant: $\frac{1}{2}$ in., $\frac{3}{4}$ in., $\frac{1}{4}$ in., $\frac{1}{2}$ in., $\frac{3}{4}$ in.

Draw a line plot to show the data.

Name ______________________________

LESSON 20.4
More Practice/ Homework

ONLINE
Video Tutorials and Interactive Examples

Solve Problems Using Measurements

1 (MP) **Construct Arguments** Jaime is helping her brother make pasta for dinner. The recipe makes 8 quarts of baked ziti. If they each eat 1 pint of baked ziti, will they have enough left over to give their grandmother 6 pints? Why or why not?

2 (MP) **Use Repeated Reasoning** Alex's landscaping company orders 2 tons of stones to put around the houses where they are working. If they use 400 pounds of stones at each house, how many houses can they finish? Explain your thinking.

3 (MP) **Reason** Jenny is making lemonade for the pep rally after school. She needs to make 8 liters. If one package of lemonade mix makes 2,500 milliliters, how many packages of mix does Jenny need to use? Explain your thinking.

4 (MP) **Model with Mathematics** A bookcase is 5 feet tall. Janelle is $\frac{1}{2}$ foot taller than the bookcase. How tall is Janelle in inches? Explain. Use an equation to model your thinking.

Test Prep

5 Sean fills three containers that each hold 24 fluid ounces of iced tea. Matt fills four containers that each hold 1 pint of iced tea. Whose containers hold more liquid, Sean's or Matt's?

__________ containers hold more liquid.

6 Mike jogged $1\frac{4}{10}$ kilometers on Tuesday, $2\frac{1}{10}$ kilometers on Thursday, and $1\frac{3}{10}$ kilometers on Friday. How many meters did Mike jog over the course of the week?

Ⓐ $4\frac{8}{10}$ meters
Ⓑ 48 meters
Ⓒ 480 meters
Ⓓ 4,800 meters

7 Liz's cat weighs 187 ounces. She owns a pet carrier for cats that can safely carry up to 12 pounds. How much more weight can the carrier safely hold when Liz's cat is in the pet carrier?

Ⓐ 5 ounces
Ⓑ 8 ounces
Ⓒ 10 ounces
Ⓓ 15 ounces

Spiral Review

8 Use benchmarks to decide which metric unit you would use to measure the length of a crayon.

____

9 Cheyanne borrows $\frac{4}{5}$ of a can of paint to finish her art project. She only uses $\frac{3}{5}$ of the can. How much paint does Cheyanne have left?

____

ONLINE
Video Tutorials and
Interactive Examples

Name ______________________________

Compare Units of Time

1 (MP) **Reason** Keli spends 200 minutes reading her favorite book over the weekend. Luke spends 3 hours playing his favorite sport. Who spends more time doing their favorite activity over the weekend? Explain.

____

____

____

2 (MP) **Use Tools** Lucy runs a lap around the track in 4 minutes. Vera runs the lap in 260 seconds. Who runs the lap in the fastest time? Use the table to support your explanation.

Lap Times	
Minutes	**Seconds**
1	60
2	
3	
4	
5	

____

____

3 **Math on the Spot** How many minutes are in a day? Explain.

____

____

Complete.

4 2 hours = _____ minutes

5 3 minutes = _____ seconds

6 9 minutes = _____ seconds

7 6 hours = _____ minutes

Write whether you would use *hours, minutes,* or *seconds* to measure how long it takes to complete each activity.

8 jog in the park __________

9 dial a phone number __________

10 drive 500 miles __________

11 walk the dog __________

Test Prep

12 Misha watches a movie that is $2\frac{1}{2}$ hours long. Fran watches a movie that is 195 minutes long. Who watches the longer movie?

____

13 What time is shown on the clock at the right?

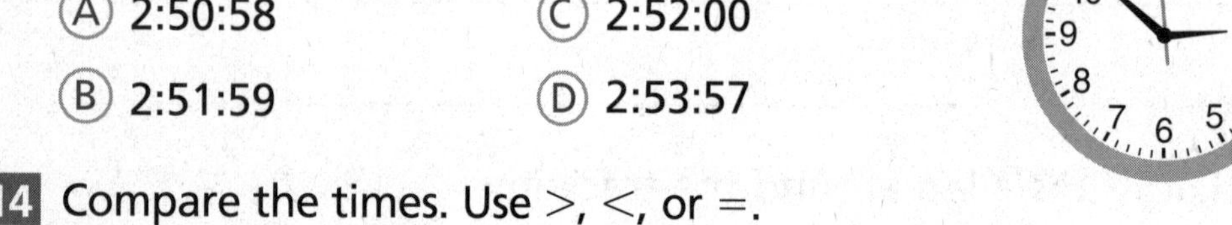

Ⓐ 2:50:58 Ⓒ 2:52:00

Ⓑ 2:51:59 Ⓓ 2:53:57

14 Compare the times. Use >, <, or =.

3 hours ◯ 170 minutes

5 hours ◯ 305 minutes

7 minutes ◯ 400 seconds

120 seconds ◯ 2 minutes

15 Joanie has 3 hours 45 minutes before swim practice. She wants to go to the store, which will take 220 minutes. She also wants to take her brother to the park for 230 minutes. Which activity does Joanie have time to do before practice?

Ⓐ Take her brother to the park

Ⓑ Go to the store

Ⓒ She has time to do both activities.

Ⓓ She does not have time to do either activity.

Spiral Review

16 Regina times herself climbing a rope. Her first climb is $\frac{6}{8}$ minute. Her second climb is $\frac{3}{10}$ minute. Which climb takes her the least amount of time?

$\frac{6}{8}$ ◯ $\frac{3}{10}$

____

17 Mike studies for $\frac{3}{6}$ hour. Rick studies for $\frac{8}{12}$ hour and Jon studies for $\frac{2}{3}$ hour. Which two students study for the same amount of time? Explain.

____

____

Name ______________________

Solve Problems Involving Elapsed Time

1 **Use Repeated Reasoning** Zed begins his homework at 3:52 p.m. and finishes at 4:18 p.m. Show how to find the elapsed time.

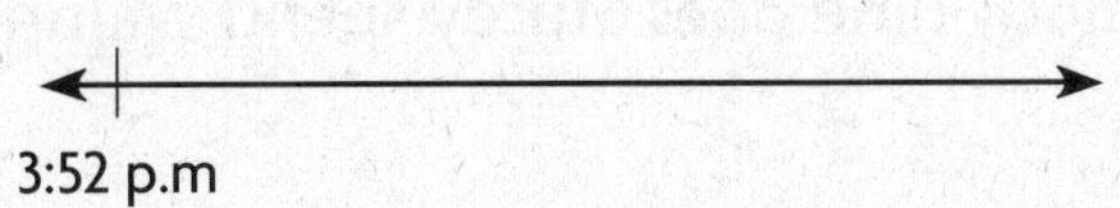

How many minutes does Zed spend doing his homework?

____

MP **Attend to Precision** **Find the elapsed time.**

2 Start time: 11:16:42 a.m.

End time: 12:35:18 p.m.

Elapsed time: __________

3 Start time: 07:42:25 a.m.

End time: 09:28:31 a.m.

Elapsed time: __________

4 **STEM Find the elapsed time. Use information from Natalie's experiment.**

The freezing point of water is 32 degrees Fahrenheit. Salt will lower the freezing point of water. The freezing point of seawater is 28.4 degrees Fahrenheit. Natalie filled one ice cube tray with fresh water and one ice cube tray with salt water. She placed both trays into the freezer at 1:43 p.m. She regularly checked on the trays and noticed the freshwater tray was completely frozen at 5:11 p.m and the saltwater tray was completely frozen at 5:14 p.m.

A. The tray filled with fresh water was frozen in ______________.

B. The tray filled with salt water was frozen in ______________.

Test Prep

5 A band begins performing at 2:54 p.m. The band finishes performing at 4:22 p.m. How long did the band perform?

Ⓐ 1 hour 28 minutes
Ⓑ 1 hour 32 minutes
Ⓒ 2 hours 28 minutes
Ⓓ 2 hours 32 minutes

6 Stacey arrives at the bus stop at 7:49 a.m. She gets on the bus at 8:12 a.m. How much time does Stacey spend waiting for the bus?

Ⓐ 11 minutes
Ⓑ 23 minutes
Ⓒ 37 minutes
Ⓓ 53 minutes

7 Finn begins walking to the park at 9:54 a.m. He arrives at the park at 10:07 a.m. How long does it take Finn to walk to the park?

____

8 Find the unknown time.

Start time: 9:28:25 a.m.

Elapsed time: __________

End time: 10:14:37 a.m.

Spiral Review

9 Use the fraction strips to help you complete the equations.

1			
$\frac{1}{6}$	$\frac{1}{6}$	$\frac{1}{6}$	$\frac{1}{6}$

____ + ____ + ____ + ____ $= \frac{4}{6}$

____ × ____ $= \frac{4}{6}$

10 Find the product.

$4 \times \frac{5}{8} =$ ____

Name ______________________________

ONLINE
Video Tutorials and
Interactive Examples

Solve Problems Involving Start Time and End Time

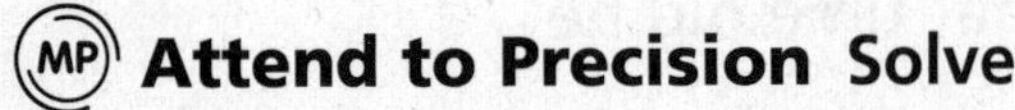
Attend to Precision Solve.

1 Zac leaves for the airport at 6:52:10 a.m. He drives for 1 hour 15 minutes 47 seconds. At what time does Zac arrive at the airport?

____

2 The bus left the school and arrived at the museum at 9:10:40 a.m. The bus traveled for 55 minutes 10 seconds. At what time did the bus leave the school?

____

3 **Math on the Spot** Bethany finished her math homework at 7:30 p.m. She did 12 multiplication problems in all. If each problem took her 4 minutes to do, at what time did Bethany start her math homework?

____

4 Sasha starts her book report at 5:15 p.m. She works for 57 minutes, takes a 35 minute break to eat dinner, and then starts working on her book report again. At what time will she start working on her book report again?

____

5 Jimmy took a nap for 3 hours 20 minutes. He woke up at 7:40 p.m. What time did he start his nap?

____

Test Prep

6 After working on his computer for 5 hours 35 minutes, Mr. Shorn stops working at 4:18 p.m. At what time did he start working?

Ⓐ 10:43 a.m.
Ⓑ 11:43 a.m.
Ⓒ 10: 43 p.m.
Ⓓ 11: 43 p.m.

7 Sheila and her friends arrived at the beach at 10:45 a.m. They were in the water for 1 hour 20 minutes before they decided to eat a snack. At what time did they eat their snack?

Ⓐ 12:05 a.m.
Ⓑ 11:05 a.m.
Ⓒ 12:05 p.m.
Ⓓ 11:05 p.m.

8 Robbie and his family left town and drove for 4 hours 35 minutes before stopping to get gas at 1:37 p.m. At what time did they leave town?

____

9 Find the end time.

Start time: 2:43:18 p.m.

Elapsed time: 0:19:35

End time: ____________________

Spiral Review

10 Are the fractions $\frac{2}{3}$ and $\frac{4}{6}$ equivalent? How do you know?

____

11 Generate two equivalent fractions for the fraction.

$\frac{8}{12} = \frac{\square}{\square} = \frac{\square}{\square}$

Name ______________________

Practice with Mixed Measures

1 (MP) **Reason** Gina jogs 4,120 meters. Meg jogs $2\frac{1}{2}$ kilometers. Evan jogs twice as far as Meg. How much farther than Gina does Evan jog? Explain.

____

____

2 (MP) **Use Structure** Jonah runs in a race and finishes 45 seconds before Chris, whose finish time is shown on the clock. Rick finishes 23 seconds after Jonah. How long does it take Rick to finish the race? Show your solution steps.

____

3 (MP) **Attend to Precision** Denise is designing 3 new windows for a kitchen. She has 8 feet 9 inches of wood frame to use. If she uses 4 feet 3 inches of wood frame for the first window, how much wood frame can she use for the other 2 windows? Show all your work.

____

____

____

____

4 **Math on the Spot** Jackson has a rope that is 2 feet 6 inches long. He cuts it into 6 equal pieces. How many inches long is each piece?

____

Test Prep

5 Mark is trying to figure out if a 1 ton 600 pound truck can drive over the new bridge. The weight limit on the bridge is 3,200 pounds. How many pounds does the truck weigh?

(A) 1,600 pounds
(B) 2,400 pounds
(C) 2,600 pounds
(D) 3,400 pounds

6 Jin is building a fence around a new garden. He uses 7 feet 3 inches of fencing and has 38 inches left over. How much fencing did Jin start with?

(A) 3 feet 2 inches
(B) 8 feet 6 inches
(C) 9 feet 10 inches
(D) 10 feet 5 inches

7 The directions of a recipe say to cook on low for 4 hours 25 minutes. Margo cooks it on high for 127 minutes. How much faster does Margo cook the meal?

____

8 Complete.

4 hours 26 minutes = _____ minutes

7 feet 9 inches = _____ inches

6 quarts 4 pints = _____ pints

9 pounds 14 ounces = _____ ounces

Spiral Review

9 Write the pair of fractions as a pair of fractions with a common denominator.

$\frac{3}{4}$ and $\frac{3}{8}$ ______________

$\frac{3}{12}$ and $\frac{1}{4}$ ______________

10 Find one number that makes both statements true.

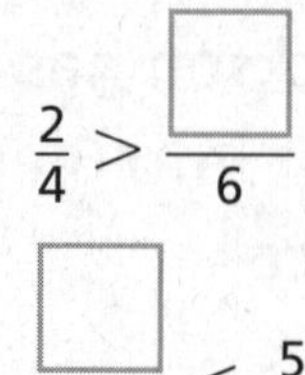

$\frac{2}{4} > \frac{\square}{6}$

$\frac{\square}{5} < \frac{5}{10}$

HMH | into Math™

My Journal

My Progress on Mathematics Standards

The lesson in your ***Into Math*** book provides instruction for Mathematics Standards for Grade 4. You can use the following pages to reflect on your learning and record your progress through the standards.

As you learn new concepts, reflect on this learning. Consider inserting a check mark if you understand the concepts or inserting a question mark if you have questions or need help.

	Student Edition Lessons	My Progress
Domain: OPERATIONS AND ALGEBRAIC THINKING		
Cluster: Use the four operations with whole numbers to solve problems.		
Interpret a multiplication equation as a comparison, e.g., interpret $35 = 5 \times 7$ as a statement that 35 is 5 times as many as 7 and 7 times as many as 5. Represent verbal statements of multiplicative comparisons as multiplication equations.	3.1	
Multiply or divide to solve word problems involving multiplicative comparison, e.g., by using drawings and equations with a symbol for the unknown number to represent the problem, distinguishing multiplicative comparison from additive comparison.	3.1, 3.2, 3.3, 3.4, 3.5	

	Student Edition Lessons	My Progress
Solve multistep word problems posed with whole numbers and having whole-number answers using the four operations, including problems in which remainders must be interpreted. Represent these problems using equations with a letter standing for the unknown quantity. Assess the reasonableness of answers using mental computation and estimation strategies including rounding.	3.5, 5.7, 6.3, 7.4, 8.7	
Cluster: Gain familiarity with factors and multiples.		
Find all factor pairs for a whole number in the range 1–100. Recognize that a whole number is a multiple of each of its factors. Determine whether a given whole number in the range 1–100 is a multiple of a given one-digit number. Determine whether a given whole number in the range 1–100 is prime or composite.	10.1, 10.2, 10.3, 10.4	
Cluster: Generate and analyze patterns.		
Generate a number or shape pattern that follows a given rule. Identify apparent features of the pattern that were not explicit in the rule itself.	10.5, 18.3	

	Student Edition Lessons	My Progress
Domain: NUMBER AND OPERATIONS IN BASE TEN		
Cluster: Generalize place value understanding for multi-digit whole numbers.		
Recognize that in a multi-digit whole number, a digit in one place represents ten times what it represents in the place to its right.	1.1, 1.3	
Read and write multi-digit whole numbers using base-ten numerals, number names, and expanded form. Compare two multi-digit numbers based on meanings of the digits in each place, using $>$, $=$, and $<$ symbols to record the results of comparisons.	1.2, 1.4	
Use place value understanding to round multi-digit whole numbers to any place.	1.5, 4.3, 8.2	
Cluster: Use place value understanding and properties of operations to perform multi-digit arithmetic.		
Fluently add and subtract multi-digit whole numbers using the standard algorithm.	2.1, 2.2, 2.3	
Multiply a whole number of up to four digits by a one-digit whole number, and multiply two two-digit numbers, using strategies based on place value and the properties of operations. Illustrate and explain the calculation by using equations, rectangular arrays, and/or area models.	4.1, 4.3, 4.5, 5.1, 5.2, 5.3, 5.4, 5.5, 5.6, 8.1, 8.3, 8.4, 8.5, 8.6	

	Student Edition Lessons	My Progress
Find whole-number quotients and remainders with up to four-digit dividends and one-digit divisors, using strategies based on place value, the properties of operations, and/or the relationship between multiplication and division. Illustrate and explain the calculation by using equations, rectangular arrays, and/or area models.	4.2, 4.4, 4.5, 6.1, 6.2, 6.3, 6.4, 6.5, 6.6, 7.1, 7.2, 7.3	
Domain: NUMBER AND OPERATIONS—FRACTIONS		
Cluster: Extend understanding of fraction equivalence and ordering.		
Explain why a fraction $\frac{a}{b}$ is equivalent to a fraction $\frac{(n \times a)}{(n \times b)}$ by using visual fraction models, with attention to how the number and size of the parts differ even though the two fractions themselves are the same size. Use this principle to recognize and generate equivalent fractions.	11.3, 11.4, 11.5	
Compare two fractions with different numerators and different denominators, e.g., by creating common denominators or numerators, or by comparing to a benchmark fraction such as $\frac{1}{2}$. Recognize that comparisons are valid only when the two fractions refer to the same whole. Record the results of comparisons with symbols $>$, $=$, or $<$, and justify the conclusions, e.g., by using a visual fraction model.	11.1, 11.2, 11.6, 11.7	

Interactive Standards

	Student Edition Lessons	My Progress
Cluster: Build fractions from unit fractions by applying and extending previous understandings of operations on whole numbers.		
Understand a fraction $\frac{a}{b}$ with $a > 1$ as a sum of fractions $\frac{1}{b}$.		
• Understand addition and subtraction of fractions as joining and separating parts referring to the same whole.	14.2, 14.4	
• Decompose a fraction into a sum of fractions with the same denominator in more than one way, recording each decomposition by an equation. Justify decompositions, e.g., by using a visual fraction model.	14.1, 15.2	
• Add and subtract mixed numbers with like denominators, e.g., by replacing each mixed number with an equivalent fraction, and/or by using properties of operations and the relationship between addition and subtraction.	15.3, 15.4, 15.5	
• Solve word problems involving addition and subtraction of fractions referring to the same whole and having like denominators, e.g., by using visual fraction models and equations to represent the problem.	14.3, 14.5, 15.1, 15.6	

	Student Edition Lessons	My Progress
Apply and extend previous understandings of multiplication to multiply a fraction by a whole number.		
• Understand a fraction $\frac{a}{b}$ as a multiple of $\frac{1}{b}$.	16.1	
• Understand a multiple of $\frac{a}{b}$ as a multiple of $\frac{1}{b}$, and use this understanding to multiply a fraction by a whole number.	16.2, 16.3	
• Solve word problems involving multiplication of a fraction by a whole number, e.g., by using visual fraction models and equations to represent the problem.	16.2, 16.3, 16.4	

	Student Edition Lessons	My Progress
Cluster: Understand decimal notation for fractions, and compare decimal fractions.		
Express a fraction with denominator 10 as an equivalent fraction with denominator 100, and use this technique to add two fractions with respective denominators 10 and 100.	12.3, 14.6	
Use decimal notation for fractions with denominators 10 or 100.	12.1, 12.2, 12.3, 12.5	
Compare two decimals to hundredths by reasoning about their size. Recognize that comparisons are valid only when the two decimals refer to the same whole. Record the results of comparisons with the symbols >, =, or <, and justify the conclusions, e.g., by using a visual model.	12.4	

	Student Edition Lessons	My Progress
Domain: MEASUREMENT AND DATA		
Cluster: Solve problems involving measurement and conversion of measurements from a larger unit to a smaller unit.		
Know relative sizes of measurement units within one system of units including km, m, cm; kg, g; lb, oz.; l, ml; hr, min, sec. Within a single system of measurement, express measurements in a larger unit in terms of a smaller unit. Record measurement equivalents in a two-column table.	19.1, 19.2, 19.3, 19.4, 20.1, 20.2, 20.3, 21.1	
Use the four operations to solve word problems involving distances, intervals of time, liquid volumes, masses of objects, and money, including problems involving simple fractions or decimals, and problems that require expressing measurements given in a larger unit in terms of a smaller unit. Represent measurement quantities using diagrams such as number line diagrams that feature a measurement scale.	12.6, 20.4, 21.2, 21.3, 21.4	
Apply the area and perimeter formulas for rectangles in real world and mathematical problems.	2.4, 9.1, 9.2, 9.3, 9.4	
Cluster: Represent and interpret data.		
Make a line plot to display a data set of measurements in fractions of a unit ($\frac{1}{2}$, $\frac{1}{4}$, $\frac{1}{8}$). Solve problems involving addition and subtraction of fractions by using information presented in line plots.	19.5	

	Student Edition Lessons	My Progress
Cluster: Geometric measurement: understand concepts of angle and measure angles.		
Recognize angles as geometric shapes that are formed wherever two rays share a common endpoint, and understand concepts of angle measurement:		
• An angle is measured with reference to a circle with its center at the common endpoint of the rays, by considering the fraction of the circular arc between the points where the two rays intersect the circle. An angle that turns through $\frac{1}{360}$ of a circle is called a "one-degree angle," and can be used to measure angles.	13.2, 13.3, 13.4	
• An angle that turns through *n* one-degree angles is said to have an angle measure of *n* degrees.	13.4	
Measure angles in whole-number degrees using a protractor. Sketch angles of specified measure.	13.5, 17.5	
Recognize angle measure as additive. When an angle is decomposed into non-overlapping parts, the angle measure of the whole is the sum of the angle measures of the parts. Solve addition and subtraction problems to find unknown angles on a diagram in real world and mathematical problems, e.g., by using an equation with a symbol for the unknown angle measure.	13.6, 13.7	

	Student Edition Lessons	My Progress
Domain: GEOMETRY		
Cluster: **Draw and identify lines and angles, and classify shapes by properties of their lines and angles.**		
Draw points, lines, line segments, rays, angles (right, acute, obtuse), and perpendicular and parallel lines. Identify these in two-dimensional figures.	13.1, 13.5, 17.1, 17.2 17.3, 17.4, 17.5	
Classify two-dimensional figures based on the presence or absence of parallel or perpendicular lines, or the presence or absence of angles of a specified size. Recognize right triangles as a category, and identify right triangles.	17.2, 17.3, 17.4	
Recognize a line of symmetry for a two-dimensional figure as a line across the figure such that the figure can be folded along the line into matching parts. Identify line-symmetric figures and draw lines of symmetry.	18.1, 18.2	

My Learning Summary

As you learn about new concepts, complete a learning summary for each module. A learning summary can include drawings, examples, non-examples, and terminology. It's your learning summary, so show or include information that will help you.

At the end of each module, you will have a summary you can reference to review content for a module test and help you make connections with related math concepts.

Name

My Learning Summary

Name

My Learning Summary

Name

My Learning Summary

Name

Module 4
Mental Math and Estimation Strategies

My Learning Summary

Name

My Learning Summary

Name

My Learning Summary

Name

My Learning Summary

Name ______________________

My Learning Summary

Name

My Learning Summary

Name

Module 10
Algebraic Thinking: Number Theory

My Learning Summary

Name

My Learning Summary

Name

My Learning Summary

Name ______________________________

My Learning Summary

Name

Module 14
Understand Addition and Subtraction of Fractions with Like Denominators

My Learning Summary

Name

My Learning Summary

Name ______________________

Module 16
Multiply Fractions by Whole Numbers

My Learning Summary

Name

My Learning Summary

Name

My Learning Summary

Name

Module 19
Relative Sizes of Customary Measurement Units

My Learning Summary

Name

My Learning Summary

Name

My Learning Summary

Interactive Glossary

As you learn about each new term, add notes, drawings, or sentences in the space next to the definition. Doing so will help you remember what each term means.

Pronunciation Key

a	**a**dd, m**a**p	ē	**e**qual, tr**ee**	m	**m**ove, see**m**	o͞o	p**oo**l, f**oo**d	u̇	p**u**ll, b**oo**k
ā	**a**ce, r**a**te	f	**f**it, hal**f**	n	**n**ice, ti**n**	p	**p**it, sto**p**	û(r)	b**ur**n, t**er**m
â(r)	c**are**, **air**	g	**g**o, lo**g**	ng	ri**ng**, so**ng**	r	**r**un, poo**r**	yo͞o	f**u**se, f**ew**
ä	p**a**lm, f**a**ther	h	**h**ope, **h**ate	o	**o**dd, h**o**t	s	**s**ee, pa**ss**	v	**v**ain, e**v**e
b	**b**at, ru**b**	i	**i**t, g**i**ve	ō	**o**pen, s**o**	sh	**s**ure, ru**sh**	w	**w**in, a**w**ay
ch	**ch**eck, cat**ch**	ī	**i**ce, wr**i**te	ô	**o**rder, j**aw**	t	**t**alk, si**t**	y	**y**et, **y**earn
d	**d**og, ro**d**	j	**j**oy, le**dg**e	oi	**oi**l, b**oy**	th	**th**in, bo**th**	z	**z**est, mu**s**e
e	**e**nd, p**e**t	k	**c**ool, ta**k**e	ou	p**ou**t, n**ow**	th̲	**th**is, ba**th**e	zh	vi**s**ion, plea**s**ure
		l	**l**ook, ru**l**e	o͝o	t**oo**k, f**u**ll	u	**u**p, d**o**ne		

ə the schwa, an unstressed vowel representing the sound spelled *a* in *above*, *e* in *sicken*, *i* in *possible*, *o* in *melon*, *u* in *circus*

Other symbols:
- • separates words into syllables
- ′ indicates stress on a syllable

A

My Vocabulary Summary

acute angle [ə•kyo͞ot′ ang′gəl] An angle that measures greater than 0° and less than 90°

ángulo agudo Un ángulo que mide más de 0° y menos de 90°

acute triangle [ə•kyo͞ot′ trī′ang•gəl] A triangle with three acute angles

triángulo acutángulo Un triángulo con tres ángulos agudos

My Vocabulary Summary

addend [a′dend] A number that is added to another in an addition problem

sumando Un número que se suma a otro en una suma

angle [ang′gəl] A shape formed by two line segments or rays that share the same endpoint

ángulo Una figura formada por dos segmentos o semirrectas que comparten un extremo

area [âr′ē•ə] The measure of the number of unit squares needed to cover a surface

área La medida del número de unidades cuadradas que se necesitan para cubrir una superficie

array [ə•rā′] An arrangement of objects in rows and columns

matriz Una disposición de objetos en hileras y columnas

Associative Property of Addition
[ə•sō′shē•āt•iv präp′ər•tē əv ə•dish′ən]
The property that states that you can group addends in different ways and still get the same sum

propiedad asociativa de la suma
La propiedad que establece que los sumandos se pueden agrupar de diferente manera sin cambiar el total

My Vocabulary Summary

Associative Property of Multiplication [ə•sō′shē•ə•tiv präp′ər•tē əv mul•tə•pli•kā′shən] The property that states that you can group factors in different ways and still get the same product

propiedad asociativa de la multiplicación La propiedad que establece que los factores se pueden agrupar de diferente manera sin cambiar el producto

B

base [bās] A polygon's side

base Uno de los lados de un polígono

benchmark [bench′märk] A known size or amount that helps you understand a different size or amount

punto de referencia Un tamaño o una cantidad que se conoce y que permite comprender otro tamaño o cantidad

C

capacity [kə•pas′i•tē] The amount a container can hold when filled

capacidad Cantidad que puede contener un recipiente cuando se llena

My Vocabulary Summary

---

common denominator [käm′ən dē•näm′ə•nāt•ər] A common multiple of two or more denominators

denominador común Múltiplo común de dos o más denominadores

---

common factor [käm′ən fak′tər] A number that is a factor of two or more numbers

factor común Un número que es factor de dos o más números

---

common multiple [käm′ən mul′tə•pəl] A number that is a multiple of two or more numbers

múltiplo común Un número que es un múltiplo de dos o más números

---

Commutative Property of Addition [kə•myo͞ot′ə•tiv präp′ər•tē əv ə•dish′ən] The property that states that when the order of two addends is changed, the sum is the same

propiedad conmutativa de la suma La propiedad que establece que, cuando cambia el orden de dos sumandos, el total es el mismo

---

Commutative Property of Multiplication [kə•myo͞ot′ə•tiv präp′ər•tē əv mul•tə•pli•kā′shən] The property that states that when the order of two factors is changed, the product is the same

propiedad conmutativa de la multiplicación La propiedad que establece que, cuando cambia el orden de dos factores, el producto es el mismo

My Vocabulary Summary

compatible numbers [kəm•pat′ə•bəl num′berz] Numbers that are easy to compute mentally

números compatibles Números con los que es fácil hacer cálculos mentales

composite number [kəm•päz′it num′bər] A number having more than two factors

número compuesto Un número que tiene más de dos factores

cup (c) [kup] A customary unit used to measure capacity and liquid volume; 1 cup = 8 fluid ounces

taza (tz) Una unidad del sistema usual con la que se mide la capacidad y el volumen de un líquido; 1 taza = 8 onzas fluidas

D

decimal [des′ə•məl] A number with one or more digits to the right of the decimal point

decimal Número con uno o más dígitos a la derecha del punto decimal

decimal point [des′ə•məl point] A symbol used to separate dollars from cents in money amounts, and to separate the ones and the tenths places in a decimal

punto decimal Un símbolo que se usa para separar los dólares de los centavos en cantidades de dinero y el lugar de las unidades del lugar de los décimos en un número decimal

My Vocabulary Summary

decimeter (dm) [des′i•mēt•ər] A metric unit for measuring length or distance; 1 meter = 10 decimeters

decimetro (dm) Una unidad del sistema métrico con la que se mide la longitud o la distancia; 1 metro = 10 decímetros

degree (°) [di•grē′] The unit used for measuring angles and temperatures

grado (°) La unidad con la que se miden los ángulos y la temperatura

denominator [dē•näm′ə•nāt•ər] The number below the bar in a fraction that tells how many equal parts are in the whole or in the group

denominador El número que está debajo de la barra en una fracción y que indica cuántas partes iguales hay en el entero o en el grupo

Distributive Property [di•strib′yoo•tiv präp′ər•tē] The property that states that multiplying a sum by a number is the same as multiplying each addend by the number and then adding the products

propiedad distributiva La propiedad que establece que multiplicar una suma por un número es igual que multiplicar cada sumando por ese número y luego sumar los productos

divide [də•vīd′] To separate into equal groups; the opposite operation of multiplication

dividir Separar en grupos iguales; la operación opuesta a la multiplicación

My Vocabulary Summary

dividend [dəv′ə•dend] The number that is to be divided in a division problem

dividendo El número que se divide en una división

divisible [də•viz′ə•bəl] A number is divisible by another number if the whole-number quotient is a counting number and the remainder is zero.

divisible Un número es divisible entre otro número si el cociente de número entero es un número natural y el residuo es cero.

divisor [də•vī′zer] The number that divides the dividend

divisor El número entre el que se divide el dividendo

E

elapsed time [ē•lapst′ tīm] The time that passes from the start of an activity to the end of that activity

tiempo transcurrido El tiempo que pasa desde el comienzo hasta el final de una actividad

endpoint [end′point] The point at either end of a line segment or the starting point of a ray

extremo El punto ubicado en cada punta de un segmento o el punto de inicio de una semirrecta

My Vocabulary Summary

equal parts [ē′kwəl pärts] Parts that are exactly the same size

partes iguales Partes que tienen exactamente el mismo tamaño

---

equilateral triangle [ē•kwi•lat′ər•əl trī′ang•gəl] A triangle with three sides of equal length

triángulo equilátero Triángulo con tres lados de la misma longitud

---

equivalent decimals [ē•kwiv′ə•lənt des′ə•məlz] Two or more decimals that name the same amount

decimales equivalentes Dos o más decimales que representan la misma cantidad

---

equivalent fractions [ē•kwiv′ə•lənt frak′shənz] Two or more fractions that name the same amount

fracciones equivalentes Dos o más fracciones que indican la misma cantidad

---

estimate (noun) [es′tə•mit] A number that is close to the exact amount

estimación Un número cercano a la cantidad exacta

---

estimate (verb) [es′tə•māt] To find an answer that is close to the exact amount

estimar Hallar un resultado cercano a la cantidad exacta

My Vocabulary Summary

expanded form [ek•span'did fôrm] A way to write numbers by showing the value of each digit

forma desarrollada Una manera de escribir los números mostrando el valor de cada dígito

F

factor [fak'tər] A number that is multiplied by another number to find a product

factor Un número que se multiplica por otro número para hallar un producto

factor pair [fak'tər pâr] Two factors that make a product

par de factores Dos factores que forman un producto

fluid ounce (fl oz) [flo͞o'id ouns] A customary unit used to measure liquid capacity and liquid volume; 1 cup = 8 fluid ounces

onza fluida (oz fl) Una unidad del sistema usual con la que se mide la capacidad y el volumen líquido; 1 taza = 8 onzas fluidas

foot (ft) [fo͝ot] A customary unit used to measure length or distance; 1 foot = 12 inches

pie Unidad del sistema usual que se usa para medir la longitud o la distancia; 1 pie = 12 pulgadas

formula [fôr'myo͞o•lə] A set of symbols that expresses a mathematical rule

fórmula Un conjunto de símbolos que expresa una regla matemática

My Vocabulary Summary

G

gallon (gal) [gal'ən] A customary unit for measuring capacity and liquid volume; 1 gallon = 4 quarts

galón (gal) Una unidad del sistema usual con la que se mide la capacidad y el volumen líquido; 1 galón = 4 cuartos

gram (g) [gram] A metric unit for measuring mass; 1 kilogram = 1,000 grams

gramo (g) Una unidad del sistema métrico con la que se mide la masa; 1 kilogramo = 1,000 gramos

H

height [hīt] The measure of a perpendicular from the base to the top of a two-dimensional figure

altura La medida de una recta perpendicular desde la base hasta la parte superior de una figura bidimensional

hundredth [hun'drədth] One of one hundred equal parts

centésimo Una de cien partes iguales

My Vocabulary Summary

I

inch (in.) [inch] A customary unit used to measure length or distance

pulgada (pulg) Unidad del sistema usual que se usa para medir la longitud o la distancia

---

intersecting lines [in•tər•sekt′ing līnz] Lines that cross each other at exactly one point

líneas secantes Líneas que se cruzan entre sí en un único punto

---

inverse operations [in′vûrs äp•ə•rā′shənz] Operations that undo each other, such as addition and subtraction or multiplication and division

operaciones inversas Operaciones que se cancelan entre sí, como la suma y la resta o la multiplicación y la división

---

isosceles triangle [ī•säs′ə•lēz trī′ang•gəl] A triangle with at least two sides of equal length

triángulo isósceles Triángulo con al menos dos lados de la misma longitud

---

K

kilogram (kg) [kil′ō•gram] A metric unit for measuring mass;
1 kilogram = 1,000 grams

kilogramo (kg) Una unidad del sistema métrico con la que se mide la masa;
1 kilogramo = 1,000 gramos

My Vocabulary Summary

kilometer (km) [kə•läm′ət•ər] A metric unit for measuring length or distance; 1 kilometer = 1,000 meters

kilómetro (km) Una unidad del sistema métrico con la que se mide la longitud o la distancia; 1 kilómetro = 1,000 metros

L

line [līn] A straight path of points in a plane that continues without end in both directions with no endpoints

línea Trayectoria recta que se extiende infinitamente en direcciones opuestas

line of symmetry [līn əv sim′ə•trē] An imaginary line on a figure about which the figure can be folded so that its two parts match exactly

eje de simetría Una línea imaginaria a lo largo de la cual se puede plegar una figura de manera que sus dos partes coincidan totalmente

line plot [līn plät] A graph that records each piece of data on a number line

diagrama de puntos Una gráfica en la que cada dato se registra sobre una recta numérica

My Vocabulary Summary

line segment [līn seg′mənt] A part of a line that includes two points called endpoints and all the points between them

segmento Una parte de una recta que incluye dos puntos llamados extremos y todos los puntos que hay entre ellos

line symmetry [līn sim′ə•trē] What a figure has if it can be folded about a line so that its two parts match exactly

simetría axial Lo que tiene una figura si se puede plegar a lo largo de una línea de manera que sus dos partes coincidan totalmente

liquid volume [lik′wid väl′yo͞om] The measure of the space a liquid occupies

volumen de un líquido La medida del espacio que ocupa un líquido

liter (L) [lēt′ər] A metric unit for measuring capacity and liquid volume; 1 liter = 1,000 milliliters

litro (l / L) Una unidad del sistema métrico con la que se mide la capacidad y el volumen líquido; 1 litro = 1,000 mililitros

M

mass [mas] The amount of matter in an object

masa La cantidad de materia que hay en un objeto

My Vocabulary Summary

meter (m) [mēt′ər] A metric unit for measuring length or distance; 1 meter = 100 centimeters

metro (m) Una unidad del sistema métrico con la que se mide la longitud o la distancia; 1 metro = 100 centímetros

mile (mi) [mīl] A customary unit for measuring length or distance; 1 mile = 5,280 feet

milla (mi) Una unidad del sistema usual con la que se mide la longitud o la distancia; 1 milla = 5,280 pies

milligram (mg) [mil′i•gram] A metric unit for measuring mass; 1,000 milligrams = 1 gram

miligramo Una unidad del sistema métrico con la que se mide la masa; 1,000 miligramo = 1 gramos

milliliter (mL) [mil′i•lēt•ər] A metric unit for measuring capacity and liquid volume; 1 liter = 1,000 milliliters

mililitro (mL) Una unidad del sistema métrico con la que se mide la capacidad y el volumen líquido; 1 litro = 1,000 mililitros

millimeter (mm) [mil′i•mēt•ər] A metric unit for measuring length or distance; 1 centimeter = 10 millimeters

milímetro (mm) Una unidad del sistema métrico con la que se mide la longitud o la distancia; 1 centímetro = 10 milímetros

My Vocabulary Summary

minute (min) [min′it] A unit used to measure short amounts of time; 1 minute = 60 seconds

minuto (min) Una unidad con la que se miden períodos breves de tiempo; 1 minuto = 60 segundos

mixed number [mikst num′ber] An amount given as a whole number and a fraction

número mixto Una cantidad que se da como un número entero y una fracción

multiple [mul′tə•pəl] A number that is the product of two counting numbers

múltiplo Número que es el producto de dos número naturales

N

numerator [no͞o′mər•āt•ər] The number above the bar in a fraction that tells how many parts of the whole or group are being considered

numerador El número que está arriba de la barra en una fracción y que indica cuántas partes del entero o del grupo se consideran

My Vocabulary Summary

O

obtuse angle [äb•to͞os′ ang′gəl] An angle that measures greater than 90° and less than 180°

ángulo obtuso Un ángulo que mide más de 90° y menos de 180°

---

obtuse triangle [äb•to͞os′ trī′ang•gəl] A triangle with one obtuse angle

triángulo obtusángulo Un triángulo con un ángulo obtuso

---

order of operations [ôr′dər əv äp•ə•rā′shənz] A special set of rules which gives the order in which calculations are done

orden de las operaciones Un conjunto especial de reglas que establece el orden en que se hacen los cálculos

---

ounce (oz) [ouns] A customary unit for measuring weight;
1 pound = 16 ounces

onza (oz) Una unidad del sistema usual con la que se mide el peso;
1 libra = 16 onzas

P

parallel lines [pâr′ə•lel līnz] Lines in the same plane that never intersect and are always the same distance apart

líneas paralelas Líneas ubicadas en un mismo plano que nunca se intersecan y siempre están a la misma distancia entre sí

My Vocabulary Summary

parallelogram [pâr•ə•lel′ə•gram]
A quadrilateral whose opposite sides are parallel and of equal length

paralelogramo Un cuadrilátero con lados opuestos paralelos y de igual longitud

partial product [pär′shəl präd′əkt]
A method of multiplying in which the ones, tens, hundreds, and so on are multiplied separately and then the products are added together

producto parcial Un método de multiplicación en el que las unidades, decenas, centenas, etc., se multiplican por separado y luego se suman los productos

partial quotient [pär′shəl kwō′shənt]
A method of dividing in which multiples of the divisor are subtracted from the dividend and then the quotients are added together

cociente parcial Un método de división en el que los múltiplos del divisor se restan del dividendo y luego se suman los cocientes

pattern [pat′ərn] An ordered set of numbers or objects; the order helps you predict what will come next

patrón Un conjunto ordenado de números u objetos; el orden permite predecir qué sigue a continuación.

perimeter [pə•rim′ə•tər] The distance around a figure

perímetro La distancia alrededor de una figura

My Vocabulary Summary

period [pir′ē•əd] Each group of three digits in a multi-digit number; periods are usually separated by commas or spaces.

período Cada grupo de tres dígitos en un número de varios dígitos; por lo general, los períodos suelen separarse con comas o espacios.

perpendicular lines [pər•pən•dik′yo͞o•lər līnz] Two lines that intersect to form four right angles

líneas perpendiculares Dos líneas que se intersecan y forman cuatro ángulos rectos

pint (pt) [pīnt] A customary unit for measuring capacity and liquid volume; 1 pint = 2 cups

pinta (pt) Una unidad del sistema usual con la que se mide la capacidad y el volumen líquido; 1 pinta = 2 tazas

place value [plās val′yo͞o] The value of a digit in a number, based on the location of the digit

valor posicional El valor que tiene un dígito en un número según su ubicación

plane [plān] A flat surface that extends without end in all directions

plano Una superficie plana que se extiende sin fin en todas direcciones

point [point] An exact location in space

punto Una ubicación exacta en el espacio

My Vocabulary Summary

pound (lb) [pound] A customary unit for measuring weight;
1 pound = 16 ounces

libra (lb) Una unidad del sistema usual con la que se mide el peso;
1 libra = 16 onzas

prime number [prīm num′bər] A number that has exactly two factors: 1 and itself

número primo Un número que tiene exactamente dos factores: 1 y él mismo

product [präd′əkt] The answer to a multiplication problem

producto El resultado de una multiplicación

protractor [prō′trak•tər] A tool for measuring the size of an angle

transportador Un instrumento con el que se mide el tamaño de un ángulo

My Vocabulary Summary

Q

quart (qt) [kwôrt] A customary unit for measuring capacity and liquid volume; 1 quart = 2 pints

cuarto (ct) Una unidad del sistema usual con la que se mide la capacidad y el volumen líquido;
1 cuarto = 2 pintas

quotient [kwō′shənt] The number that results from dividing

cociente Número que resulta de una división

R

ray [rā] A part of a line; it has one endpoint and continues without end in one direction.

semirrecta Una parte de una recta; tiene un extremo y continúa sin fin en una sola dirección.

rectangle [rek′tang•gəl] A quadrilateral with two pairs of parallel sides, two pairs of sides of equal length, and four right angles

rectángulo Un cuadrilátero con dos pares de lados paralelos de igual longitud y cuatro ángulos rectos

My Vocabulary Summary

reflex angle [re′fleks′ ang′gəl] An angle that measures greater than 180° and less than 360°

ángulo de reflexión Ángulo cuya medida es mayor que 180° y menor que 360°

---

regroup [rē•gro͞op′] To exchange amounts of equal value to rename a number

reagrupar Intercambiar cantidades de igual valor para convertir un número

---

regular polygon [reg′yə•lər päl′i•gän] A polygon that has all sides that are equal in length and all angles equal in measure

polígono regular Un polígono en el que todos los lados tienen la misma longitud y todos los ángulos tienen la misma medida

---

remainder [ri•mān′dər] The amount left over when a number cannot be divided equally

residuo La cantidad que queda cuando no se puede dividir un número en partes iguales

---

rhombus [räm′bəs] A quadrilateral with two pairs of parallel sides and four sides of equal length

rombo Un cuadrilátero con dos pares de lados paralelos y cuatro lados de igual longitud

---

right angle [rīt ang′gəl] An angle that forms a square corner

ángulo recto Un ángulo que forma una esquina cuadrada

My Vocabulary Summary

right triangle [rīt trī′ang•gəl] A triangle with one right angle

triángulo rectángulo Un triángulo con un ángulo recto

---

round [round] To replace a number with another number that tells about how many or how much

redondear Reemplazar un número con otro número que indica una cantidad aproximada

---

S

scale [skāl] Numbers or marks arranged at regular intervals that are used for measurement or to establish position

escala Números o marcas dispuestos a intervalos regulares que se emplean para medir o establecer una posición

---

scalene triangle [skā′lēn trī′ang•gəl] A triangle with no sides of equal length

triángulo escaleno Triángulo cuyos lados no son de la misma longitud

My Vocabulary Summary

second (sec) [sek'ənd] A small unit of time;
1 minute = 60 seconds

segundo (s) Una unidad de tiempo pequeña;
1 minuto = 60 segundos

square [skwâr] A quadrilateral with two pairs of parallel sides, four sides of equal length, and four right angles

cuadrado Un cuadrilátero con dos pares de lados paralelos, cuatro lados de igual longitud y cuatro ángulos rectos

square unit [skwâr yo͞o'nit] A unit of area with dimensions of 1 unit × 1 unit

unidad cuadrada Una unidad de área con dimensiones de 1 unidad × 1 unidad

standard form [stan'dərd fôrm] A way to write numbers by using the digits 0–9, with each digit having a place value

forma normal Una manera de escribir números usando los dígitos 0 a 9, en laque cada dígito ocupa un valor posicional

straight angle [strāt ang'gel] An angle that measures 180°

ángulo llano Ángulo que mide 180°

My Vocabulary Summary

T

tenth [tenth] One of ten equal parts

décimo Una de diez partes iguales

term [tûrm] A number or object in a pattern

término Un número u objeto en un patrón

ton (T) [tun] A customary unit used to measure weight;
1 ton = 2,000 pounds

tonelada (t) Una unidad del sistema usual que se usa para medir el peso;
1 tonelada = 2,000 libras

trapezoid [trap′i•zoid] *exclusive* A quadrilateral with exactly one pair of parallel sides

trapecio *exclusivo* Cuadrilátero con exactamente un par de lados paralelos

trapezoid [trap′i•zoid] *inclusive* A quadrilateral with at least one pair of parallel sides

trapecio *inclusivo* Cuadrilátero con al menos un par de lados paralelos

My Vocabulary Summary

U

unit fraction [yo͞o′nit frak′shən] A fraction that has a numerator of one

fracción unitaria Una fracción que tiene un numerador de uno

V

vertex [vûr′teks] The point at which two rays of an angle meet or two (or more) line segments meet in a two-dimensional figure

vértice El punto en el que se unen dos semirrectas de un ángulo o dos (o más) segmentos de una figura bidimensional

W

weight [wāt] How heavy an object is

peso Cuán pesado es un objeto

whole [hōl] All of the parts of a figure or group

entero Todas las partes de una figura o de un grupo

My Vocabulary Summary

word form [wûrd fôrm] A way to write numbers by using words

en palabras Manera de escribir los números usando palabras

yard (yd) [yärd] A customary unit for measuring length or distance;
1 yard = 3 feet

yarda (yd) Una unidad del sistema usual con la que se mide la longitud o la distancia;
1 yarda = 3 pies

Table of Measures

LENGTH

Metric	Customary
1 centimeter (cm) = 10 millimeters (mm)	1 foot (ft) = 12 inches (in.)
1 meter (m) = 1,000 millimeters	1 yard (yd) = 3 feet
1 meter = 100 centimeters	1 yard = 36 inches
1 meter = 10 decimeters (dm)	1 mile (mi) = 1,760 yards
1 kilometer (km) = 1,000 meters	1 mile = 5,280 feet

CAPACITY AND LIQUID VOLUME

Metric	Customary
1 liter (L) = 1,000 milliliters (mL)	1 cup (c) = 8 fluid ounces (fl oz)
	1 pint (pt) = 2 cups
	1 quart (qt) = 2 pints
	1 quart = 4 cups
	1 gallon (gal) = 4 quarts

MASS/WEIGHT

Metric	Customary
1 gram (g) = 1,000 milligrams (mg)	1 pound (lb) = 16 ounces (oz)
1 kilogram (kg) = 1,000 grams	1 ton (T) = 2,000 pounds

MONEY

1 penny = 1¢, or \$0.01	1 quarter = 25¢, or \$0.25
1 nickel = 5¢, or \$0.05	1 half dollar = 50¢, or \$0.50
1 dime = 10¢, or \$0.10	1 dollar = 100¢, or \$1.00

TIME

1 minute (min) = 60 seconds (sec)
1 half hour = 30 minutes
1 hour (hr) = 60 minutes
1 day (d) = 24 hours
1 week (wk) = 7 days

1 year (yr) = about 52 weeks
1 year = 12 months (mo)
1 year = 365 days
1 leap year = 366 days
1 decade = 10 years
1 century = 100 years

SYMBOLS

$<$	is less than
$>$	is greater than
$=$	is equal to
$\neq$	is not equal to
¢	cent or cents
$	dollar or dollars
°	degree or degrees
$\perp$	is perpendicular to
$\parallel$	is parallel to
$\overleftrightarrow{AB}$	line *AB*
$\overrightarrow{AB}$	ray *AB*
$\overline{AB}$	line segment *AB*
$\angle ABC$	angle *ABC*, or angle *B*
$\triangle ABC$	triangle *ABC*

FORMULAS

Perimeter

Polygon $P =$ sum of the lengths of sides

Rectangle $P = l + w + l + w$, or $P = 2 \times l + 2 \times w$

Square $P = 4 \times s$

Area

Rectangle $A = l \times w$, or $A = b \times h$